THE

UNWRITTEN SONG

THE

UNWRITTEN SONG

POETRY OF THE PRIMITIVE AND
TRADITIONAL PEOPLES OF THE WORLD
EDITED, IN PART RETRANSLATED,
AND WITH AN INTRODUCTION BY

WILLARD R. TRASK

VOLUME I

The Far North / Africa / Indonesia
Melanesia / Australia

THE MACMILLAN COMPANY · NEW YORK
COLLIER-MACMILLAN LTD · LONDON

Library of Congress Catalog Card Number: 66-24053

First Printing

The Macmillan Company, New York
Collier-Macmillan Canada Ltd., Toronto, Ontario

Printed in the United States of America

Table of Contents

Introduction / vii

Notes to Introduction / xxiii

Acknowledgments / xxix

THE FAR NORTH

Greenland / 3

Canada / 9

Alaska / 31

Europe / 33

AFRICA

Western Africa and the Congo / 37

Southern Africa / 69

Eastern Africa and Madagascar / 90

North Africa / 121

INDONESIA

Borneo / 141

(*Indonesia cont'd.*)

Sumatra / 156

Nias / 159

Lesser Sundas / 166

Celebes / 170

Moluccas / 175

Philippines / 178

MELANESIA

New Guinea / 187

D'Entrecasteaux Islands / 196

Trobriand Islands / 203

Bismarck Archipelago / 207

Solomon Islands / 211

Banks Islands and New Hebrides / 216

New Caledonia / 218

Fiji Islands / 227

AUSTRALIA

Australia / 241

Sources / 263

Index of Peoples / 283

Introduction

I

Herodotus reported that the Pygmies were "wizards," but he had nothing to say of their poetry.[1]* Tacitus, somewhat nearer to his subject, knew that the Germani had "ancient songs," but he recorded none.[2] So, too, Antiquity in general.† So, too, the Middle Ages, whose learned men regarded the popular oral poetry even of their own culture as "obscene and foul jingles."[3]

It was the curiosity of the Renaissance which first thought it worth putting into writing poems of what were then called "savage" peoples. André Thevet, in his account of travels in northeastern South America, published at Paris in 1558, gave a translation of an Indian fightingman's songs of defiance to his captors.[4] Twenty years later, Montaigne quoted a very similar song and followed it by the beginning of a love song.[5]

In 1673, Johann Scheffer in his description of Lapland did what Thevet and Montaigne had failed to do: he published a Lapp poem not only in translation but also in the original text.[6]

Scheffer's translation, like his book, was in Latin. In 1815, Johann Gottfried von Herder included a German retranslation of it among the "Songs from the Far North" in his ground-breaking anthology of "folk" poems, *Stimmen der Völker in Liedern*.‡ The same section

* Numbered notes will be found after the Introduction and Acknowledgments.

† Catullus' *Attis* may possibly have been inspired by what he saw of Cybele worship during his visit to Bithynia (cf. Tenney Frank, *Catullus and Horace: Two Poets in Their Environment* [New York, Henry Holt & Co., 1928], pp. 71 ff.). Ovid said that he wrote a poem in Getic, but it was in Roman meter (*ex Ponto*, IV, 13, 19–20).

‡ Herder coined the term *Volkslied* (folk song, folk poem), as Montaigne before him had coined its French equivalent, *poésie populaire*. Herder's anthology both indicated and went far toward consolidating the new Romantic admiration for folk poetry.

It was in Herder that Longfellow read Scheffer's Lapp poem, two lines of which included an Eskimo "Threnody" from Greenland and, in a section entitled "Songs of the Savages," Herder put two Inca poems.[7]

Unfortunately, he put with them nine so-called "Poems from Madagascar." Unfortunately, for they were straight from Paris: sheer inventions by a contemporary minor French poet, the Chevalier de Parny. Parny at least had the excuse that he was born in Réunion. There seems to have been none for the greatest hoax of the kind ever perpetrated. Its inventors, two young French seminarians named Parisot and Dejouy, made up an American Indian language out of whole cloth and, with the blessings of two eminent French linguists, published a grammar and vocabulary of it, with illustrative poems!*

II

Thevet had quoted his Indian song simply as another of his "curiosities." It was the embracing mind of Montaigne which first found value in the culture and the poetry of "cannibals."

> And lest anyone think [he writes in the same essay] that what they do is done out of mere servile compliance with their usages and under the compulsion of their ancient code, without reflection or judgment, their souls being so stupefied that they cannot do otherwise, I must cite some examples of their capacity. In addition to the example I have given of one of their fighting-men's songs, I have another, a love song. . . . I have enough acquaintance with poetry to declare that not only is there nothing barbaric in such a product of the imagination, but that it is the perfection of the Anacreontic.

Anacreon's reputation has become sadly tarnished in this day, still more so that of the *Anacreontica* which were formerly foisted on him. But in the Renaissance no higher praise could be bestowed on a lyric love poem than to call it Anacreontic. Montaigne continues:

> In addition, their language is sweet, and pleasant to the ear, with a likeness to Greek terminations.[1]

---

he later turned into the well-known refrain of his "My Lost Youth": "A boy's will is the wind's will / And the thoughts of youth are long, long thoughts."

* *Grammaire et Vocabulaire de la Langue Taensa, avec textes traduits et commentés* . . . (Paris, 1882). The hoax was exploded by D. G. Brinton, *Essays of an Americanist* (Philadelphia, 1890), pp. 452 ff., though some years earlier, in an essay on American Indian poetry, he had written that the faked poems "appear to be accurate translations" (*Aboriginal American Authors and Their Productions; especially those in the native languages* [Philadelphia, 1883], p. 49).

Nor could the Renaissance bestow any higher praise on a language than to say it was like Greek.*

III

But what is there in common among Pygmy, ancient Germanic, tribal South American Indian, Lapp, Inca, and—supposing they had been genuine—Madagascan poems? Obviously, from the point of view of Western culture, they are all "exotic." But then, so are Japanese and Chinese and Sanskrit poems. What have they in common that differentiates them from both Western and extra-Western literary products? The answer lies in the word "literary": those "literatures" are *literally* such—that is, they are *written.* The verbal art products of the Pygmies, the ancient Germans, the South American Indians, the Lapps, and the Incas are *unwritten.* However much their cultures may differ in other respects, they have it in common that they have no writing.†

And what term are we to apply to peoples of these orders? Literally, again, they are *illiterate,* that is, "without letters." But "illiterate" has acquired a pejorative meaning among us: an "Anthology of Illiterate Poetry" (which this one literally is) would hardly attract many readers.

Thevet and Montaigne and even Herder could innocently refer to their exotic peoples as "barbarians," "cannibals," and "savages." These terms too—and very rightly—have become "dirty words." Among the many proposed substitutes, I have thought it best to stay with "primitive" and "traditional."‡ The first is applied to peoples whose material culture remains essentially that of the Stone Age. The second is applied

* After Montaigne, except for some of his imitators (Sidney, Puttenham), specific praise gave place to the generalities of the Rousseauists and the Pre-Romantics. I shall return to the question of value judgments toward the end of this Introduction and, more fully, in the Introduction to Volume II.

† Means of recording events are found among some peoples of the same orders. The Maya had their glyphs; the Tuareg have an alphabet. But in none of these exceptional cases are they used in either the composition or the recording of verbal art products.

‡ For a well-argued ostracism of the term "primitive," see A. A. Gerbrands, *Art as an Element of Culture, especially in Negro-Africa* (Leiden, E. J. Brill, 1957). But the fact remains that when a gallery announces an exhibition of "primitive art," one knows that if one goes to it one will find tribal sculptures from Africa, New Guinea, Polynesia, and so on. I do not see why "primitive poetry" should not be equally indicative—and equally inoffensive. "Traditional" has not yet been so heavily attacked; but no doubt the time is not far off.

to peoples who, though their cultures are more elaborate, hand them on orally. They may or may not be in close contact with "literate" peoples and, in the former case, may or may not be influenced by their cultures.*

IV

Obviously, poetry among peoples without letters cannot be what it has become for us—something one reads from a printed page. But the difference is far greater than that. Only very rarely is a poem even recited. Almost always it is sung, either to a traditional melody or to one composed for the occasion by the poet.†

> The words and the music . . . come to him.[1]

> Melody and its words seem to be conceived together by the primitive composer-poet.[2]

> Words fitted to music are the songs and poetry of the people. . . . There is no conception of poetry without a tune.[3]

In many cases, and among many peoples, yet a third element goes to make up the complete creation. This element is rhythmic motion. With the addition of it, we have

> gesture song, combining the arts of poetry, music, and dance.[4]

> Verse is wedded to the dance and to some extent depends on it.[5]

> Singing and dancing went together. The vocal part with the words received its distinctive name according to theme. The accompanying movements varied in extent and energy. Some songs were sung by singers sitting on the ground, movements being restricted to the arms. . . . When, however, the performers stood up to sing, movements of the body and feet were made, and the performance became a dance.[6]

Finally, musical instruments, including those simplest forms of percussion, clapping hands and stamping feet, are often added to reinforce the rhythm, or indeed to counterpoint it.

> The fundamental rhythm is despotically marked by the big, low-pitched drums and by the hands of the audience; visually, too, by the dancer's steps

* In selecting the poems for this anthology, I have tried to avoid those which too clearly show the influence of extraneous cultures.

† The same conception obtained even among the literate poets of the medieval West: at least the earlier generations of troubadours and trouvères in France, and of their followers in Germany and Portugal, composed both the words and the melodies of their lyrics.

and gestures. Other, lighter drums and other clapping hands embroider on this rhythm, in counterpoint and syncopation.[7]

Singing, clapping, dancing and drumming are not separate entities but may be said to constitute *one homogeneous art form.*[8]

V

Whether in this most complete manifestation, or reduced to the minimum of words and tune, this poetry is incomparably more a part of the fabric of life than poetry is among us. Its occasions are innumerable.

When some remarkable event occurs, the launching of a canoe, a visit of strangers, or a feast, song-makers are engaged to celebrate it . . . or the occasion produces a song.[1]

The principal subjects on which songs are composed are pig-hunting, fish-shooting, turtle and dugong spearing, fighting, making boats, bows. . . .[2]

Songs express their life, songs mark its course at every turn.[3]

If I attempt to give an English rendering of a few . . . songs . . . it is . . . to convey an idea of the function of poetry in Konyak life. The songs not only reflect the Konyak's attitude to many aspects of life, they are the principal and recognized medium through which the individual as well as the group express their most intense emotions.[4]

A glance through the titles of the songs in this collection will not only confirm such statements but will show to how many of the peoples represented they can be applied.*

One flourishing occasion for poetry, and one which the West formerly possessed but has allowed to sink into disuse, is the song contest.†

When villages or clans meet on great occasions it is a common practice for champions on either side to sing songs of mockery at one another. These are listened to with roars of delight by the audience.[5]

Of such song contests elsewhere, one writer has remarked:

Properly speaking, they represented the court of justice.[6]

* Most primitive and traditional poems have no titles. Those given either stem from the collector or have been supplied by the compiler from the data accompanying the collection. (For an exception, see Te Rangi Hiroa's remarks on Mangarevan gesture and dance songs, cited in the previous section.)

† A late and piquant Western example is "The Flyting of Dunbar and Kennedie," of *ca.* 1500 (*The Poems of William Dunbar,* ed. W. M. Mackenzie, Edinburgh, 1932, pp. 5–20).

But the elements of personal mockery and of litigation are not necessarily present: poem is simply pitted against poem in a purely "literary tournament."[7]

Halfway between contest and courtship are the songs exchanged between young men and girls.

> When men were wooing women, the women met them beside rivers. There they spread mats and sat down. When the couples had come together in this way the girl began singing. . . . When the girl had sung, the young man answered.[8]

> When at dawn the young people return from work in the fields, they assemble on raised platforms specially built for the purpose . . . : boys and girls, leaning affectionately on each other, sing alternative songs. . . . Boys and girls sing in turn, each vying with the other in appropriate responses . . . sometimes sentimental, sometimes taunting.[9]

> When the rice harvest has been gathered and work in the fields is temporarily suspended the chief occupation of the young men is to court the girls. . . . Squatting in a row before their lady-loves the young men compose verses in their honour, and the ladies reply. . . . Each couple keeps up the exchange of vocal repartee before a public only too ready to record its approval when one party or the other scores a point.[10]

The last example is from southeast Asia, where this kind of alternative singing has reached a particularly high stage of development.[11]

VI

With the more numerous occasions for poetry, there is a far greater range of subject matter. Among the various poetic genres known to the Mnong Gar are "law-court verses," in which either party to a suit summarizes the arguments and precedents for his side.[1] Who ever heard of a Western poem on fertility or pregnancy? They are "common among the Kawar."[2] Or on "the development of the body after its conception by the parents"? The Uraon have them.[3]

> A number of songs enumerate various parts of the human body. . . . In the Tuamotuan songs the ordinary physiological function is given with each, but the Mangarevan songs are erotic in that the verb associated with each of the nine parts has something to do with love.[4]

> Songs are a part of everyday life. Everything is sung, everything is improvised on: personal griefs, torn clothes, a sprain, good weather, tiredness, etc.[5]

> Mapuche songs cover a wide range of topics, including . . . grief resulting from . . . failure to have offspring.[6]

> So desirable is corpulence as a sexual trait that I have frequently heard men make up songs about the merits of a fat vulva.[7]

Songs on abortion and the death of illegitimate infants, a song sung by a woman during childbirth, songs in praise of cattle appear in this anthology, not as "ethnological curiosities" but because they are, quite simply, poetry.[8] Again, a glance through titles will serve the purpose of a further listing, as it will show what unpromising material, from the Western point of view, can be made to yield poems of a very high order.*

VII

But be their subjects and their occasions what they may, poems nowhere arise of their own motion. Who are the poets of these poems, the song makers of these songs? They are professional poets on the one hand; on the other they are anyone and everyone.†

To take anyone and everyone first:

> Every one composes songs. A man or woman would be thought little of who could not do so. Even the small children compose their own songs. Each person composes his own.[1]

> Every man, and most of the women, have their own songs with which they have been inspired and then composed themselves.[2]

> All the women have a talent for singing and are able to make up songs on the spot about any laughable behavior.

This last is from a description of Madagascar published in 1686.[3] Two and a quarter centuries later another observer says almost the same thing of continental Africa:

> Fang women have a very caustic wit: in their songs they contrive to say the most biting things without seeming to.[4]

> The Nuer . . . are poetic and most men and women compose songs which are sung at dances and concerts and are composed for the creator's own pleasure and chanted by him in lonely pastures. . . . Youths break into song, praising their kinsmen, sweethearts, and cattle, when they feel happy, wherever they may be.[5]

* In theory, the subject matter of a Western poem is of no consequence; it is only the "poetry" that counts. But in practice, subject matter weighs quite heavily. Witness the praises bestowed, in their several times, on Baudelaire and on Eliot for extending the range of poetry.

† The smallness of many of the populations from which great numbers of songs have been collected is remarkable. The Copper Eskimo numbered about 800, the Netsilik Eskimos about 300, in 1922; the population of Ifaluk Atoll was 260 in 1953.

My ascription of the authorship of the song poems to the people of Ifaluk . . . is almost literally true. Most of the song poems that make up the bulk of the text were indeed composed by one of the people or, as they tell it, by one of their gods.[6]

A great number of . . . songs are improvised at public gatherings by men or women.[7]

When someone of either sex is injured or ill, dying or dead, both men and women . . . "compose" and sing, individually, various appropriate songs. . . . Illness and death do not provide the only occasions for this type of singing.[8]

Every Dobuan is a song-maker.[9]

The Meo, a people of poets.[10]

VIII

Improvisation may be largely a reshaping of traditionary material:

Songs, remembered over long periods, provide a basis upon which each person constructs his or her own. . . . There are a number of conventional subjects. . . . They . . . serve as a sort of accepted framework which is used as a medium for expressing the desired sentiments; and to this each singer, building on the remembered phrases of others, adds something of his or her own experience and emotion.[1]

So, too, may composition.
But not necessarily:

Any interesting event calls forth a number of songs. There is very little imitation, very little use of poetic verbal counters. The form is more or less stereotyped as in our sonnet form; and there is as much emphasis on originality of content and of words used for expression as in our own literary tradition. The song-maker is proud of his creation, proud of its originality.[2]

IX

But in all things involving technique there are differences in aptitude and accomplishment. Where "everyone" is a poet, some will be better poets than others.

The Toda name for [funeral] laments is . . . *kunedsti,* and certain men have great reputations as composers both for funerals and on other occasions.[1]

With recognition of differences in accomplishment, the ground is laid for specialization.

A poet or poetess more or less distinguished is probably found in every considerable village throughout the islands.[2]

Every village has its own poet, or sometimes several. . . . This song is known all over the Gilbert group and is highly esteemed.[3]

From specialization it is only a step to professionalism.

When some remarkable event occurs . . . song-makers are engaged to celebrate it and rewarded.[4]

When one hired the services of a poet, he brought a basket of flowers and leaves to him.[5]

The song-maker . . . has rights to prevent others from using his song, at least for a while. He must give his permission before his song is used for the dance.[6]

X

Or, as they tell it, by one of their gods . . .[1]

There is a widespread conception that poems are dictated to the poet by powers outside him.

They say that, while asleep, they visit the world of spirits, where a poetic divinity teaches them a poem, while, at the same time, they learn a dance corresponding to the song.[2]

Poetry and song was the gift of the gods; and poets professed to have received their songs from them or from the spirits of the dead.[3]

I found an interesting example of the "inspired song" in the Wurunjerri tribe. . . . In this case it is Bunjil [the "tribal All-father"] himself who "rushes down" into the breast of the singer.[4]

[The poet will] chant his *tabunea* or invocation. . . . The words and the music then come to him.[5]

Eskimo magicians may compose their songs during trances.[6] Songs also come in dreams:

Towards midnight, as Rata slept, he dreamed about his ship, and as he dreamed he chanted.[7]

XI

But this is only one side of the medal.

Some bards profess to be inspired. Others make no such pretensions.[1]

A man composes his song as he cuts a canoe or a bow or as he paddles a canoe, singing it over softly to himself until he is satisfied with it. He then awaits an opportunity to sing it in public.[2]

His songs are polished and repolished with loving care, according to the canons of a technique as exacting as it is beautiful.[3]

One of the very few detailed accounts of composition that I have been able to find describes a process in which the elements of inspiration and conscious technique both play a part:

It is only when the poet feels the divine spark of inspiration once more strong within him that he deviates from the ordinary course of village life. . . . He removes himself to some lonely spot, there to avoid all contact with man or woman. He eats nothing but the flesh of coconuts, and drinks nothing but water. . . . For three days he thus purges his body of its vicious humours. On the fourth morning he marks out a twelve-foot square on the ground. . . . This is his "house of song," wherein he will sit in travail with the poem that is yet unborn. All the next night he sits there, bolt upright, facing east. . . . Dawn breaks. As the edge of the sun's disc appears over the eastern sea, the poet lifts his hands at arms' length . . . and intones [his invocation to the sun[4]]. . . . This incantation . . . he repeats three times, then rinses his mouth with salt water, thereby making his tongue "pure for song." Immediately after . . . he goes to the village to seek five friends. . . . He brings them back to his "house of song." They carry with them . . . withered dancing wreaths, together with the feathers of frigate birds, and of this strange fuel they make a small, acridly smoking fire in the middle of the "house." The poet sits, in such a position that the smoke may be blown upon him . . . , and his five friends face him in a semiciricle. . . . Without further preamble, he begins to recite the "rough draft" of his poem. . . . His friends . . . interrupt, criticize, interject suggestions, applaud, or howl down, according to their taste. . . . They will remain without food or drink . . . until night falls, searching for the right word, the balance and music to convert [the poem] into a finished work of art. . . . When all their wit and wisdom has been poured out upon him, they depart. He remains alone again—probably for several days—to reflect upon their advice, accept, reject, accommodate, improve, as his genius dictates. The responsibility for the completed song will be entirely his.[5]

In short:

When the two met, they both sat down to have a cry together. Rehua cried simple, but Tane cried, with a meaning, in verses.[6]

XII

But if poetry is, at least in some measure, a conscious art among these peoples, what does the poet think about his function?

When I began this investigation, this was one of the problems to which I most hoped to find an answer. Unfortunately, the material for an answer has turned out to be extremely meager.

An African poet says: "We were born under an evil star, we poets. . . . We were given a thankless trade." An African poetess, singing her death song, gives as her last credential the fact that she has "sung so many songs" to her people. Another African poets asks: "Is there anything better than a gifted poet?"[1] But such references to poets and poetry in the poems themselves are extremely scarce.

What of the investigators? All but a very few seem simply not to have been interested; they have not asked the right questions.[2] But when the right questions are asked, the illumination is astonishing. Here, for example, is what Knud Rasmussen learned from the Netsilik Eskimo poet and shaman Orpingalik:

> Songs are thoughts, sung out with the breath when people are moved by great forces and ordinary speech no longer suffices.
>
> Man is moved just like the ice floe sailing here and there out in the current. His thoughts are driven by a flowing force when he feels joy, when he feels fear, when he feels sorrow. Thoughts can wash over him like a flood, making his breath come in gasps and his heart throb. Something, like an abatement in the weather, will keep him thawed up. And then it will happen that we, who always think we are small, will feel still smaller. And we will fear to use words. But it will happen that the words we need will come of themselves. When the words we want to use shoot up of themselves—we get a new song.[3]

Rasmussen also questioned an old Eskimo woman on little Diomedes Island. She answered:

> In the old days—every autumn—we used to hold great festivals for the soul of the whale, and these festivals were always opened with new songs which the men made up. The spirits had to be summoned with fresh words—worn-out songs must never be used when men and women danced and sang in homage to this great prize of the huntsman—the whale. And while the men were thinking out the words for these hymns, it was the custom to put out all the lights. The feast house had to be dark and quiet—nothing must disturb or distract the men. In utter silence all these men sat there in the gloom and thought, old and young—ay—down to the very smallest urchin, provided he was old enough to speak. It was that silence we called *karrtsiluni*. It means waiting for something to break forth. For our forefathers believed that songs are born in such a silence. While everyone is trying hard to think fair thoughts, songs are born in the minds of men, rising like bubbles from the depths—bubbles seeking breath in which to burst.
>
> So come all holy songs.[4]

XIII

There is no formulated literary criticism among primitive and traditional peoples. That standards of some sort exist is shown by the existence of song contests: without them, one poem could not "win" over another. There is also some form of selectivity, which preserves one poem for generations while another is allowed to perish almost at once. But none of all this is codified.

It would be of the utmost interest if it were possible to grade poems by indigenous standards. Unfortunately, it is not.

Instead, I offer some value judgments of collectors. They represent, of course, the application of Western literary criteria.

> The poetry and charm of the songs . . .[1]

> [The song] is far more beautiful than the translation suggests, full of fine sound effects both in rhyme and rhythm. The allusions and the refrains are admirable in their simplicity.[2]

> Yet other tribes of a similar economic status evince a remarkable artistic sense, if not in the field of plastic art, then in poetry and music. The songs of the Baigas spring from genuine and often profound poetic feeling, and among the Dires . . . I have heard choral singing of fascinating beauty.[3]

> I have thought it well to publish this *mengap* without any abbreviation. It is, as far as I know, the first time that a Dyak *mengap* is published, and to obtain a true idea of Dyak mythology and especially of Dyak poetry, it is indispensable to study its creations in their full integrity. With regard to what we might call insistent repetitions, we must consider that these peoples do not know the hurried life of European civilization and therefore listen all the more, not only with religious devotion, but also with a kind of true esthetic enjoyment, to these creations of their national poetic genius. Moreover, these passages are repetitions only with regard to the content of the poem, but not as to the mode of representing its content. And as to this mode, it is a very high degree of formal art which displays itself here, in expressing the same idea, the same event, in the most varied manners, like a precious gem turned in all directions. . . . And we must confess that often the beauty of the language, not only in its splendid poetical images, but also in expressing deep and sincere feeling, reaches a very high level.[4]

And, for the musical side of the song-dance-poem:

> This man was the first crack drummer I saw perform, and certainly he did not fall beneath my expectations. The weaving into and out of each other, with each hand, of the most complicated rhythms, and all with the most amazing speed and mathematical precision, far surpassed anything of the kind I have ever heard. . . . If only we could import Malekulans for the

ballet! . . . I confess to experiencing the most exquisite delight in Malekulan gong-rhythms. There is about them a mathematical beauty, translated somehow into a most intoxicating and exhilarating bodily experience.[5]

XIV

But, apart from whatever the literary value of these poems may be (and I think it is of the highest), there is another, and perhaps a more profound reason for such an anthology as this. In its small way, it is a contribution to human solidarity.

Here I give the word to some who, having most keenly felt the need for the collection of primitive poetry, have expressed it most eloquently:

> Only through its songs do the attitudes of a tribe or caste become clear and it is not until the poetry has been understood that a tribe is understood.[1]

> Oral literature may be said to be the Cinderella of anthropological studies. One of the great tasks of the future is to bring together and classify the native literary records of the peoples of the world. . . . The evidence of these native literatures is essential to a comprehensive survey of Man's intellectual history.[2]

> Among the most rewarding of studies on this continent [Africa] is the collecting of original and authentic songs, provided always that adequate translations can be made into a world language from the plethora of vernaculars with which centuries of isolation have vexed their human relations.[3]

> The Editors . . . propose in the next few years to give emphatic attention to the place that poetry and art hold in Indian village life and should have in ethnographic studies. "More and more," said Matthew Arnold, "mankind will discover that we have to turn to poetry to interpret life for us, to console us, to sustain us. Without poetry, our science will appear incomplete; and most of what now passes for religion and philosophy will be replaced by poetry." To the aboriginal, religion is often a nightmare but poetry ever consoles and sustains him. Over against the false interpretations of the magician and the priest is the pure vision of the poet. This is true even of the so-called "primitive" and "savage." To surprise that vision and to learn from it is the privilege of the ethnographer.[4]

XV

It has been a chief purpose of this Introduction to make the poetry of primitive and traditional peoples more immediately comprehensible by showing the differences between it and the poetry of the West. It is my hope that the poems which follow will show what they have in common, both on the plane of inspiration and on the plane of accomplishment.

As to the more specific purposes of this anthology:

There is ample evidence for assuming that all peoples would be found to have songs. However, one student of a people—ethnographer, anthropologist, missionary, traveler—will record dozens of songs; another will not even mention their existence. Within the limitations imposed by this irregularity of collecting, I have sought to make this anthology both representative and comprehensive.*

I have also sought—in addition to presenting material of general literary interest—to serve some of the needs of the scholar. Specifically, in every case where the collector has given either the original text or the melody (or both) I have indicated the fact in the section on Sources.† I hope that these references may provide the beginning of a basis for further study.

This anthology was originally to have been published in one volume. Manufacturing considerations have dictated that, instead, it should appear in two—the second, it is hoped, some six months after the first.

This has necessitated some revision of the original geographical arrangement. The present volume begins with poetry of the Eskimos in the Far North, then proceeds to Africa, Indonesia, Melanesia, and Australia. Volume II will comprise primitive and traditional poetry of Asia, Polynesia, Micronesia, and the Americas. Under the geographical divisions and subdivisions, the arrangement is by peoples. The name of the people (in boldface) is followed by an indication of locality (in small capitals). When the collector gives only the place of collection, the locality appears in boldface with a footnote to that effect.

That part of the original Introduction which is devoted to present-

* So far as I have been able to ascertain, there have been only two previous general anthologies in the field: G. Ragusa Moleti, *La Poesia dei Selvaggi* (Naples, 1897) and Eckart von Sydow, *Dichtungen der Naturvölker: religiöse, magische und profane Lyrik* (Vienna, 1935; revised edition, Zurich, 1954). The latter, which is also more extensive, contains 188 poems. The present volume contains some 360 poems; the second volume of this anthology will contain as many more. It was a review of the first edition of Von Sydow's book that—now more than thirty years ago—first awakened my interest in primitive and traditional poetry.

† These indications are given in the form of symbols following the bibliographical references. Inclusion of the original text in the source cited is shown by an asterisk (*); inclusion of both the original text and the melody is shown by two asterisks (**). Two other symbols show whether the translation given was made directly from the original language or is a retranslation from one of the modern Western languages.

ing primitive and traditional poetry in their own terms appears as the Introduction to the present volume. The Introduction to Volume II will point out certain correspondences between those poetries and Western poetry and treat them more generally in terms of Western literary aesthetics.

Brooklyn, New York
February 1966

Notes to Introduction

I

1. *Histories,* II, 32–33.
2. *Germania,* II: *carminibus antiquis.*
3. *Obscina et turpea cantica,* Council of Châlons (639–54), quoted in Carl Voretzsch, *Einführung in das Studium der altfranzösischen Sprache* (Halle a. S., Max Niemeyer, 1905), where also much more of the same tenor.
4. *Les Singularitez de la France Antarctique, autrement nommée Amerique* (ed. Paul Gaffarel, Paris, Maisonneuve, 1878), pp. 199–200.

I pass over the sixteenth-century Spanish collecting of Aztec poems in Mexico: Sahugun's *Historia General* was not published until 1829, the manuscript known as *Cantares Mexicanos* not until the present century. They had the inestimable advantage of recording the original Nahuatl texts. But they might as well not have existed, for any effect that they could have on contemporary literary perception in Europe.

5. "Des Cannibales," *Essais,* 3 vols., ed. P. Villery, (Paris, Alcan, 1930), I, 411–12. Montaigne seems not to have drawn on Thevet, but on a friend or acquaintance "who had lived among the Tupis of Brazil" (D. G. Brinton, *Aboriginal American Authors and their Productions; especially those in the native languages* [Philadelphia, 1883], p. 49). Montaigne's essay was probably written in 1579.
6. Joan. Schefferi *Lapponia,* Frankfurt, 1673, p. 283, quoted in O. Donner, *Lieder der Lappen* (Helsingfors, 1876), pp. 114–15.
7. Herder ascribes them, vaguely, to the *Allgemeine Reisen.* Their ultimate source is Garcilasso de la Vega's *Commentarios reales.*

II

1. Montaigne, *op. cit.,* 412.

IV

1. Gilbert Islands: P. B. Laxton, "A Gilbertese Song," *Journal of the Polynesian Society,* LXII (1953), 344.
2. George Herzog, *Research in Primitive and Folk Music in the United States* (American Council of Learned Societies, Bulletin No. 24) (Washington, D.C., 1936), p. 9.
3. Melanesia: R. H. Codrington, *The Melanesians: Studies in Their Anthropology and Folklore* (Oxford, Clarendon Press, 1891), p. 334.
4. Ifaluk Atoll, Caroline Islands: Edwin Grant Burrows, *Flower in My Ear: Arts and Ethos of Ifaluk Atoll* (University of Washington Publications in Anthropology, Vol. 14) (Seattle, University of Washington Press, 1963), p. 7.

5. India: Verrier Elwin and Shamrao Hivale, *Folk-Songs of the Maikal Hills* (Madras, published for *Man in India* by Humphrey Milford, Oxford University Press, 1944), p. xv.
6. Mangareva: Te Rangi Hiroa (Peter H. Buck), *Ethnology of Mangareva* (Bernice P. Bishop Museum Bulletin 157) (Honolulu, published by the Museum, 1938), p. 396.
7. Africa: Léopold Sédar Senghor, "La Poésie Négro-Africaine," *Problèmes d'Afrique Centrale,* IV (1951), p. 113.
8. Africa: Lord Hailey, ed., *An African Survey* (rev. ed., London, Oxford University Press, 1957), p. 67 (italics mine).

V

1. Melanesia: R. H. Codrington, *op. cit.,* pp. 334–35.
2. Andaman Islands: M. V. Portman, "Andamanese Music," *Journal of the Royal Asiatic Society,* n. s. XX (1888), 184.
3. Indochina: G. Condominas, "Chansons Mnong Gar," *France-Asie,* IX (1953), 648.
4. Assam: Christoph von Fürer-Haimendorf, "The Role of Songs in Konyak Culture," *Man in India,* XXIII (1943), 70.
5. Assam: J. P. Mills, *The Ao Nagas* (London, Macmillan & Co., 1926), p. 330.
6. Greenland: Henry Rink, *Tales and Traditions of the Eskimo, with a sketch of their habits, religion, language and other peculiarities* (Edinburgh and London, William Blackwood & Sons, 1875), p. 33.
7. Tuareg, Sahara: André Leroi-Gourhan *et al., Ethnologie de l'Union Française (Territoires extérieurs),* 2 vols. (Paris, Presses Universitaires de France, 1953), I, 234.
8. New Guinea: Georg F. Vicedom, in Vicedom and Herbert Tischner, *Die Mbowamb: Die Kultur der Hagenberg-Stämme im Östlichen Zentral-Neuguinea,* Vol. II: *(I) Gesellschaft, (II) Religion und Weltbild* (Monographien zur Völkerkunde herausgegeben vom Hamburgischen Museum für Völkerkunde, I) (Hamburg, Friederichsen, De Gruyter & Co., 1943), p. 190.
9. Assam: C. von Fürer-Haimendorf, *loc. cit.,* pp. 70–71.
10. Laos: Henry Baudesson, *Indo-China and Its Primitive People,* trans. E. Appleby Holt (London, Hutchinson & Co., n. d.), pp. 212–13.
11. Cf. Nguyen Van Huyen, *Les Chants alternés des garçons et des filles en Annam* (Paris, Paul Geuthner, 1933).

VI

1. G. Condominas, *loc. cit.,* p. 648 ("dits de justice").
2. India: V. Elwin and S. Hivale, *op. cit.,* p. 246.
3. India: *ibid.*
4. Te Rangi Hiroa, *op. cit.,* p. 397.
5. Southern China: Paul Vial, *Les Lolos* (Shanghai, Imprimerie de la Mission Catholique, 1898), p. 20.
6. South America: Mischa Titiev, *Social Singing Among the Mapuche* (Anthropological Papers, Museum of Anthropology, University of Michigan, No. 2) (Ann Arbor, University of Michigan Press, 1949), p. 2.
7. South America: A. R. Holmberg, *The Siriono* (unpublished Ph.D. dissertation, Yale University, 1946), p. 181, quoted in Clellan S. Ford and Frank A. Beach, *Patterns of Sexual Behavior* (New York, Harper & Bros. and Paul B. Hoeber, Inc., 1951), p. 89.
8. Songs on the first two of these subjects will be found in Vol. II.

VII

1. Andaman Islands: M. V. Portman, *loc. cit.*, p. 184.
2. Eskimo, Canada: Knud Rasmussen, *Intellectual Culture of the Copper Eskimos* (Report of the Fifth Thule Expedition 1921–24, Vol. IX) (Copenhagen, Gyldendalske Boghandel, Nordisk Forlag, 1932), p. 130.
3. Dapper, *Description de l'Afrique* (Amsterdam, 1686) quoted in Erich M. von Hornbostel, "Wanyamwezi-Gesänge," *Anthropos*, IV (1909), 785, n. 2.
4. H. Trilles, *Le Totémisme chez les Fâñ* (Collection Internationale de Monographies Ethnologiques, Bibliothèque-Anthropos, I, 4) (Münster i. W., Aschendorffsche Verlagsbuchhandlung, 1912), p. 267, n. 1.
5. Africa: E. E. Evans-Pritchard, *The Nuer: A description of the modes of livelihood and political institutions of a Nilotic people* (Oxford, Clarendon Press, 1940), p. 46.
6. Micronesia: E. G. Burrows, *op. cit.*, p. 7.
7. Mapuche, South America: M. Titiev, *op cit.*, p. 2.
8. Australia: Catherine H. Berndt, "Expressions of Grief Among Aboriginal Women," *Oceania*, XX (1949–50), p. 289.
9. Melanesia: R. F. Fortune, *Sorcerers of Dobu: The social anthropology of the Dobu Islanders of the Western Pacific* (Australasian National Research Council Expedition to New Guinea, 1927–8) (New York, E. P. Dutton & Co., Inc., 1932), p. 251.
10. Laos: G. Morechand, in A. Leroi-Gourhan *et al.*, *op. cit.*, II, 656.

VIII

1. Australia: C. H. Berndt, *loc. cit.*, p. 290. The passage quoted refers to "composition." But the context makes it clear (e.g., "when her husband dies, she will 'compose' other songs . . . *at the burial*," *ibid.*, p. 289 [italics mine]) that the term here includes, if it does not stand for, improvisation.
2. Melanesia: R. F. Fortune, *op. cit.*, p. 251.

IX

1. India: W. H. R. Rivers, *The Todas* (London, Macmillan & Co., 1906), p. 385.
2. Melanesia: R. H. Codrington, *op. cit.*, p. 334.
3. Micronesia: R. Parkinson, "Beiträge zur Ethnographie der Gilbert-Insulaner," *Internationales Archiv für Ethnographie*, II (1889), 95.
4. Melanesia: R. H. Codrington, *op. cit.*, pp. 334–35.
5. Polynesia: Gunn, *The Gospel in Futuna* (London, 1914), p. 238, quoted in Felix Speiser, *Ethnographische Materialen aus den Neuen Hebriden und den Banks-Inseln* (Berlin, C. W. Kreidel's Verlag, 1923), p. 425.
6. Melanesia: R. F. Fortune, *op. cit.*, p. 251.

X

1. Ifaluk Atoll: E. G. Burrows, *op. cit.*, p. 7. (Already quoted in Section VII.)
2. Fiji: Thomas Williams and J. Calvert, *Fiji and the Fijians* (New York, Appleton, 1859) p. 89.
3. Futuna: Gunn, *op. cit.*, p. 238, quoted in F. Speiser, *op. cit.*, p. 425.
4. Australia: A. W. Howitt, *The Native Tribes of South-East Australia* (London, Macmillan & Co., 1904), p. 418. (The song is given in the Australian section. See p. 261.)

5. Gilbert Islands: P. B. Laxton, *loc. cit.*, pp. 343–44. (The Invocation, together with further circumstances, is given in the Micronesian section, in Vol. II.)

6. William Thalbitzer, *Les magiciens esquimaux,* p. 102, cited in Mircea Eliade, *Le Chamanisme et les techniques archaïques de l'extase* (Paris, Payot, 1951), p. 263.

7. Tuamotus: Teuira Henry, *Ancient Tahiti: Based on material collected by J. M. Orsmond* (Bernice P. Bishop Museum Bulletin 48) (Honolulu, Published by the Museum, 1928), p. 500. (The song is given in the Polynesian section, in Vol. II.) Songs "received . . . in dreams" also among the Australian Yuin (A. W. Howitt, *op. cit.*, p. 422) and Murring (*ibid.*).

XI

1. Fiji: Basil Thomson, *The Fijians: A Study of the Decay of Custom* (London, William Heinemann, 1908), p. 315.

2. Andaman Islands: A. R. Radcliffe-Brown, *The Andaman Islanders* (Glencoe, Ill., The Free Press, 1948), p. 132.

3. Gilbert Islands: Sir Arthur Grimble, *Return to the Islands: Life and Legend in the Gilberts* (New York, William Morrow & Co., 1957; John Murray Ltd., London), p. 200. With permission of the publishers.

4. The text of the invocation, omitted here, is given in the Micronesian section, in Vol. II.

5. Gilbert Islands: Sir Arthur Grimble, *op. cit.*, pp. 204–05.

6. New Zealand: J. F. H. Wohlers, "The Mythology and Traditions of the Maori in New Zealand," *Transactions and Proceedings of the New Zealand Institute,* VII (1874), 8.

XII

1. All three poems are given in full in the African section. See pp. 50, 51, 92.

2. E. G. Burrows, for example, who collected a whole volume of magnificent poems (*Flower in My Ear*, Seattle, 1963) on the tiny atoll of Ifaluk and whose native informants gave him the names of the composers of many of them, reports absolutely nothing concerning the poets' attitude to poetry and to themselves as poets.

3. Knud Rasmussen, *The Netsilik Eskimos: Social Life and Spiritual Culture* (Report of the Fifth Thule Expedition 1921–24, Vol. VIII, No. 1–2), trans. W. E. Calvert (Copenhagen, Gyldendalske Boghandel, Nordisk Forlag, 1931), pp. 320–21.

4. *Idem, The Eagle's Gift: Alaska Eskimo Tales,* trans. Isobel Hutchinson (Garden City, N.Y., Doubleday, Doran & Co., 1932), pp. 6–7.

XIII

1. Polynesia: Samuel H. Elbert, "Chants and Love Songs of the Marquesas Islands, French Polynesia" *Journal of the Polynesian Society,* L (1941), 85.

2. Laos: G. Morechand, *loc. cit.*, p. 656.

3. India: Christoph von Fürer-Haimendorf, *The Reddis of the Bison Hills: A Study in Acculturation* (The Aboriginal Tribes of Hyderbad, Vol. II) (London, Macmillan & Co., 1945), pp. 45–46.

4. Borneo: F. W. Schmidt, in E. Dunn, "The *Mengap Bungai Taun,* the 'Chant of the Flowers of the Year,' a sacred chant used by the Sea-Dyaks on the occasion of a sacrificial feast to invoke a blessing on the fruits of the field," Part I, *Anthropos,* VII (1912), 136. (I have silently corrected some of the quainter expressions in Schmidt's Germanic English.) Part of this very long *mengap* is given in the Indonesian section.

5. New Hebrides: A. Bernard Deacon, *Malekula: A Vanishing People in the New Hebrides,* ed. Camilla H. Wedgwood (London, George Routledge & Sons, 1934), p. 506.

XIV

1. W. G. Archer, "Comment," *Man in India,* XXIII (1943), 1.
2. Nora Chadwick, (untitled paragraph), *Man in India,* XXIII (1943), 122.
3. Hugh Tracey, "Behind the Lyrics," *African Music* (Journal of the African Music Society), III (1963), No. 2, p. 17.
4. Verrier Elwin, "Comment," *Man in India,* XXII (1942), 197.

Acknowledgments

I wish to express my gratitude first of all to the Bollingen Foundation for granting me two Bollingen Fellowships, which freed me to accomplish much of the work of compilation. My friend Professor Mircea Eliade, of the University of Chicago, has generously encouraged the undertaking from the beginning and has been so good as to discuss various specific points with me. Professor Charles H. Long, of the same university, kindly supplied me with some African references.

Acknowledgments to authors and publishers for permissions to reprint are duly made in the Sources. However, there is one book which, since it is nowhere directly quoted, is not included there. I refer to George Peter Murdock's *Outline of World Cultures* (New Haven, Human Relations Area Files, 1958), without which I do not know if I could have found my way through the maze. Specifically, I have followed its geography, benefited by its synonymy, and largely adhered to its spellings.

Such a work as this cannot even be conceived, much less executed, without great libraries. I have gathered material at a number of them. But I am particularly indebted to Harvard College for extending the privileges of the Widener Library to a former frequenter of its halls, and to Harvard University for allowing me to use the Peabody Museum Library. At Widener, I am especially grateful to Mrs. A. M. Decker, at Peabody to Miss Currier, for their most generous help. The Bollingen Foundation also kindly allowed me to use material from its Paul Radin Anthropological Library.

THE FAR NORTH

⤙ 3 ⤚

Greenland

Eskimo GREENLAND

MAGIC SONG FOR HIM WHO WISHES TO LIVE

Day arises
From its sleep,
Day wakes up
With the dawning light.
Also you must arise,
Also you must awake
Together with the day which comes.

TAUNT SONG AGAINST A CLUMSY KAYAK-PADDLER

Oh, how I envy him for his singing
Every time I hear it—
What a sad failure I am, compared with him,
In the art of composing songs,
In the art of handling a kayak!

A SALMON TROUT TO HER CHILDREN

There by the promontory the kayak is coming out,
yayee . . .

The kayak-man's oars are red with blood,
yayee . . .
The white bone edges are red with blood,
yayee . . .
Oh, they have killed your father,
yayee . . .

LULLABY

It's my fat baby
I feel in my hood,
Oh, how heavy he is!
Ya ya! Ya ya!

When I turn my head
He smiles at me, my baby,
Hidden deep in my hood,
Oh, how heavy he is!
Ya ya! Ya ya!

How pretty he is when he smiles
With his two teeth, like a little walrus!
Oh, I'd rather my baby were heavy,
So long as my hood is full!

Eskimo EAST GREENLAND

A SONG FROM ARSUT[1]

The great Koonak mount yonder south, . . .
I do behold it; . . .
the great Koonak mount yonder south, . . .
I regard it; . . .

[1] In performance, each line is followed by an interjectional burden, such as: "imakayah hayah, imakayah hah—hayah!"

the shining brightness yonder south, . . .
I contemplate. . . .
Outside of Koonak . . .
it is expanding, . . .
the same that Koonak towards the seaside . . .
doth quite encompass. . . .
Behold how in the south . . .
they shift and change. . . .
Behold how yonder south . . .
they tend to beautify each other, . . .
while from the seaside the mountain-top is enveloped . . .
in sheets still changing, . . .
from the seaside enveloped, . . .
to mutual embellishment.

ANOTHER SONG FROM ARSUT

Towards the south I ever turn my gaze, . . .
for at the point of Isua land, . . .
for near the strand of Isua, . . .
yonder from the south he will appear; . . .
that way he certainly will come. . . .
Korsarak is sure to clear the point, . . .
no doubt Korsarak will be equal to it in his kayak. . . .
But if still he did not happen to come, . . .
not until the season of the halibuts, . . .
not before the halibut-fishing begins, . . .
not until the men are hauling up the halibuts.

MUTUAL NITH-SONG BETWEEN SAVDLADT AND PULANGITSISSOK[2]

Savdladt:
The south, the south, oh the south yonder. . . .
When settling on the midland coast I met Pulangitsissok, . . .

[2] "Nith-song" is Rink's term for the satirical songs of a song contest. Of them he says that "properly speaking, they represented the court of justice" (H. Rink, as cited, p. 33. See Sources).

who had grown stout and fat with eating halibut. . . .
Those people from the midland coast they don't know speaking, . . .
because they are ashamed of their speech. . . .
Stupid they are besides. . . .
Their speech is not alike, . . .
some speak like the northern, some like the southern; . . .
therefore we can't make out their talk.

Pulangitsissok:
There was a time when Savdladt wished that I should be a good kayaker, . . .
that I could take a good load on my kayak. . . .
Many years ago one day he wanted me to put a heavy load on my kayak. . . .
when Savdladt had his kayak tied to mine for fear of being capsized. . . .
Then he could carry plenty on his kayak. . . .
When I had to tow you, and you cried most pitifully, . . .
and you grew afraid, . . .
and nearly upset, . . .
and had to keep hold by help of my kayak strings.

Ammassalik Eskimo EAST GREENLAND

KAYAK SONG IN DIALOGUE[3]

First man (on the rocks):
Listen, you out there, listen!
Listen, kayak, kayak, listen!
Where, where, where is your wife?

Second man (in his kayak):
I abandoned her, I abandoned her!

First man:
But where, where, where?

[3] "The words are repeated because of the distance [between the speakers]" (W. Thalbitzer, as cited. See Sources).

Second man:
In the women's boat, in the women's boat!

First man:
But why, why, why?

Second man:
She was almost dead from cold
And she was pregnant.
She had her sealskin coat
And I gave her a piece of fat.

First man:
May the current carry her away,
May the current carry her away,
Far away,
Into the distance!

THE KAYAK PADDLER'S JOY AT THE WEATHER

When I'm out of the house in the open, I feel joy.
When I get out on the sea on hap-hazard, I feel joy.
If it is really fine weather, I feel joy.
If the sky really clears nicely, I feel joy.
May it continue thus for the good of my sealing!
May it continue thus for the good of my hunting!
May it continue thus for the good of my singing-match!
May it continue thus for the good of my drum-song!

PADDLER'S SONG ON BAD HUNTING WEATHER

I got my poem in perfect order.
On the threshold of my tongue
Its arrangement was made.
But I failed, indeed, in my hunting.

≺ 9 ≻

Canada

Iglulik Eskimo NORTHWEST TERRITORIES

MAGIC PRAYER

I arise from rest with movements swift
As the beat of a raven's wings
I arise
To meet the day
Wa–wa.
My face is turned from the dark of night
To gaze at the dawn of day,
Now whitening in the sky.

MAGIC WORDS

Earth, earth,
Great earth,
Round about on earth
There are bones, bones, bones,
Which are bleached by the great Sila*
By the weather, the sun, the air,
So that all the flesh disappears,
He–he–he.

Spirit, spirit, spirit,
And the day, the day,
Go to my limbs
Without drying them up,

* Glosses will be found at the foot of the page on which the song ends.

Without turning them to bones
Uvai, uvai, uvai.

THE SHAMAN AUA'S SONG TO CALL HIS SPIRITS

Joy, joy,
Joy, joy!
I see a little shore spirit,
A little aua,
I myself am also Aua,
The shore spirit's namesake,
Joy, joy!

SUNG BY A LITTLE GIRL TO SOOTHE A CRYING BABY

Do not weep, little one,
Your mother will fetch you,
Mother is coming for you
As soon as she has finished
Her new kamiks.

Do not weep, little one,
Your father will fetch you,
Father is coming as soon as he has made
His new harpoon head,
Do not weep, little one,
Do not weep!

OLD DANCE SONG

Aja–ja–japape!
Aja–ja–japape!
Bring out your hair ornaments!
We are but girls
Who will keep together.

Sila: the spirit that threatens mankind through the powers of nature.

Aja . . .
Aja . . .

Hard times, dearth times
Plague us every one,
Stomachs are shrunken,
Aja . . .
Aja . . .

Joy bewitches
All about us,
Skin boats rise up
Out of their moorings,
The fastenings go with them,
Earth itself hovers
Loose in the air.
Aja . . .
Aja . . .

Mark you there yonder?
There come the men
Dragging beautiful seals
To our homes.
Aja . . .
Aja . . .

Now is abundance
With us once more,
Days of feasting
To hold us together.
Aja . . .
Aja . . .

Know you the smell
Of pots on the boil?
And lumps of blubber
Slapped down by the side bench,
Aja–ja–japape!

Hu–hue! Joyfully
Greet we those
Who brought us plenty!

HUNTING SONGS

I *Walrus Hunting*

I could not sleep,
for the sea lay so smooth
near at hand.
So I rowed out,
and a walrus came up
close beside my kayak.
It was too near to throw,
and I thrust the harpoon into its side,
and the hunting float bounded over the water.
But it kept coming up again
and set its flippers angrily
like elbows on the surface of the water,
trying to tear the hunting float to pieces.
In vain it spent its utmost strength,
for the skin of an unborn lemming
was sewn inside as a guardian amulet,
and when it drew back, blowing viciously,
to gather strength again,
I rowed up and stabbed it
with my lance.
And this I sing
because the men who dwell
south and north of us here
fill their breathing with self-praise.

II *Bear Song*

It chanced that I caught sight of
one wearing the skin of a bear
out in the drifting pack ice.
ajajaija aja ajaija.
It came not threateningly.

Turning about
was the only thing that seemed to hamper it.
ajajaija aja ajaija.
It wore out its strength against me,
and I thrust my lance
into its body.
ajajaija aja ajaija.
ajajaija aja ajaija.
I call this to mind
merely because they are ever breathing self-praise,
those neighbours of ours to the south and to the north.

III *Caribou Hunting*

All unexpected I came and took by surprise
The heedless dweller of the plains,
All unexpected I came and took by surprise
The heedless dweller of the plains,
And I scattered the herd
In headlong flight.

IMPROVISATION[4]

Ajaja—aja—jaja,
The lands around my dwelling
Are more beautiful
From the day
When it is given me to see
Faces I have never seen before.
All is more beautiful,
All is more beautiful,
And life is thankfulness.
These guests of mine
Make my house grand,
Ajaja—aja—jaja.

[4] Improvised in greeting to Rasmussen by an old woman of the Iglulik.

Caribou Eskimo BARREN GROUNDS

KIBKARJUK CALLS TO MIND THE TIMES WHEN SHE WAS HER HUSBAND'S FAVOURITE WIFE AND WAS ALLOWED TO HUNT CARIBOU HERSELF

Away up inland
Iya–yi–ya . . .
Mournful it is
That I never more shall move
From my place on the bench,
For I can still feel the wish to go wandering
Away up inland . . .
Iya–ye–ya
Yai–ye–ya
Ayai–ya–ayai–ya
Iya–ya
Away up inland . . .
Iya–ye–ya
Iya–aya–aye–aya
My thoughts play ever with something that seems
Like the flesh of beasts
And yet I shall never move again
From my place on the bench,
Though I feel the old wish to go out and away
Up inland
Iya–ye–ya
Iya–aiya aiye aiya.
It is I who am here–
Never again to go out with the rest–
And yet it was I that shot
Both the old bull with the wide-spreading antlers
And the young bull, as well,
Once on a time
When the twilight of the heavens
Lay over the land.

Away up inland
Iya—ye—ya
Iya—ye—ya
Away up inland
Aya—aiya—aiye
All this I cannot forget,
All this I think of . . .
From that hunting, when I added to my gains
A caribou cow with its calf,
While the earth
Turned white with snow.
Away up inland
Ya—iya—ye—ya
Ayai—ya ayi—ya
Iya—ya iya
Away up inland.

AKJARTOQ'S SONG OF THE OLDEN DAYS

I call forth the song . . .
I draw a deep breath . . .
My breast breathes heavily
As I call forth the song.

I hear of distant villages
And their miserable catch
And draw a deep breath . . .
As I call forth the song
—From above—
Aya—haye
Ayia.
I forget altogether
The heavy breathing of my breast
When I call to mind the olden days
When I had strength enough
To cut up mighty caribou bulls.
I call forth the song
Ayaya—aya

I call forth the song.
I call forth the song
Aya—aya.
Three great caribou bulls I could cut up
—And have the clean meat all laid out to dry—
While the sun was on his upward way
Across the sky.
A song I call forth
As I draw a deep breath
Aya aye.

Netsilik Eskimo NORTHWEST TERRITORIES

IT IS DIFFICULT TO PUT WORDS TOGETHER

Avayaja
I recognize what I want to put into words,
But it does not become well arranged,
It does not become worth listening to;
Something that is well arranged, avayaja!
Something well worth hearing hastily to put *that* together
That is often difficult.
An awkward one—may be so—I have put together
Avayaja!

UVLUNUAQ'S SONG[5]

Eya—eya.
I recognize
A bit of song
And take it to me like a fellow being.
Eyaya—eya.

[5] "A year or two before, [her] son had murdered a hunting companion in a fit of temper, and now he lived an outlaw in the mountains. . . . And so his mother had made [this] song through sorrow over her son's fate" (K. Rasmussen, as cited, p. 16. See Sources).

Should I be ashamed
At the child I once carried
With me in my back-pouch,
Because I heard of his flight
From the haunts of man?
Eyaya—eya.

Truly I was ashamed:
But only because he had not
A mother who was blameless as the blue sky,
Wise and without foolishness.
Now people's talk will educate him
And gossip complete the education.
I should perhaps be ashamed,
I, who bore a child
Who was not to be my refuge;
Instead, I envy those
Who have a crowd of friends behind them,
Waving on the ice,
When after festive leave-taking they journey out.
Oh, I remember a winter,
We left the island "The squinting eye":
The weather was mild,
And the feet sank, gently creaking, into the thawing snow.
I was then as a tame animal among men;
But when the message came
Of the killing and the flight,
Then I staggered,
Like one unable to get a foothold.

ORPINGALIK'S SONG: MY BREATH

[This is what I call this song, for it is just as necessary to me to sing it as it is to breathe.]

I will sing a song,
A song that is strong.
Unaya—unaya.

Sick I have lain since autumn,
Helpless I lay, as were I
My own child.

Sad, I would that my woman
Were away to another house
To a husband
Who can be her refuge,
Safe and secure as winter ice.
Unaya—unaya.

Sad, I would that my woman
Were gone to a better protector
Now that I lack strength
To rise from my couch.
Unaya—unaya.

Dost thou know thyself?
So little thou knowest of thyself.
Feeble I lie here on my bench
And only my memories are strong!
Unaya—unaya.

Beasts of the hunt! Big game!
Oft the fleeting quarry I chased!
Let me live it again and remember,
Forgetting my weakness.
Unaya—unaya.

Let me recall the great white
Polar bear,
High up its back body,
Snout in the snow, it came!
He really believed
He alone was a male
And ran towards me.
Unaya—unaya.

It threw me down
Again and again,

Then breathless departed
And lay down to rest,
Hid by a mound on a floe.
Heedless it was, and unknowing
That I was to be its fate.
Deluding itself
That he alone was a male,
And unthinking
That I too was a man!
          Unaya—unaya.

I shall ne'er forget that great blubber-beast,
A fjord seal,
I killed from the sea ice
Early, long before dawn,
While my companions at home
Still lay like the dead,
Faint from failure and hunger,
Sleeping.
With meat and with swelling blubber
I returned so quickly
As if merely running over ice
To view a breathing hole there.
And yet it was
An old and cunning male seal.
But before he had even breathed
My harpoon head was fast
Mortally deep in his neck.

That was the manner of me then.
Now I lie feeble on my bench
Unable even a little blubber to get
For my wife's stone lamp.
The time, the time will not pass,
While dawn gives place to dawn
And spring is upon the village.
          Unaya—unaya.

But how long shall I lie here?
How long?

And how long must she go a-begging
For fat for her lamp,
For skins for clothing
And meat for a meal?
A helpless thing—a defenceless woman.
Unaya—unaya.

Knowest thou thyself?
So little thou knowest of thyself!
While dawn gives place to dawn,
And spring is upon the village.
Unaya—unaya.

Copper Eskimo VICTORIA ISLAND; KENT PENINSULA; BERNARD HARBOUR

RELIGIOUS HYMN TO BE SUNG WEARING A HEAD DECORATION OF THE SKIN OF THE GREAT NORTHERN DIVER

Here I stand,
Humble, with outstretched arms,
For the spirit of the air
Let glorious food sink down to me.

Here I stand
Surrounded with great joy.
For a caribou bull with high antlers
Recklessly exposed his flanks to me.
—Oh, how I had to crouch
In my hide.

But, scarcely had I
Hastily glimpsed his flanks
When my arrow pierced them
From shoulder to shoulder.

And then, when you, lovely caribou
Let the water go
Out over the ground
As you tumbled down,
Well, then I felt surrounded with great joy.

Here I stand,
Humble, with outstretched arms,
For the spirit of the air
Lets glorious food sink down to me.

Here I stand
Surrounded with great joy.
And this time it was an old dog seal
Starting to blow through his breathing hole.
I, little man,
Stood upright above it.
And with excitement became
Quite long of body,
Until I drove my harpoon in the beast
And tethered it to
My harpoon line!

DEAD MAN'S SONG[6]

I am filled with joy
When the day peacefully dawns
Up over the heavens,
ayi, yai ya.

I am filled with joy
When the sun slowly rises
Up over the heavens,
ayi, yai ya.

But else I choke with fear
At greedy maggot throngs;

[6] Original title: "Aijuk, after his death, his song, dreamt by Paulinaq."

They eat their way in
At the hollow of my collarbone
And in my eyes,
ayi, yai ya.

Here I lie, recollecting
How stifled with fear I was
When they buried me
In a snow hut out on the lake.
ayi, yai ya.

A block of snow was pushed to,
Incomprehensible it was
How my soul should make its way
And fly to the game land up there,
ayi, yai ya.

That door-block worried me,
And ever greater grew my fear
When the fresh-water ice split in the cold,
And the frost-crack thunderously grew
Up over the heavens,
ayi, yai ya.

Glorious was life
In winter.
But did winter bring me joy?
No! Ever was I so anxious
For sole-skins and skins for kamiks,
Would there be enough for us all?
Yes, I was ever anxious,
ayi, ya ya.

Glorious was life
In summer.
But did summer bring me joy?
No! Ever was I so anxious
For skins and rugs for the platform,
Yes, I was ever anxious,
ayi, yai ya.

Glorious was life
When standing at one's fishing hole
On the ice.
But did standing at the fishing hole bring me joy?
No! Ever was I so anxious
For my tiny little fish-hook
If it should not get a bite,
        ayi, yai ya.

Glorious was life
When dancing in the dance-house,
But did dancing in the dance-house bring me joy?
No! Ever was I so anxious,
That I could not recall
The song I was to sing.
Yes, I was ever anxious,
        ayi, yai ya.

Glorious was life . . .
Now I am filled with joy
For every time a dawn
Makes white the sky of night,
For every time the sun goes up
Over the heavens.
        Ayi, yai, ya.

MEN'S IMPOTENCE

Perhaps—well
It may not matter!
Perhaps—well.
I sing merely of him,
"The boiling one,"
Who sat, fearful, his mouth fast closed,
Among women.

Perhaps—well
It may not matter!

Perhaps—well.
I sing merely of him,
"Caribou Stomach,"
Who sat, fearful, his mouth fast closed,
Among women.
His two eyes ill-boding,
Bent like a horn
To be cut into leisters!

Perhaps—well
It may not matter!
Perhaps—well.
I sing merely of him,
"The Axe,"
Who sat, fearful, his mouth fast closed,
Far, far away from man,
In solitude.

Perhaps—well
It may not matter!
Perhaps—well.
My tongue merely joins words
Into a little song.
A little mouth,
Curling downwards at the corners,
Like a bent twig
For a kayak rib.

THE SONG OF ULIPSHIALUK'S WIFE

There is fear in
Turning the mind away,
Longing for loneliness,
Amid the joyous
People's throng.
    Iyaiya—ya—ya.

There is joy in
Feeling the warmth
Come to the great world
And seeing the sun
Follow its old footprints
In the summer night.
Iyaiya—ya—ya.

There is fear in
Feeling the cold
Come to the great world
And seeing the moon
—Now new moon, now full moon—
Follow its old footprints
In the winter night.
Iyaiya—ya—ya.

Where does it all go?
I long for the east!
And yet, no more shall I see my uncle,
To whom my mind would fain be revealed.

HUNGER

Fear was about me . . .
In my little house
Remaining was intolerable.

Hungry and starving
I staggered in over land
For ever stumbling forwards.

At "the little musk-ox lake"
The trout made fun of me.
I got no bite.

Onward then I toiled
To "the young man's broad"—
I had caught salmon there once.

I did so wish to see
Swimming caribou or fish in a lake.
That joy was my one wish.

My thought ended in nothing.
It was like a line
That all runs out.

Would I ever, I wondered,
Have firm ground to stand on?
Magic words I mumbled all the way.

SONG OF CARIBOU, MUSK OXEN, WOMEN, AND MEN WHO WOULD BE MANLY

Glorious it is to see
The caribou flocking down from the forests
And beginning
Their wandering to the north.
Timidly they watch
For the pitfalls of man.
Glorious it is to see
The great herds from the forests
Spreading out over plains of white,
Glorious to see.
Yayai—ya—yiya.

Glorious it is to see
Early summer's short-haired caribou
Beginning to wander.
Glorious to see them trot
To and fro
Across the promontories,
Seeking a crossing place.
Yai—ya—yiya.

Glorious it is
To see the great musk oxen
Gathering in herds.

The little dogs they watch for
When they gather in herds.
Glorious to see.
        Yai—ya—yiya.

Glorious it is
To see young women
Gathering in little groups
And paying visits in the houses—
Then all at once the men
Do so want to be manly.
While the girls simply
Think of some little lie.
        Yayai—ya—yiya.

Glorious it is
To see long-haired winter caribou
Returning to the forests.
Fearfully they watch
For the little people.
While the herd follows the ebb-mark of the sea
With a storm of clattering hooves.
Glorious it is
When wandering time is come.
        Yayai—ya—yiya.

SONG

And I thought over again
My small adventures
As with a shore-wind I drifted out
In my kayak
And thought I was in danger.

My fears,
Those small ones
That I thought so big
For all the vital things
I had to get and to reach.

And yet, there is only
One great thing,
The only thing:
To live to see in huts and on journeys
The great day that dawns
And the light that fills the world.

DANCE SONGS

I

My song, that one, it begins to want to come out,
It begins to want to go out to my companions, there being a request for singing,
There being a request for dancing.
My song, that one, it only, it also comes back, that one, my companions
Asking to be made happy.

II

Let me recall them to mind,
The lands that I have reached,
Game as I do not even wish to find.

Kugyuaq river and Pingoq hill
And Ukpilik river and Kissigaq,
Usungnaqsiorvik and Isoqtoq's muddy water,
Maqiqsarvik and Mangaqtorvik.

III

Let me go and dance beside him,
Let me go and dance beside him.

Let me go and dance beside him,
Let me go and dance beside him.
Of whatever place he is,
That man, let me go and dance beside him.
He from Puivliq,
That man, let me go and dance beside him.

Whether he will shoot—whether he will stab me or not,
Since I cannot help it, let me go and dance beside him.

Let me go and dance beside him,
Let me go and dance beside him.
He from Kanghiryuaq,
That man, let me go and dance beside him.
Whether he will stab me or not,
Since I cannot help it, let me go and dance beside him.

IV

Let me sing in opposition to him, let me sing in opposition to him,
Let me sing in opposition to him, let me sing in opposition to him.

The ice down here though I walked on it,
The ice down here though I walked on it,
It did not seem like real ice.

The land down here though I walked on it,
The land down here though I walked on it,
It did not seem like real land.

The lake down here though I visited it,
The lake down here though I visited it,
It did not seem like a real lake.

The ptarmigan down here though I approached it,
The ptarmigan down here though I approached it,
It did not seem like a real ptarmigan.

The woman down here though I visited her,
The woman down here though I visited her,
She did not seem like a real woman.

Mackenzie Eskimo MACKENZIE

SONG FROM A STORY

The long-tailed duck:
My husband it is—jai, jai, jai,
My husband I weep for
because he was eager to go hunting
because he was good at bringing me meat
he, the short-necked one
he, the short-legged one!

The owl:
Me, me, take me for your husband!

The long-tailed duck:
Who would want you for a husband,
you with the thick eyebrows,
you with eyes full of sleep—
if you got me for a wife and I dived down
what would you do?

Alaska

Nunivak Island Eskimo

SONG COMPOSED AT THE BEGINNING OF AN AUTUMN FESTIVAL IN HONOR OF THE RIBBON SEAL

The autumn comes blowing;
Oh, I tremble, I tremble at the harsh northern wind
That strikes me pitilessly in its might
While the waves threaten to upset my kayak.
The autumn comes blowing;
Ah, I tremble, I tremble lest the storm and the seas
Send me down to the clammy ooze in the depths of the waters.
Rarely I see the water calm,
The waves cast me about;
And I tremble, I tremble at the thought of the hour
When the gulls shall hack at my dead body.

Upper Koyukuk Eskimo WISEMAN, ALASKA

SONG FOR A CHRISTMAS CELEBRATION[7]

I am lonesome,
I want to feel better.

[7] Composed to the tune of an old dance song.

I want to warm myself,
So I go to Wiseman.
I go.
All of us go.
All of us sing.
My arms aren't washed.
Take my arm in the dance.
Shake my hand in the dance.
Christmas comes pretty soon.
Roadhouse man,
Busy all the time.
Everyone drinks coffee.

NOTE Songs of the Siberian Eskimo will be found in Volume II.

Europe

Lapp LAPLAND

HYMN TO THE SOUTHERN MOUNTAINS

The mountain range in the south
is a range from ancient times to the south of Varanger Fjord.
There the Reindeer Lapps
used to gather their reindeer.
There too they used
to slaughter their reindeer.

SONGS

I *The Wolf*

The wolf, yes the wolf,
the wolf, yes the wolf:
"Ho ho-o-o."

Through nine wooded valleys
at twilight,
he runs, runs, runs.

II *The Reindeer Herd*

The reindeer herd on the Varanger Peninsula
Runs over cliffs and stony uplands.
The fine beasts swing their heels
About the tops of cliffs.

The great white reindeer shines
On the top of Mount Emitoaivve
Near Annijokka.
Proudly he carries his great antlers.

COMPLAINT

With tears I mourn for my reindeer-cows on the mountains,
In vain I look for them, here in this cold house.

No longer is it given me
To run up hill and down,
Nor to see the white-spotted reindeer.

How can I thrive here
Where I no longer milk my reindeer
But must live all my days on the milk of long-tailed cows?

If this is my fate, I must bear it
And run no more after reindeer in the mountains.

AFRICA

Western Africa and the Congo

Bambara FORMER FRENCH SUDAN

SONG AFTER DEFEAT[1]

Old woman:
Diossé has lost men for nothing.
Where did you leave your men?
Where did you leave your fighting men?

Spirit of Diossé:
Let me alone. I am trying to find my way.
Go ask the Whites,
Go ask their soldiers,
And look at the bank of the dry watercourse.

Old woman:
Diossé did not run away, but he lost his fame.
Samba ran away. Whites are brave men.
Samba was afraid,
Samba of Massantola is not a man.

Girls:
Samba and Diossé unleashed war for no reason,
They took our elder brothers to be killed for nothing.

[1] Composed in 1915. The chiefs Samba and Diossé had revolted against the French and were defeated on the bank of a dry watercourse. Diossé escaped to a stronghold with some followers, then blew it up, killing himself and them. The song was composed by an old woman whose only son was killed in the revolt.

Old woman:
Now I have no son; now I shall have nothing to eat,
I shall have no clothes . . . and I am old.

Girls:
Old woman, don't cry.
We will marry, we will feed you.
Don't cry, we will take good care of you.
Forget Samba and Diossé, they are criminals.

Dogon FORMER FRENCH SUDAN

SONG ENCOURAGING A MASKER DANCING THE PART OF A GIRL

Hail, girl
The drums are your drums
May Amma protect your body, your legs
Agile legs, agile arms, come to the drums
Pretty head
All have their eyes on you
You have good milk
All have their eyes on you
You have beautiful sandals
A calabash in your hand
A pretty calabash
All the men have their eyes on you
All the women have their eyes on you
All the children have their eyes on you
All your lovers have their eyes on you
You have beautiful flesh
You have beautiful legs
You have beautiful arms
All of you is beautiful
You have done beautiful things, you have done beautiful things, girl, you have done beautiful things

The voice of the drums is in your ears
Come, young men
To the girl, pay over cowries
It is well
She is a beautiful girl

Peul (Fulani) MACINA, FORMER FRENCH SUDAN; UPPER VOLTA

HERDER'S SONG

Greeting, joyous night! You appear before the sun dawns, shines, rises. You dim, then put out his light.

So long as you continue, the calves remain hobbled, the youngest of them stay lying down.

Greeting, joyous night! You are a chance to set the drums beating, the thighs of the Negroes throbbing.

You are my favorite time—the time when I like to put my lance and my herder's crook across my shoulder, bend my head down a little to keep them from falling off, grasp and twang the cords of my guitar.

I make my way through narrow paths, I trot along to the night pastures. Greeting, joyous night! I pass through you to the high brush, there to sing a beautiful song for you.

I spread my cloak on a termites' nest. My oxen, which have gone through the hedge, will scatter through the high grass. There are neither flies nor millet spikes nor swarms of stinging insects.

The noise of the village is lost in the distance; now is the time when it is pleasant to hear the guitar.

The moon has not appeared. Its light has not fired the sky nor put out the beauty of the stars.

My oxen crowd together and crop grass. Above me the stars glitter in the darkness. They shoot through space, streak the sky, brighten it.

He who pastures his cattle by night will surely fatten them.

Only my wish to fatten mine could make me leave my sleep beside Diko with her light skin and her long, smooth hair. She exhales a pleasant odor and never stinks of fish. She does not smell of sweat like the women who gather dead wood. Her head has not the bald spot that comes from carrying faggots.

Her teeth are white, her eyes like the eyes of a fawn, the first-born of a gazelle, crammed with milk from an udder that gives it for the first time.

Neither her heel nor the palm of her hand is rough; no, they are soft to the touch, like liver or even the glossy down of silk cotton.

My ox who is leading the rest has bellowed. He suddenly comes out from the herd and stops, raises his tail and lowers his head. He springs and strikes the ground with his four legs, goes forward, then back, looks right and left, sidles this way and that.

I soothe him with the word *dial* and then he digs into the ground with his hoofs.

Meanwhile my little guitar sends out a thread of sounds, which the night echo returns. A pleasant breeze rumples my hair.

No human being is beside me. Before me, I see the dome of a baobab tree, it makes me think of a crouching genie.

He whose heart is easily startled does not pasture at night, for fear of receiving visits. . . .

But he who is not afraid of visits obtains women's favors—they flirt with him, sing for him, give him welcoming presents. For him the guitars will play. The Peul women will sing his praises and those of the damp-nosed beasts who sway as they walk and, rearing up, set a fat, well-fleshed hump swinging.

WAR SONG[2]

At Djibo there is a pool:
He who brings good with him may quench his thirst and bathe there,
he who brings evil shall drink his fill of blood.

It has been surrounded with stallions:
God watches from dark to dawn and lances watch from dawn to dark.
Its banks will be covered with entrails, no longer with washed women's
clothes.

[2] "Refers to a foray into the Djilgodi made by the Mossi emperor Boukari Kouto about 1890, in the course of which he was turned back by the Peul near the pool at Djibo" (M. Delafosse, as cited. See Sources).

Around the pool, hedges of spiny mimosa have been set;
Traitorous lances are in the pool, there are arms in the pool;
It will be planted with skulls, no longer with water lilies.

Boukari Kouto has surrounded us,
He has surrounded us with thousands of stallions, he has stationed canoes in a circle, filled with rifles. . . .
Let every man who has come here in anger depart!
Let him leave the birds of the pool in the pool!
Kyende-kyende, great son of the Mossi!
It is not *kyende-kyende* that we want, it is *milla-milla* that makes us glad.

LOVE SONG

The sky darkens with the deep blue of Guinea-cloth,
The mist drops a dew of fresh milk;
The hyena roars, the Elder of the Brush answers. . . .
It is the time when it is good to be with a light-skinned lover, whispering.

Mossi UPPER VOLTA

DRUM SONG

The blindman's stew is a black stew, a stew of tears.

Kyende-kyende: Mossi formula of greeting. *Milla-milla:* Peul formula of greeting.
Elder of the Brush: the lion.

Former French Guinea or Sudan*

SONG TO THE XYLOPHONE AT A FIGHTING MAN'S FUNERAL

The grievousness of death will not hold death off. Woe if the dead man has no sons; well if he has, to continue his brave deeds.

Ibo NIGERIA

GIRLS' SONG[3]

Ants lament son,
Lizards lament child.
To whom it happens, lament.

Hausa NIGER TERRITORY; NIGERIA

DEVICES

I *For a Hunter*

It is not for the meat
But for the sport of it that we hunt.
If you think we are out for meat,
We will go back!
Meat is something you find at home or at the butcher's.

* People not identified.
3 Literal translation.

II *For a Prostitute*

A little pool without water!
Yet men drown in it.

"PRAISE-SONG" BY A WOMAN POSSESSED BY A SPIRIT

We are the end,
We are meningitis,
We are all the other illnesses,
We own the bit of earth behind the hut,
Laughing one, there's no cure for this illness,
Reveller, there is no rejoicing without us.

Tukolor SENEGAL

SONG

Bandya is on the banks of the Yame,
Bandyagara is on the banks of the Yame,
Sintyu is on the banks of the Yame,
Sintyarma is on the banks of the Yame.

Bandya is a pleasanter place than Kayes,
Bandyagara is a pleasanter place than Kayes,
Sintyu is a pleasanter place than Kayes,
Sintyarma is a pleasanter place than Kayes.

Clapping hands pleases me,
Dyagu's laugh pleases me,
The laugh of Kadidyata, Baba's daughter,
And the smile of Fatimata, daughter of Samba.

As for you, Fadima, daughter of Tyamel Allah,
All your father's horses, many as they are,
All your father's camels, many as they are,
Didn't prevent you from carrying a bastard on your back!

GIRLS' SONG

Between Gesene and Nema
I met thirty fighting men.
I chose you, you who were riding Sileme.
Sileme is a white horse.
The Soninkes call him Sileme,
The Peuls call him Molubara.
It's you, young Dyallo, son of Dyeri,
My ruddy-faced lover, Tyillo's young brother.

Mende SIERRA LEONE

PROLOGUE TO A YOMEH BALLAD[4]

I know the Yomeh as Europeans know the English book—they make lorries that can fly in the sky.

I know the Yomeh as the prostitute knows the night. She walks about without stumbling against anybody; she never steps on a snake, and no one recognizes her.

I know the Yomeh as the alligator knows the river. It has a nose, but it breathes under water. I know the Yomeh as the guinea fowl knows the bush. It has a check garment and yet it stays in the bush.

There are some who say there are no riches in the bush. Look at an ant hill: it has a helmet that shelters it from the rain. Look at the beetle: he has a coat that does not go round him and yet has three buttons. A bird lives away there in the bush, and it has a wooden house—who is the carpenter? The bush cow wears boots like those of a soldier. The baboon has a black coat like a policeman, and the king-

[4] Sung by a professional musician in the service of a chief. Free translation.

fisher has a silk gown. Why, then, do people say there are no riches in the bush?

I know the Yomeh as the snail knows the bush. It goes "on patrol" with its house on its back. I know the Yomeh as the deer knows the bush: it has a pattern gown which does not get torn even going through thorns.

Some people say there is no civilization in the bush. But there is a priest [crow] who spends his time on the palm trees.

Now listen, all of you, to me, and let me tell you about . . .

HOME-SICK SONGS

I

Let us return to Njama.
Oh! let us return to Njama.
O [friend] Yumbe come.
Oh! let us return to Njama.

II

Oh, they are delightful,
Bawuiya and Bandajuma.
You were at Bawuiya very long ago.

Temne SIERRA LEONE

LOVE SONG

If I beat up cassava leaf
And mix it with green-green
And eat my fill of it,
And then take my drum
And beat it with a will,
Ah! then my mind goes back
And I remember your caresses

Ah! How sweet it was—
In that little room—
Where we first told our love!
Breathe it to no one!

Baule IVORY COAST

SONG OF A WANDERING STORY-TELLER

In times past lute and drum
were played together for dancing.
Now only I can play the lute to my story-telling.
I am a young man,
my lute is beautiful,
because of my lute I have planted no crop,
because of my lute I have nothing to eat.

SONG OF A WOMAN WHOSE HUSBAND HAD GONE TO THE COAST TO EARN MONEY

Whenever I go out of the village
and see a stone
or a tree in the distance,
I think:
It is my husband.

WOMEN'S SONG

O handsome Sokoti, O handsome Sokoti, O pretty youth,
Take me and let us go, yes, O master, take me and let us go!
Take me and let us go to the ford across the Agbagnian,
Take me and let us go quietly as far as the ford across the Agbagnian.
O Sokoti, O pretty youth,
O master, take me and let us go, take me and let us go as far as the ford across the Agbagnian.

Akan GHANA

DIRGES

I

Duodu,
The king's servant,
Who was killed through his valor.
See! the rain washes his house away.
Duodu, I am grieved by your death.
Alas! it has always been so:
Once dead, you are useless,
And all is decay.

II *On a ruler*

Yes, Adummaa Duro,
Osekyeredu, the fighter,
Slaughterer of sheep on the Adowa drums,
Alas, alas!
To be in the hands of Death is
To be in the hands of someone indeed.

Ashanti GHANA

ADDRESS ON THE TALKING DRUMS TO ASASE YAA, THE SPIRIT OF EARTH

Earth, condolences,
Earth, condolences,

Earth and dust,
The Dependable One,
I lean upon you.
Earth, when I am about to die,
I lean upon you.
Earth, while I am alive,
I depend upon you.
Earth, while I am alive,
I depend upon you.
Earth that receives dead bodies,
The Creator's drummer says,
From wherever he went,
He has roused himself,
He has roused himself.

SONG TO INSTRUMENTS[5]

First woman:
My husband likes me too much,
He is good to me,
But I cannot like him,
So I must listen to my lover.

First man:
My wife does not please me,
I tire of her now;
So I will please myself with another
Who is very handsome.

Second woman:
My lover tempts me with sweet words,
But my husband always does me good,
So I must like him well
And I must be true to him.

[5] Collected before 1819. The collector comments: "I never heard this sung without its recalling Horace's beautiful little dialogue ode . . . 'Donec gratus eram tibi' " (T. Bowditch, as cited. See Sources).

Second man:
Girl, you surpass my wife in handsomeness,
But I cannot call you wife;
A wife pleases her husband only,
But when I leave you, you go to others.

Ewe TOGO

THE DEAD MAN ASKS FOR A SONG[6]

Sing me a song of the dead,
That I may take it with me.
A song of the underworld sing me,
That I may take it with me
And travel to the underworld.

The underworld says,
Says the underworld:
It is beautiful in the grave.
Beautiful is the underworld
But there is no wine to drink there.
So I will take it with me
And travel to the underworld
And travel to the underworld.

Sing me a song of the dead,
That I may take it with me.
A song of the underworld sing me,
That I may take it with me
And travel to the underworld.

[6] "After the corpse is buried, the mourners shoot and sing and drum and make merry over the dead man. He takes all this with him on his journey to the underworld. Here is one such song" (J. Spieth, as cited. See Sources).

DEATH SONG[7]

I have sung until I wept bitterly.
The world is immeasurably vast.
I say: on my death day
Let the ferryman only bring his boat to shore!
Then I will wave my left hand to the living:
I am already on the way!
Listen! I am already on the way!
Then the boat of death comes rocking nearer,
I am already on the way,
I who have sung my people so many songs.

DIRGE

He died; no song, no drumming, no sport, he is a poor man and his clan is poor.
One dies in fire, one dies in water. So do we all belong to death and go to our place.
I was at home alone, and I heard a bitter wailing; I went and found my brother dead and drummed in grief.

SONG

The beautiful playground goes quickly to ruin,
The beautiful game field goes quickly to ruin,
Dense jungle soon becomes grass steppe, grass steppe,
Our beautiful town returns to open plain,
Our beautiful town returns to open plain.

Let the grave-diggers not bury me,
Let one bury my feet and leave my body free;
So that my kindred may come and see my face,
Come and look in my face.

[7] By the poetess Dzenavo.

The drum does not beat to joy,
The drum does not beat to joy,
"Misery, misery," beats the drum,
Only to misery the drum beats.

If Death were game, a hunter would kill him, and I would be given a thigh,
Would kill him, and I would be given a thigh,
A hunter would kill him, and I would be given an arm,
The slayer of my dear father,
A hunter would kill him, and I would be given an arm,
The slayer of my dear mother,
A hunter would kill him, and I would be given an arm,
The slayer of my dear brother.
Could not King Death be a game animal, so that a hunter would kill him and I be given a thigh?

SONG TO THE *SIKELI* DRUM

The bad woman struts at the door. But we are not led astray, even though the bad woman struts at our door. Our natural gifts make our true happiness. Is there anything better than a [gifted] poet? Oh, we are not led astray. I will not let my drum be played before a whore.

SONG OF THE TELEGRAPH[8]

The European's hand goes into the book when the telegraph calls him, the telegraph calls him.

Be given a thigh: damage caused by an ox is compensated by the gift of a thigh when the animal is slaughtered.

The bad woman: a whore who comes knocking at men's doors at night. *We are not led astray:* literally, "We come from Alada."

Goes into the book: i.e., to write.

[8] Composed and sung by Chlogo from Anecho.

GIRLS' SONG DERIDING WHITE MEN'S EWE SERVING BOYS

White man's serving boy! O you Red-belt, ayo!
White man's serving boy! O you Red-belt!
White man's serving boy! O you Red-belt, ayo!
White man's serving boy! O you Red-belt!
The white man will go back home!
The white man will go back home, go back home!
White man's serving boy! O you Red-belt, *ayo*!

Dahomean (Fon) DAHOMEY

TO THE SUN-GOD

Softly, softly, Lisa—o,
Softly, O Sun-God,
Do not ravish the world.
Ram pawing the earth with hooves of flame,
Ram pounding the earth with horns of fire,
Do not ravish the world,
Do not destroy us.

FOR THE EARTH GOD

Thy need is great,
And great our need to sing,
For days of trouble are upon us.

The bullock of Abomey
Says to him of Cana,
It is the day of trouble;

The carrier of grain
Says to the bearer of salt,
Thy load is heavy, brother,
And this the day for carrying;
The bearer of the dead
Says to the carrier of ladders,
It is the day for carrying loads,
It is the day of trouble.

TO THE ENVIOUS

The Giver of Life
Placed the Sun in great space,
And said: No hand
Shall be the length to reach it;
Though clouds disappear,
And we become a mountain,
Immovable and high,
It will not be that the hand obeys not.

The Giver of Life
Placed the Sun in the heavens,
And said: No eye
Shall have the cunning to see within;
Though clouds disappear,
And we become a mountain,
Immovable and high,
It will not be that the eye obeys not.

SONG FOR THE DEAD

Leader:
Do not weep,
Nothing stays death,
Nor the day of its coming.

Chorus:
Death troubles us—o!
Death troubles us.

As the flies fret our backs,
Returning, and returning,
So Death troubles us—o!
Death troubles us.

As the pigeons alight
On a housetop,
And dance, and dance,
So Death dances—o!
Death dances.

Ai-yo!
Ai-yo-o!

SONG IN PRAISE OF BOW AND ARROW

The sword does not run the elephant through,
Fire does not devour the King's house,
The wind does not pass through stones, through stones;
A reed cartridge-pouch drops:
The bow sends an arrow,
The game falls in a heap;
It is like a pearl on a manure pile.

Few men try to grasp iron red-hot from the fire;
The earth does not bring forth the crocodiles of the lagoon;
Until a beast is dead, it has not done dying;
Cities that are too great perish;
A horse does not travel in a reed boat:
The wind does not pass through stones, through stones;
A reed cartridge-pouch drops;
An arrow . . . and the game falls in a heap;
It is like a pearl on a manure pile.

THE SONG OF KING AGONGOLO[9]

If I had money
I should buy drinks to drink,
One for seventy-five centimes.
Son of Xolo, drink.
Let all of you hear-O. . . .
To have a pleasant thought,
Yes, yes, yes.
He who has money
And hoards all for the future
Of him I do not think well.
Remember that Gbeko, too, was destroyed.
In the coffers of the houses of the dead are many drinks.
Had he for whom this was bought drunk of it?
No, no, no, no.
Seller of drinks, give me drinks to drink
For today my head is turning.
I see it: There is no pleasure for the dead.
I say: What you eat in this world, the pleasure of it goes with you.
I say: The wives you had, the pleasure you had of them goes with you.
I say: The meat you ate, the pleasure of it goes with you.
I say: The drinks you drank, the pleasure of them goes with you.
I say: The pipe you smoked, the pleasure of it goes with you.

Duala CAMEROON

MOCK LAMENT OVER A DEAD SLAVE

We have come to mourn for Mbangwe.
Mbangwe did not want to die.
The noble family of Nanjo a Mbela already lies among the ghosts—
Only the slave does not want to die.

Gbeko: a kingdom that was thought to be invincible.

[9] "Agongolo said that after every burial this song is to be sung" (M. Herskovits, as cited. See Sources). The first seven lines are repeated.

The masters of the land lie among the ghosts—
Only Mbangwe does not want to die.

Ewondo CAMEROON

DRUM SONG IN THREE PARTS FROM THE FUNERAL CEREMONY FOR A HERO[10]

1

The dead man:
I began with convulsive shakings
And I ended by turning cold all over.
Get up, get up,
For pity's sake, dear brothers,
Come and bid me farewell—
I am about to walk away
With the gait of a man in distress.
I am about to walk away
All alone, like an old, solitary boar.
I am about to lose all my dignity
And mingle with fruit-guzzling chimpanzees.
I am already a beast that men scorn.
Dear brothers, for pity's sake,
Get up, come and bid me farewell.
You will never see me again.
In daily life, when something attacks you in the morning,
That very evening you take your revenge.
But this thing—death—is for everyone.
The only right you have is to wait for it in your turn.
It is dreadful, dear brothers.
And now I begin to walk away
With the gait of a man in distress.

[10] "The drum song . . . commemorating . . . the exploits of a hero is in three parts. In the first the dead man bewails his undeserved fate; in the second the mourners console him by telling him that his present state allows him to explore places that he could not see before; in the third they make him responsible for his own situation" (T. Tsala, as cited, p. 106. See Sources).

2

Mourners:
Climb the steepest heights,
Climb the steepest heights!

3

Mourners:
When you were told
"Avoid this"—did you avoid it?
"Drink this medicine"—did you drink it?
Now here you are with an eye like the eyeball of a kid.

Fang CAMEROON AND CONGO

SONG AT A DEATHBED

Solo:
The son has gone to the plantations
To see if the fruits are fully ripe.

Response:
The fruits have ripened.
The spirits are abroad.
The time has come.
Night begins.
The prisoner is free.

Solo:
The son has gone . . .

Response:
The prisoner is freed.
He crosses to the opposite shore.
His eyes stare ahead.
He no longer looks back.

Solo:
The son has gone . . .

Response:
He can no longer look behind him.

Solo:
The shade has brushed past the wall of the house.
I see a spark that passes,

Response:
Like a firefly flitting,
Circling the palmtrees.

SONG OF THE LAST MOMENTS[11]

O Father, *yi, yi,* why, O Father, are you forsaking your hearth?
A man has killed you, O Father.
You [men who are present] shall avenge his death. . . .
Now your shade will cross to the opposite shore.
O Father, why are you forsaking your hearth!
The sky has brightened, the eyes have darkened.
The water has fallen from the tree drop by drop, the rat has left its hole.

Look you, it is our Father's house.
Pick the funeral herbs.
[Sprinkle] to the right, [sprinkle] to the left. . . .
Now a man sees things invisible.

The fruits: that is, his father's life.

The opposite shore: the dead must cross a river. *The sky has brightened:* life is a flame that shines in the eye; at death the eye grows dull, and the flame of life, which is immortal, remains in the air. *The water . . . the rat:* images for the departed life.

[11] Women's dirge, from "The Legend of Separation."

FIRE SONG AT AN EXPIATION CEREMONY

Fire, fire, fire of the hearth below, fire of the hearth above,
Light that shines in the moon, light that shines in the sun,
Star that sparkles at night, star that cleaves the light,
Spirit of the thunder, shining eye of the storm,
Fire of the sun that gives us light,
I summon you for expiation, fire, fire,
Fire that passes, and everything dies behind your track,
Fire that passes, and everything lives behind you,
The trees are burned, ashes and ashes,
The grasses have grown up, the grasses have set seed.
Fire friend to man, I summon you, fire, for expiation.
Fire, I summon you, fire guardian of the hearth,
You pass, they are conquered, none overcomes you,
Fire of the hearth, I summon you for expiation.

SONG OF THE WILL-O'-THE-WISP[12]

Fire that men see only at night, dark night,
Fire that burns without warming, that shines without burning,
Fire that flies without body and without support, that knows neither
house nor hearth,
Transparent fire of palmtrees, a man without fear calls you.

Fire of sorcerers, your mother is where? your father where? Who
nursed you?
You are your father, you are your mother, you pass without a trace.
Dry wood does not beget you, you have not ashes for daughters, you
die without death.
The wandering soul is changed into you and no man knows it.

Fire of sorcerers, spirit of the waters underground, spirit of the upper
airs,

Star that cleaves the light: shooting star.

[12] From the "Legend of the Snake and the Turtle." The Snake sings it as one of the "songs that call the sorcerers' fire" (H. Trilles, as cited, p. 964. See Sources).

Flash that shines, firefly that lights the swamp,
Bird without wings, thing without body, spirit of the strength of fire,
Hear my words, a man without fear calls you.

OMBRURE CALLS UP THE FOREST SPIRITS[13]

You who rule the forests, spirits of the forests,
All you who obey me, it is I who call you.
Come, come, to the call of your chief.
Answer without lingering, answer now.
I will send the Lightning that passes and splits the sky.
I will send the Thunder that shatters everything.
I will send the Storm Wind that rips the banana trees.
I will send the Rainstorm that drops from the clouds and sweeps everything before it.
All must answer the voice of their chief.

All you who obey me, show me the road,
The road taken by those who have run away.
Spirits of the forest, answer. . . .

You who rule the forests, spirits of the forests,
All you who obey me, it is I who call.
Where are men, have they gone by your roads?

THE HONEY BIRD'S SONG[14]

Like the wind among the trees,
The bee flits around his nest,
Their song is the same,
Their humming is the same.

Ombrure: the Great Crocodile from whose depredations the first ancestors of the Fang had fled.

[13] From the "Legend of Ngurangurane."

[14] The honey bird (*Cuculus indicator*) is reputed to guide people to wild bees' nests, expecting a share of the honey in return.

Azande CONGO

SONG

Desire for a woman took hold of me in the night oo like madness,
desire for a woman took hold of me in the night oo like madness.

Bakongo CONGO

KIMPA (RHYTHM)

The old man takes all that he can,
The young man does the same.
But above all things reigns Nzambi Mpungu.
If we men fish only once, we go hungry,
If we draw wine from only one palm-tree, we go thirsty.
The ancestors come to eat with us.
She who eats us—Death—does not eat with men,
She wanders in deep valleys, in far lands.

SONG OF A MOTHER WHOSE CHILD HAS BEEN LEFT BEHIND ON THE CARAVAN TRAIL

I heard a sound of footsteps outside.
Is it my child coming back?
Oh, it is another footstep!
They have delivered him to the White Man, alas!
They have given him as a gift to the foreigners,
Alas for me!
What is in store for us?
Alas, I am orphaned of my child!

Pygmy CAMEROON; GABON

SONG OF A MARRIAGEABLE GIRL

Will a man come for me?
The good spirit of the forest knows.
He could tell little Medje;
But he will not tell.
There are things it is not right to know:
If there will be dew on the grass tomorrow,
If the fish will come to the trap and be caught,
If a spell put on the gazelle
Will let my father kill it?

RITUAL SONG

The light becomes darkness,
The night becomes greater night.
Tomorrow's day, hunger,
Creator angry against us!

The men of old have passed,
Their bones are far away,
Their spirits are wandering,
Where are their spirits?

The wind that passes knows perhaps.
Their bones are far away,
Their spirits are wandering,
Are they there far away, are they here close by?
Do they want the blood of sacrifices?
Are they far, are they near?
The wind that passes, the will-o'-the-wisp
Know perhaps.

INVOCATION TO THE RAINBOW

Rainbow, O Rainbow,
You who shine away up there, so high,
Above the forest that is so vast,
Among the black clouds,
Dividing the dark Sky,

You have overturned,
You have wrestled down
The thunder that roared,
Roared so loud, in rage!
Was it angry against us?

Among the black clouds,
Dividing the dark sky,
As a knife cuts through an overripe fruit,
Rainbow, Rainbow!

And it fled,
The thunder killer of men,
Like the antelope from the panther,
Rainbow, Rainbow!

Strong bow of the Hunter above,
The Hunter who hunts down the herd of the clouds
Like a herd of elephants in terror,
Rainbow, speak our thanks to him.
Say to him: "Be not angry!"
Say to him: "Be not wrathful!"
Say to him: "Kill us not!"
For we are greatly afraid,
Rainbow, tell him so!

SONG OF EXPIATION

Spirits of the forest, night-walking ghosts
Who during the bright day,
Like bats that suck men's blood,
Hang hooked to the slippery walls of great caves,
Behind the green moss, behind the great white stones—
Tell us: Who has seen them, the night-walking ghosts?
Tell us: Who has seen them?

DIRGE IN DIALOGUE

[The eldest son, answered by the maternal uncle]

Son: The animal runs, it passes, it dies. And then the great cold.
Uncle: The great cold of night, the dark.
Son: The bird flies, it passes, it dies. And then the great cold.
Uncle: The great cold of night, the dark.
Son: The fish flees, it passes, it dies. And then the great cold.
Uncle: The great cold of night, the dark.
Son: Man eats and sleeps. He dies. And then the great cold.
Uncle: The great cold of night, the dark.
Son: And the sky has brightened, the eyes have lost their light, the star glitters.
Uncle: Cold below, light above.
Son: The man has passed, the shadow has vanished, the prisoner is free. Khmvum, Khmvum, to thee we call!

SONG

Many days have passed—
They will wake and come again.
We are a master people, a free people.

SONG SUNG BY A WOMAN WHILE GIVING BIRTH

My heart is joyful,
My heart flies away, singing,
Under the trees of the forest,
Forest our home and our mother,
In my net I have caught
A little bird.
My heart is caught in the net,
In the net with the bird.

SATIRE IMPROVISED BEFORE WHITES AGAINST THE TRIBE'S NEGRO OVERLORDS

The forest is vast, the wind is right.
Forward, the tribe, bow on arm!
This way, that way, that way and this.
A pig!—Who kills the pig?—
The Pygmy.—But who'll eat it?—Poor Pygmy!
Still, cut it up: you'll get the entrails to chew on. . . .

Wham! an elephant down!
—Who killed it?—The Pygmy.—
Who'll get its fine tusks?—Poor Pygmy!—
Still, kill it—they'll leave you its tail. . . .

Without a house, like the monkeys,
Who gathers honey?—The Pygmy.—
And who guzzles it and gets fat?—Poor Pygmy!—
Still, bring it down; they'll leave you the wax! . . .

The Whites have come here, kind Whites.
Who is dancing?—The Pygmy.—
But who'll smoke his tobacco?—Poor Pygmy!
Still, sit down, and hold out your hand!

SONG OF THE ANIMAL WORLD

Refrain

SOLOIST: The fish goes .... CHORUS: Hip!
The bird goes .... Viss!
The monkey goes .... Gnan!

SOLOIST [*mimicking*]:
I jump to the left,
I turn to the right,
I'm being the fish
That slips through the water, that slips,
That twists, that springs!
Everything lives, everything dances, everything chirps. . . .

The fish .... Hip!
The bird .... Viss!
The monkey .... Gnan!

SOLOIST [*mimicking*]:
The bird flies away,
Flies, flies, flies,
Goes, comes back, passes,
Rises, floats, swoops,
I'm being the bird.
Everything lives, everything dances, everything chirps. . . .

The fish .... Hip!
The bird .... Viss!
The monkey .... Gnan!

SOLOIST [*mimicking*]:
The monkey—from branch to branch
He runs, hops, jumps,
With his wife and his brat,
His mouth stuffed full, his tail in the air.
Here's the monkey, here's the monkey!
Everything lives, everything dances, everything chirps. . . .

The fish .... Hip!
The bird .... Viss!
The monkey .... Gnan!

ELEPHANT SONG

On the weeping forest, under the evening wind,
Black night has lain down joyfully,
In the sky the stars have fled, trembling,
Fireflies that shine vaguely and go out.
Up there, the moon is dark, its white light has gone out.
The spirits are wandering.
Elephant hunter, take your bow!
CHORUS:
Elephant hunter, take your bow!

In the frightened forest the tree sleeps, leaves are dead,
Monkeys have shut their eyes, hanging high in the branches,
Antelopes slip along with silent steps,
Crop the fresh grass, prick up their ears, intent,
Raise their heads and listen, startled.
The cicada falls silent, shutting in its rasping song.
Elephant hunter, take your bow!
CHORUS:
Elephant hunter, take your bow!

In the forest lashed by a great rain,
Father Elephant walks, heavily, *bau, bau,*
At ease and fearless, sure of his strength,
Father Elephant whom none can overcome,
Breaking through the forest, he stops, starts off again.
He eats, trumpets, knocks down trees, and seeks his mate.
Father Elephant, you are heard from far away.
Elephant hunter, take your bow!
CHORUS:
Elephant hunter, take your bow!

In the forest through which no man except you goes,
Hunter, lift up your heart, slip, run, jump, walk!
Meat is before you, the huge mass of meat,
The meat that walks like a hill,
The meat that makes the heart glad,

The meat that will roast at your fire,
The meat into which your teeth sink,
The fine red meat and the blood that is drunk smoking.
Elephant hunter, take your bow!

CHORUS:

Yo-ye, elephant hunter, take your bow!
Yo-ye, elephant hunter, take your bow!

Southern Africa

Aandonga ANGOLA AND SOUTH AFRICA

HOME-COMING SONG OF FIGHTING MEN AFTER A RAID

We men are dried meat for the vultures.
We are meat thrown out for the crows and ravens.
We men are hung up to rot.
Yet we have something as many-colored as a bird's feathers,
As the feathers of cackling guineahens,
A herd as many-colored as a feather of the horned guineahen.
You father of a coward, look not!
You mother of a boaster, dance not for joy!
Your son took fright at the ox-horns.
Every man of the other people mixes his porridge with water!

LOVE PRAISE

My dark-brown girl is like a cow,
My light-yellow girl is like Nimuene,
As beautiful as Schikuni or Ombago,
As pretty as a delicately cut thong,
As hides round the loins of a royal servant.
When I wait for her, I can eat nothing,
When I expect her, I cannot sleep,
Sleep and food matter not to me then.

Mixes his porridge with water: having no milk, his cattle having been captured and driven off by the war party.

Her fingernails are white as if they were washed,
Her fingers, as if she had just touched fat.
She is as bright as the ombimbo-root,
Ombimbo, dug up by the Bushmen,
Ombimbo, grown in the sandy desert of Amambo,
Picked up at the root of the omusati-tree.
My girl is like a copper ring in looks,
My girl is serious, she does not laugh for nothing,
She does not laugh when we are with people,
She laughs only when we are alone together.
Each time I look into her face
It is as if the sun rose newly.
When I have to leave her
It is as if night came over me.
When she goes for water, help her,
When she treads grain, tread for her too,
When she goes to sow, sow for her too,
When she walks about, carry her!
O my Nehoja, you are my adornment!
All the young men offer you their beads.
My treasure is the most beautiful among all strings of beads,
She is like a delicately cut thong.
Her mother bore her for me.
Since she was born, she has belonged only to me.
I love her dearly even when I am asleep,
But when I am awake, a thousand times more.

SONG OF A BRIDEGROOM IN PRAISE OF HIS BRIDE

Jinkono's Namujezi, Nascheja's grandchild,
Mpingana, a tree on the plain,
A palm-tree in the possession of Schinkonjo, Nepaka's son,
Belonged to our people of heroes. . . .
Namujezi, you flower from Jinkono's garden,
You plant too high to be reached!
Her noble figure is something to marvel at,

Nimuene, Schikuni, Ombago: names of cows.

Her beauty turns the heads of the Aalombe,
The people of Jikokola are ravished too.
They run in their eagerness to give Namujezi gifts.
Namujezi's beauty is indescribable.
Jinkono's flower shines like a star.
I saw her from far away, before she came to us.
Namujezi, your eyes—how fresh-new they are!
And your teeth—as if you had gotten them only yesterday!
And your eyes—like those of a hornless cow!
Namujezi, open your eyes, clear as water;
Your teeth—just laugh, laugh out,
So that we may see them all and marvel at them.

We will let our game sleep
Until the morning star appears.
I will not leave the playground so long as Namujezi is there.
Where she is, the moon becomes the sun,
Night becomes bright day.
We are favorites of glorious night,
We are court servants of the moon.
Where you, Star-Namujezi, shine,
I will follow you, no matter where you go.
Well I know the signs of your passing.
Anyone knows Namujezi, even among many women.
She shines like the spring sun rising.
You say: "No one can eat beauty."
Yet I feed on Namujezi's.

THE RAIN-MAN'S PRAISE-SONG OF HIMSELF

No house is ever too thick-built
To keep me, the rain, from getting in.
I am well known to huts and roofs,
A grandson of Never-Been-There.
I am mother of the finest grasses,
Father of green fields everywhere.

Mpingana: another name of Namujezi.

My arrows do not miss their aim,
They strike the owner of huts.
I am a terror to clay walls and the architecture of termites,
Fear-inspiring above and below.
When I pour in the morning, people say:
"He has cut off our lips and stopped our mouths,
He is giving us juicy fruits.
He has rained and brought mushrooms,
White as ivory."

Bergdama SOUTH AFRICA

LAMENT OF A WIDOW OVER HER DEAD HUSBAND

You, father of my little son,
Is the field so far?
You lie there without speaking, my husband!
Stand up, and shoot something for me!
Among the women who are eating meat, I have to wait without eating.

You, Kudu,
The wild oxen have gone by!
Get up, go, sit in the hunters' shelter, and bring down a giraffe!
I shall be without shoes!
Who now will give me shoes?

Father of my little son, black as a pigeon,
You follow the hunting paths no longer!
He was a good youth.
Werf always full of meat! My husband!
Cannot Father move any more?
On the path by which he used to come back, it is already dark.
Did a big scorpion sting him?
Was he clawed by a lion?

Cut off our lips, etc.: has made men fall silent.

The elephant has gone by!
O hunter, you who never missed,
Now all men leave you!
O Mother! Get up now, my husband,
Follow your comrades!
And may your fire burn!
Who now will kill gemsbok?
Are you still silent?
When will you go drive-hunting?
I shall become a laughing-stock!

My husband, who never beat my son,
Who did not treat an old woman stingily,
My son, who used to say: "Give the old woman something too!"
He who knew everything—
Oh, lay me in my husband's grave!

Get up now and go hunting!
The zebra have gone by.
Go out and shoot!
Is not Father the tall man?
He lies there, saying nothing.
Get up now and greet us!
Will he get up? The man only lies there.
Do you say he is dead?
Sit him up! He is a man who loves to go afield.
Who now will go out and kill giraffe?
Get up, go! . . .
Powder him with some perfume, so that he will follow the men!

Father, a tall youth,
Rising like a tree,
Lies there and speaks no more.
A widow—no man supports her. These things are the lot of mankind.
Father never laughed at a widow.
Now that he has died, whom can I have?
People looked to him alone.
To what country shall I go now? . . .[15]

Without shoes: the Bergdama's sandals are made from giraffe hide. *May your fire burn:* the fire in the werf is not lighted until the hunters bring back meat.

[15] The lament continues for ten more stanzas.

JOURNEY SONG

This is a waterless country!
Do you women know the country to which I would go?
This is a waterless country!
Do you women know the spring to which I would go?
I am sick of being ordered around.
"No, we have not seen it."
"I am going to look for it."

LEAVE-TAKING

Tomorrow I will go.
Will I reach my country?
I am a bird at the fork of the river.
The women have forsaken me, have gone down to fetch water.
Tell me, you girl without ornaments,
Tell me, you with the broad face,
O you without ornaments,
Will I reach the distant country?
Will I reach the Okawango?
That is what my harp has to say.

DESPERATION

May the days kill me, that I perish!
May the years kill me, that I perish!
I call out "Woe!"
I call the days!
Years—I do not believe that I shall live them.
Days—I do not believe that I shall live them.
Any measure of time—I do not believe that I shall live it.

Without ornaments: the epithet indicates that the singer would like to take the girl with him. On journeys no ornaments are worn. *Broad face:* "to turn a broad face"—that is, to look at a person with both eyes—is a sign that one is well disposed toward him.

THE OSTRICH

[Song to the harp]

You belly full of rock-flint,
Big-toed one, you who say *tsam-tsam* with your feathers,
You who eat wild melon seeds,
Give me a wing!

Ostrich, who gets up and flees,
Long-neck, big-toe,
Belly full of rock-flint, big bird,
Wide-mouthed ostrich,
Flying running big bird,
Give me a gray feather!

Dusty-sided ostrich,
Big bird that runs swinging your wings,
Belly that says *chou-chou,*
Man-ostrich that runs and [seems to] walk,
Give me a tail-feather!

High-staring man-ostrich,
Belly that says *chari-chari,*
Ostrich in whose entrails everything tastes bitter,
Give me a leg-bone, O ostrich!

Man-ostrich that has two bones that say *khui-khui,*
That has the best of marrow,
That says *gou-gou* with his face—
If only I could get you, my ostrich!

Bushman SOUTH AFRICA

THE BROKEN STRING[16]

People were those who
Broke for me the string.
Therefore,
The place became like this to me,
On account of it,
Because the string was that which broke for me.
Therefore,
The place does not feel to me,
As the place used to feel to me,
On account of it.
For
The place feels as if it stood open before me,
Because the string has broken for me.
Therefore,
The place does not feel pleasant to me,
On account of it.

Hottentot SOUTH AFRICA

INVOCATION[17]

Thou, O Tsui-goa!
Thou Father of the Fathers,
Thou our Father!

[16] Dictated in 1875 by the son of the composer. It is a lament on the death of the latter's friend, a magician and rain-maker, "who died from the effect of a shot he had received when going about, by night, in the form of a lion. . . . Now that 'the string is broken,' the former 'ringing sound of the sky' is no longer heard by the singer, as it was in the magician's lifetime" (Bleek and Lloyd, as cited. See Sources).

[17] Publishing this invocation in 1881, Hahn added that it was still sung "almost in the same words as George Schmidt heard it . . . in 1737" (T. Hahn, as cited. See Sources).

Let stream the thunder cloud!
Let our flocks live, please,
Let us live, please!
I am so very weak indeed,
From thirst,
From hunger!
That I may eat field fruits!
Art thou then not our Father,
Father of the Fathers?
Thou, Tsui-goa!
That we may praise thee,
That we may give thee in return!
Thou Father of the Fathers,
Thou our Lord,
Thou, O Tsui-goa!

PRAYER OF A HUNTER AT A GRAVE OF HEITSI-EIBIB

Oh, Heitsi-eibib,
Thou, our Grandfather,
Let me be lucky,
Give me game,
Let me find honey and roots,
That I may bless thee again.
Art thou not our Great-grandfather?
Thou, Heitsi-eibib!

A MOTHER PRAISES HER BABY

You son of a clear-eyed mother,
You far-sighted one,
How you will see game one day,
You, who have strong arms and legs,
You strong-limbed one,
How surely you will shoot, plunder the Herreros,

And bring your mother their fat cattle to eat,
You child of a strong-thighed father,
How you will subdue strong oxen between your thighs one day,
You who have a mighty penis,
How many and what mighty children you will beget!

PRAISE SONGS FOR THE BABOON

I

Heretse!
Heretse!
Thou thin-armed one,
Who hast thin hands!
Thou smooth bulrush mat,
Thou whose neck is bent.
Thou who art made so as to be lifted up (upon a tree),
Who liftest thyself up.
Thou who wilt not die even behind *that* hill
Which is yet beyond those hills,
That lie on the other side of this far-distant hill.

II

Thou hollow-cheeked son
Of a hollow-cheeked one,
My hollow-cheeked one!
Who hast two hip-bones,
High hip-bones,
With which thou sittest on the edge of the rock,
Thou whose face appears like the edge of a rock.

See game: Literally, "cut spoor."

Heretse: imitates the voice of the baboon. *Behind* that *hill,* etc.: referring to the baboon's ability to outrun its pursuers.

SONG OF A LIONESS WARNING HER CUB[18]

Beware of the one who has sharp weapons
And wears a tiger-tail tuft,
Of him who has white dogs,
O son of the short-haired lioness!
You my short-eared child,
Son of the lioness who devours raw flesh,
You flesh-devourer!
Son of the lioness whose nostrils are red with bloody prey,
You with blood-reddened nostrils!
Son of the lioness who laps up swamp water,
You water-lapper.

SONG OF GREETING TO A MISSIONARY'S WIFE

You who go about with long black hair,
You daughter of a black-eyed mother,
You black-eyed one;
You whose dress drags along
So that the dust is swept as with a broom
And whirls up behind you!

Zulu SOUTH AFRICA

IN HONOR OF SENZANGAKONA[19]

Thou dark grave of Nohamba!
Ever noosing the ankles of foes at home and abroad;

18 Ezra Pound included a free translation of this poem in his review of Eckart von Sydow's *Dichtungen der Naturvölker* (Vienna, 1935); his version appears in his *Guide to Kulchur* (Norfolk, Conn., New Directions Books, n.d.), pp. 209–10. Pound attributes the poem to the wrong collector and to the wrong people.

19 Senzangakona was an early Zulu king.

Black spotted beast of Zwa Ngendaba;
Thou deadly destroyer of Makanda and Unsele;
Voracious consumer of the root and the branch;
Descendant of Menzi! plundering till plunder is gone;
Thou fount of Nohamba! drinking of which,
I dropped down dead, and sunk into the shade of Punga.[20]

SONG AT SEPARATION[21]

I thought you loved me,
Yet I am wasting my time on you.
I thought we would be parted only by death,
But to-day you have disappointed me.
You will never be anything.
You are a disgrace, worthless and unreliable.
Bring my things. I will put them in my pillow.
You take yours and put them under your armpit.
You deceived me.

LOVE SONG

I walk alone.

Nohamba: one of the first of the great royal towns of the Zulu. *Menzi:* maker, creator.

[20] Collected before 1864. Fragment of a praise song composed by an ancient court poet.
[21] Woman's song. From Durban.

Basuto BASUTOLAND

SONG OF THE UNBURIED

We, men, we are the oxen of the vultures,
We are cattle to be shared by the vultures,
To be devoured by carrion crows in the veld.

HYMN OF THE AFFLICTED[22]

Older widows:
We are left outside!
We are left to grief!
We are left to despair,
Which only makes our woes more bitter!
Would that I had wings to fly up to the sky!
Why does not a strong cord come down from the sky?
I would tie it to me, I would mount,
I would go there to live.

The new widow:
O fool that I am!
When evening comes, I open my window a little,
I listen in the silence, I look:
I imagine that he is coming back!

The dead fighting man's sister:
If women, too, went to war,
I would have gone, I would have thrown darts beside him:
My brother would not be dead:
Rather, my mother's son would have turned back half way,
He would have pretended he had hurt his foot against a stone.

[22] Collected in 1836. Commenting on a similar song of the Thonga—"Oh! how I shoud love to plait a string, and go up to Heaven, I would go there to find rest"—Henri A. Junod (*The Life of a South African Tribe*, 2 vols. [Neuchatel, Attinger Frères, 1912–13], II, p. 391) writes: "An old refrain which has come down through the ages, and has in no way been inspired by the Christian religion: it is pure, authentic Bantu."

All the women:
Alas! are they really gone?
Are we abandoned indeed?
But where have they gone
That they cannot come back?
That they cannot come back to see us?
Are they really gone?
Is the underworld insatiable?
Is it never filled?

SATIRICAL SONG ON A MISSIONARY

Even if I am out in a pouring rain and get soaked,
I will not stop in at the missionary's house.
He is a liar—we have caught him at it;
He says: "I speak God's Word." He lies.

WAR SONG OF GOLOANE[23]

Goloane is going to fight,
He sets out with Letsie.
He hastens toward the enemy,
He against whom men murmur,
He whom men refuse to obey.
There are those who jibe at his small red shield,
Yet it is still the old shield
Of the ox of Tane.
What! Does not King Moshesh come and say:
Jibe no more at Goloane the veteran?
Whether or no, now the horses are coming . . .
From the battles Goloane brings back
A white horse and a roan.
They will not return to their masters.
The hornless ox will not be given back.
Today war has broken out,
More terrible than ever before . . .

[23] Composed by Goloane himself, on two of his victories.

Goloane has thrown a rock,
He has struck the fighting man with the tawny shield.
Do you see the cowardly companions of the fallen fighting man
Standing motionless beside a rock?
Why cannot their brother go and strip them
Of the feathers with which they have adorned their heads? . . .
Goloane, your praises are like the thick mist
That comes before rain.
Your songs of triumph travel through the mountains;
They reach even to the valley
Where the enemy are kneeling before you.
The cowards! . . . They are praying!
They are begging for food.
They shall see who will give them food!
Let us give to our allies,
To the fighting men of Makaba,
To those whom we never see coming to attack us.
Goloane comes back from his battles limping,
He comes back, and his leg is dripping;
A stream of black blood
Runs down the hero's leg.
The companion of Rantsoafi
Seizes a heifer by the shoulder;
It is Goloane, son of Makao,
Descendant of Molisse.
Let there be no more insolent words! . . .
Ramakamane complains,
He moans, he says that his heifer
Has broken its white shoulder.
The companion of the brave,
Goloane, has matched himself against Empapang and Kabane.
The javelin is thrown:
Skilfully Goloane avoids it,
And Kabane's dart
Goes wide and sticks in the ground.

Northern Sotho NORTHERN TRANSVAAL

OLD PRAISE SONG OF THE CROCODILE

The crocodile is the invoker of the waters of rain
The black one of the pool
The black black one lying on the water slime
It is the crocodile of the pool
The biter I go about seeking for prey
Son of the father of pools to whom tribute is paid
Tribute to the lords of the rivers
To the lords of the rivers, the hippo and the crocodile
The great torrents of rain will come thundering down
It is the black crocodile of the pool
The crocodile that drags down a beast into the depths
It drags the beast into the dark depths
The crocodile has jammed the beast down in a fork
It has taken the beast into the dark depths
The owners of the beast peer over and down into them
They open out the rushes and willows
They think they are looking right into the pool
It is the pool into which the beast has disappeared. . . .
The crocodile stays down in the weeds with the beast
It is still down in the dark pool with it
It is the one than cannot be drowned of Mmamolemana
Crocodile that must not be poked with a reed, though born in the reeds
Cruel one, killer whilst laughing,
The Crocodile is the laughing teeth that kill, for anger slays no man.

Laughing teeth, etc.: "Lit.: the crocodile is an eating up of one another of people who laugh. This latter is a phrase or proverb, which means that an enemy who can dissemble by smiling is one to be reckoned with, for an appearance of anger will be enough to put the other on his guard" (S. K. Lekgothoane, as cited. See Sources).

Matabele SOUTHERN RHODESIA

"NATIONAL SONG" OF THE MATABELE (*ca.* 1880)

Here is news, *dzi, dzi!*
Oho! oho! here is news,
Dzi, dzi, here is news,
News of the assegai, *dzi, dzi!*

Come and see us, the Zulu,
Come see the talk of other nations.
Oho! Not another nation will come, *dzi, dzi!*

Refrain

Here is news (etc.).

News of the nation of Matchoban, *dzi, dzi!*
Come and see, come and see!
Here is news of Matchoban!
No other nation will come, *dzi, dzi!*

Refrain

Here is news (etc.) .

Matchoban is the leader, the black lion,
The black lion is Matchoban, *dzi, dzi!*
The black lion is Matchoban,
The great chief Matchoban!

Refrain

Here is news (etc.).

It strikes men down, oh! oh! oh!
It strikes men down, *dzi, dzi!*
The lance of our chief, oh! oh! oh!
Yes, it strikes men down, *dzi, dzi!*

Ba-Ila NORTHERN RHODESIA

A SONG MADE BY DANCERS ON HEARING A WOMAN MOURNING FOR HER CHILD

Kachila, blood of my blood, let me think of you;
Perhaps, thinking of you, the whole world will know of my grief.
These little hair-ornaments let them be thrown into the river
That the crocodiles may wear them. Oh dear! my child.

Ndau MOZAMBIQUE

LAMENT[24]

1

Where shall I find one
Like to Bala'nku,
Mother!
Like to Bala'nku,
Mother!
Where shall I find one
Like to Bala'nku,
Mother!
Like to Bala'nku,
Mother!
Mother, Mother, Mother,
Ma—maï—ne',
Like to Bala'nku.

2

He brought me unto goodly things,
All these I did possess;

[24] "Sung by a woman who . . . was the only wife of a man named Bala'nku" (N. Curtis, as cited. See Sources).

He showed me joy,
Mother!
None like Bala'nku,
Mother, Mother, Mother,
Ma—maï—ne',
Mother!
None like Bala'nku.

3

All these sorrows have befallen me,
This misery is mine alone,
By myself I am left alone,
Mother!
None like Bala'nku,
Mother, Mother, Mother,
Ma—maï—ne',
Mother!
None like Bala'nku.

Thonga MOZAMBIQUE

PRAISE SONG FOR A CHIEF[25]

Muhlaba Shiluvane, you are like the rhinoceros who seizes a man, bites him through and through, rolls him over and cuts him in two! You are like the crocodile which lives in water; it bites a man! You are like its claws; it seizes a man by his arms and legs, it drags him into the deep pool to eat him at sunset; it watches over the entrance to prevent other crocodiles from taking its prey. . . . Muhlaba! You are like the ram; when it butts with its head, it knocks a man down; like a goat, like the son of a goat, which is herded by the boys, which is very cunning; it pricks up its ears, it prepares itself for defence, when attacked! . . .

Muhlaba Dabuka! Men are coming, oxen are coming. You are on

[25] (Extracts.) Composed by the clan herald Mawewe; the war referred to took place in 1901.

the top of the hills, you are like heaven which roars. . . . The lightning is like you, it is full of strength, it is terrible! Your saliva is white, your eyes are beaming, your face is elongated, your body is like the stone of gold; your fingers are long. You are known in every country. At Gungunyana, they know you. At Ngwana [Swaziland], they know you. The Zulu know you! At Mosilakatse, they know you. You are like the grass on the road; when people trample on it, they crush it to the ground, but when the rains come, it grows again and covers the earth. You are like the water of the river, how beautiful! The water is clear and pure, though impurities may float upon it, they pass away and the water is pure again!

The Bvesha weep at Sikokoro's kraal! They weep at Sikhukhunu's! You have taken their charms! You have sprinkled your warriors with them. Muhlaba, you have beaten them with the shaft of the assegai, your men crossed the river, they went to kill the enemy in their own kraal!

You are like the ostrich feather, the white one, very white, or the red one of the bird which cries tswe-tswe, the bird called rivi, which adorns the chiefs! . . .

DANCE SONG IN PRAISE OF A DANCER

Thou dancest, Gilela! Thou dancest and thy waist is no thicker than a string!
Son of Tshimbeni! Dance, dance!—That was too little.—We have not yet had enough!

COMPLAINT OF A JILTED LOVER

Refuse me if you will, girl!
The grains of maize you eat in your village are human eyes!
The tumblers from which you drink are human skulls!
The manioc roots you eat are human tibia!
The sweet potatoes are human fingers!
Refuse me, if you will, girl!

Thonga: Nkuna TRANSVAAL, SOUTH AFRICA

WAR SONG OF THE NKUNA CLAN

War comes from the chiefs!
It is ordered by the chiefs! We go and kill!
The spear is in our hands! Eji! Eji!
The spear kills and bends in the wound!

Eastern Africa and Madagascar

Bemba NORTHERN RHODESIA

THE PREGNANT WOMAN

[Song from the girls' initiation ceremony]

The sun has set;
The sun has already gone.
The days are fulfilled;
Let me go and honour the *musuku* tree.[26]

Tonga NORTHERN RHODESIA

MOTHER AND SLAVE RAIDERS[27]

Mother (pursuing raiders who have carried off her child):
How thick the bush is today!

Raiders:
Let us walk in the path.

[26] "The *musuku* tree . . . stands for fertility. . . . Nangoshye explained the song by saying, 'The days are over; my time has come to give birth' " (A. I. Richards, as cited. See Sources).

[27] From a tale. "One should hear . . . with what fervour the narrator sings these words. . . . She was herself, when young, taken into slavery from place to place. She knows something of the horrors of what were those raids" (J. Torrend, as cited. See Sources).

Mother:
How thick the bush is today!

Raiders:
Let us walk in the path.

Mother:
My child, I am afraid,
They are far already.

Raiders:
Let us walk in the path.

Child:
There are thorns!

Raiders:
Let us go carefully, let us walk in the path.

Child:
O master!

Raiders:
Let us go carefully, let us walk in the path.

Basumbwa FORMER TANGANYIKA

PLAINT

How scornful men are!
Just now I, Kagobozi,
I almost died
In the *pori* of Lamwiyabe munoni.
Even if I had died,
Where is he who would have said:
"Men will grow old on earth"?

When a king dies
He leaves a great country,
Elephant tusks in plenty
And many slaves.
But I, Kagobozi,
When I die
Who will weep for me?

MUGALA'S SONG

[Sung while hoeing]

We were born under an evil star, we poets,
When the jackal howls!
We were given a thankless trade.
They who are marked with python's excrement,
They are born lucky,
They are the rich.
God created me ill. I had a desire.
I do not know, but if I had stayed
In my mother's belly, it would be over and done with.
Crafts are dealt out.
I was sound asleep,
I woke—someone calls me:
"You're asleep, Mugala! Come out here and see
How the ground is ringing!"

Chagga FORMER TANGANYIKA

SONG FOR A WAR DANCE

Even if all the cattle of our country be stolen by the enemy, we shall not leave this country of ours. Even if chief Orombo carries off one and all, we shall not leave this country of ours. If we have no other food to eat, let us nibble the trunks of banana plants in this land of ours!

HER SISTER-IN-LAW ANSWERS THE GREETING SONG OF THE RETURNING DAUGHTER OF THE HOUSEHOLD

Yes indeed, be you welcome, my sister-in-law!
Rightly you pay your respects to your father in this homestead.
If there is a right-thinking brother here,
He will look after you with devotion.
And if there are little brothers here,
You teach them rightly and as they are glad to be taught.
And the Old Man listens while you sing as you do.
And those who were born after you pay heed and are glad to hear it, my sister-in-law.
Along the ways that brought you, may herb and moss spring up,
May the *kengera*-herb spring up there and soft grass.
Wherever you step, there may it spring up, my sister-in-law.
The Old Woman and the Old Man—he was strengthened by God,
God helped him then
And gave you the tongue, my sister-in-law,
That now greets the household so well.
May God remain the chieftain,
May God remain the chieftain,
He who also gave you those eyes
With which you look so pleasantly.
May God remain the chieftain,
We thank him heartily who also gave you that toenail
By the help of which you are come here to this homestead
To pay your respects to your brother so rightly.

Kibende FORMER TANGANYIKA

SONG COMMEMORATING THE DEATH OF A HUNTER

Who went about the forest like him? He alone knows the sweetness of meats. His field was the forest; it gave him all his food. What shall we have to eat henceforth?

Kifimbwe FORMER TANGANYIKA

MAN'S DANCE SONG

My friend still has his mother; but I am an orphan; no one will weep for me when I die.

Kinga FORMER TANGANYIKA

PRAISE SONG FOR A CHIEF

Yes, my master!
Yes, my friend!
Yes, my mother!
Yes, my god!
Yes, giver of good things!
Oh, you give a fat she-goat,
Yes, and straightway she bears a kid,
And you, oh, you do not claim her again;
Sooner than you would claim her again,
The world would go to ruin.
O you mother of the forests,
What you have planted
As god, it is like a stone,
Set deep in the ground, that never moves.

Bantu Kavirondo KENYA

LAMENT[28]

Yeyey ohé yeyeye . . .
I am wondering only, mother;
Yeyeye . . .

Masai KENYA

WOMEN'S SONG FOR FIGHTING MEN DELAYED ON A RAID

Solo: God! God! Tear out
Chorus: The brand-marks of the people!
Solo: Tear out, tear out
Chorus: The brand-marks of the people!

Solo: Girls, be not silent.
Chorus: It is being prayed to God.
Solo: Tear out, tear out
Chorus: The brand-marks of the people!

Solo: Venus who is rising
Chorus: And the evening star,
Solo: Tear out
Chorus: The brand-marks of the people!

Solo: The clouds of snow-capped mountains, tear out
Chorus: The brand-marks of the people!
Solo: [He] Who waits till the heavens are red, tear out
Chorus: The brand-marks of the people!

Tear out the brand-marks, etc.: break the power of the enemy. *Who waits till,* etc.: the sun.

28 "This short lament was sung by a young woman a few minutes after her mother had died. As she sang it, tears ran down her cheeks and she ran along the road, obviously in great distress" (G. Wagner, as cited. See Sources).

Pokomo KENYA

HIPPOPOTAMUS HUNTER'S SONG

O Wachi! O Mola! My heart is with Muungu!
I prayed to Wachi,
I prayed to Muungu.
May Muungu give me a very fine beast!
I went through the swamps, through the mud,
Where Muungu's oxen are.
I pushed on through the bitterness of the lake.
I went into the lake, I went praying to Muungu.
Wachi is the kindly one.
Out there in the water the beast was snorting and spouting.

O Muungu, pray for me!
O Wachi, entreat that I may have a good ox!

A stupid ox, he was bound as if with a cord.
I tied a turban round him with my spear-shaft.

You women and children, rejoice!
Rejoice with a song of meat!
I pushed on through the bitterness of the lake.
I scattered the carrion-vultures and the eagles.
Look! The birds are circling yet!
Look! How they snatch their booty from one another!

Swahili KENYA

A CARAVAN PORTER'S SONG

My love, there where you live, if you remember me,
Every time I stop at a river, I shall cross it.
(The girl is troubled.)

Wachi, Mola, Muungu: names of deities.

And come quickly, my love, that my heart may be calmed!
(The girl is troubled.)

HOME-SICK SONG

Magoboreni!
Let me tie a [nosegay] of jasmine,
That it may give out the scent of Magoboreni.

Barundi FORMER RUANDA-URUNDI

LULLABY

A heart to hate you
Is as far away as the moon.
A heart to love you
Is as close by as the door.

Ruanda FORMER RUANDA-URUNDI

TO THE NEW KING MÚTARA II RWÔGERA

[Extract][29]

As for you, Nsóro, among those whom I praise
I cannot put you in the second rank.
You are Clothed-in-Gladness;

Be calmed: literally, "go down."

Magoboreni: probably the name of a place in Unyamwezi.

29 The entire poem contains 391 lines. Mútara II Rwôgera reigned about 1825. Some 170 of these panegyrics by court poets of the Banyiginya dynasty have been preserved, dating from the end of the sixteenth century to modern times.

You are pleasantness among the drums.
You are Beautiful-Complexion, from whom the cows receive due care,
You are the appointed herder of the bulls Rusúgi and Rúsanga!
You bring us back to the times of the Leopard-spotted.
Since, still so young, you engross all prowess,
And your horn is already vigorous,
Despite your being but a bull-calf in age,
When you shall have taken on years,
A bull at the height of his powers,
O Conqueror-of-Famines—
The nations that have not served you in time,
Where will they flee from you?
O Protector-of-Cows, prolong my audience
And lend me your ear that I may render you my due of gratitude,
A messenger of your reign spent the night in my house,
Demanding that early in the morning we go to give thanks for the King,
For Ravishing-Beauty has ceded his rights to Rwôgera.
I neither hesitated nor made inquiries:
Your gladness lodges in my breast!
While man others hesitated, I knew!
I hurried to find you,
Filled with joy, O Refuge,
While your excess poured out on the people!
Oh what good things ears hear,
Eyes have been made to see!
I, who found the King's house
All smiling and radiant,
Like spotless potter's clay,
Who found, in that tabernacle, the King
Like a new moon,
His complexion purely bright
Like Beauty-in-splendor—
It put me in a gay humor!
The inspiration that is mine by nature
Increased by that with which he wreathed my head,
I danced crowned with these sacred ensigns
And was irreproachable among the band of poets!

Leopard-spotted: name of a predecessor of Mútara II. *Ravishing-Beauty:* another predecessor.

Former Mulera-Ruanda*

COURTSHIP AND WEDDING SONGS

I *After the Offer of Marriage*

1.

Chorus of women:
Today, O woe! (Repeated after every line.)

The bride:
Ah now, all of you,
And you, my friend Magalane,
My mother told me:
Come now, child, be quiet,
Go, get used to what must be.
Friend, I answered her:
No one gets used to unhappiness.
No, I don't want to go to the mountains,
I won't dress in their clothes,
Their monkey-skins!

2. (Her friends answer her)

Oh, child, hush, be quiet.
Oh, child, they are deceiving you, they are!
They're carrying you off, beyond the forest,
Beyond the forest, where there are no more people.
Oh, girl, wait till next year!
Oh, child, you don't know if the sown seed will flower,
You don't know if it will flower or die.

3. (Love song)

O child, hush,
Child, hush!

* People not identified.

I will ask your father to give you to me,
And if he sends me away, I'll take you.
Lovers go together,
Sit down, make a compact of friendship in blood
So that love will not wither from their hearts.

II *After the Wedding*

1. (Taking leave of the bride)

O darling, let me go, I must go!
Oh, hush, darling, oh, darling, hush, be quiet,
Child of my mother, let me go, I must go,
Child of my mother, oh, don't cry.
Oh, don't cry, you cry-baby,
Oh, hush, child, stop your grieving.
Oh, yes, darling, you're going where others [have gone before you].
Child of my mother, get used to it,
Oh, hush, child, stop your grieving,
Child of my mother, let me go, I must go!

2. (Her mother's advice to the bride)

Oh, child, behave like the tiger,
Behave like the tiger in the moonlight;
When it is dark, he bites.
Oh, child, behave like the tiger.
Your mother has behaved like the tiger,
She has behaved like the tiger in the moonlight.

III *Two Weeks After the Wedding*

(Final parting song of the bride's relatives)

Hush, first-born,
Hush, only child,
Hush, you are being deceived, oh!
Being carried off, oh!
Hush, darling, oh!
Into a strange land, oh!
Our child, oh!
Doesn't want to be beaten, oh!

Hush, darling, oh!
Our child, oh!
Shall not hoe, oh!
Hoe alone.
Hush, first-born,
Our child, oh!
Shall not be scolded,
Rather than scold her,
We'll take her in our arms
And bring her back to her father,
Her father who begot her.
Our child, oh!
Hush, darling.

Acholi UGANDA

BATTLE HYMN

We are poured on the enemy like a mighty torrent:
We are poured like a river in spate when the rain is in the mountains.
The water hisses down the sands, swirling, exultant, and the tree that stood in its path is torn up quivering.
It is tossed from eddy to eddy.
We are poured on the enemy and they are bewildered.
They look this way and that seeking escape, but our spears fall thickly about them.
Our spears cling to their bodies and they are routed.
They look this way and that for deliverance, but they cannot escape us, the avengers, the great killers.
God of our fathers, guide our spears, our spears which thy lilac has touched.
They are anointed with sacrifice, with the sacrifice of unblemished kids, consecrate and hallowed by the nightjar of good omen.
Help us, high Spirit. Slay with us.
Let death come to their ranks, let the villages mourn their lost warriors.
Let their villages be desolate, let them echo with the cry of mourning.
We shall return rejoicing; and the lowing of cattle is in our ears.
The lowing of innumerable cattle will make glad our hearts.

Baganda UGANDA

PRAISE OF KING MTESA (1877)

Thy feet are hammers,
Son of the forest.
Great is the fear of thee;
Great is thy wrath;
Great is thy peace;
Great is thy power.

WEDDING SONG

"Oh, you who are going by,
Stop and I'll ask you
About the one paining my soul.
What about my beloved Ndawula?"
"We met him at Namuwanda!"
"No, no, he is not there!
Where is my Ndawula?"
"We met him at Namuwanda!"

SONG COMPOSED UNDER A TYRANNICAL KING

I'll buy myself an ugly old woman.
Why, don't you see?
Every beautiful woman is for the King,
And *young* ugly women are for the Chiefs!

Son of the forest: a synonym of the lion, the emblem of royalty.

Lango UGANDA

SPEAR-BLESSING

O tree of blessing, our spears have watched the long night out under thy shadow.
The shafts are wet with dew that shall soon run with blood.
The blades glint in the sun: its first rays tinge them to redness.
They flash to the Ancient One.
The dewdrops quiver with light: they glisten like spray from a leaping fish.
Bless our spears, O holy ones:
Give us honour of battle, and to their women the tears of widowhood.

O tree of blessing, with the evening shadows brought we our spears to thy keeping,
Reverently,
Piously.
Guard them from shame and our hearts from the treachery of fear.
Let their aim be as the sure eye of an eagle;
Swift as the swiftness of an eagle, swift and sure and merciless.
Give us honour of battle, and to their women the tears of widowhood.
Bless our spears, O holy ones.

The nightjar circled round thee and its fluttering pinions brushed our spears.
Bathed in the moon, the blades took grace of its benison.
The crickets hushed to silence:
A holy silence fell on thy holiness, O tree of blessing.
Was only the beating of the nightjar's wings, its long pinions drooping over our blades.
Bless our spears, O holy ones:
Give us honour of battle, and to their women the tears of widowhood.

Brothers and warriors, the goat of sacrifice awaits you:
Its blood is shed at the crossroads that your feet may be laved with its power:

That your feet be shod with might and your arms be hot with courage:
That your spears be red with victory, and that desire shall die in the breasts of their women, save only the desire for tears.
The blessing of the lilac be on you, my children.
Lo, I strike you thus, shields covering your eyes:
I strike you thus, once, twice—
I strike you with the lilac of blessing,
I, the guardian of sanctity, warden of the shrine.

FROM THE RAIN-MAKING CEREMONY

RECITATIVE	RESPONSE
We overcome this wind.	We overcome.
We desire the rain to fall, that it be poured in showers quickly.	Be poured.
Ah! thou rain, I adjure thee fall. If thou rainest, it is well.	It is well.
A drizzling confusion.	Confusion.
If it rains and our food ripens, it is well.	It is well.
If the children rejoice, it is well.	It is well.
If it rains, it is well. If our women rejoice, it is well.	It is well.
If the young men sing, it is well.	It is well.
A drizzling confusion.	Confusion.
If our grain ripens, it is well.	It is well.
If our women rejoice.	It is well.
If the children rejoice.	It is well.
If the young men sing.	It is well.
If the aged rejoice.	It is well.
An overflowing in the granary.	Overflowing.
May our grain fill the granaries.	May it fill.
A torrent in flow.	A torrent.
If the wind veers to the south, it is well.	It is well.
If the rain veers to the south, it is well.	It is well.

Overcome this wind: the dry season wind is easterly, and the rains come when the wind veers to the south.

Didinga or Lango UGANDA

A MOTHER TO HER FIRST-BORN

Speak to me, child of my heart.
Speak to me with your eyes, your round, laughing eyes,
Wet and shining as Lupeyo's bull-calf.

Speak to me, little one,
Clutching my breast with your hand,
So strong and firm for all its littleness.
It will be the hand of a warrior, my son,
A hand that will gladden your father.
See how eagerly it fastens on me:
It thinks already of a spear:
It quivers as at the throwing of a spear.
O son, you will have a warrior's name and be a leader of men.
And your sons, and your sons' sons, will remember you long after you have slipped into the darkness.
But I, I shall always remember your hand clutching me so.
I shall recall how you lay in my arms,
And looked at me so, and so,
And how your tiny hands played with my bosom.
And when they name you great warrior, then will my eyes be wet with remembering.

And how shall we name you, little warrior?
See, let us play at naming.
It will not be a name of despisal, for you are my first-born.
Not as Nawal's son is named will you be named.
Our gods will be kinder to you than theirs.
Must we call you "Insolence" or "Worthless One"?
Shall you be named, like a child of ill fortune, after the dung of cattle?
Our gods need no cheating, my child:
They wish you no ill.
They have washed your body and clothed it with beauty.
They have set a fire in your eyes.

And the little, puckering ridges of your brow—
Are they not the seal of their finger-prints when they fashioned you?
They have given you beauty and strength, child of my heart,
And wisdom is already shining in your eyes,
And laughter.

So how shall we name you, little one?
Are you your father's father, or his brother, or yet another?
Whose spirit is it that is in you, little warrior?
Whose spear-hand tightens round my breast?
Who lives in you and quickens to life, like last year's melon seed?
Are you silent, then?
But your eyes are thinking, thinking, and glowing like the eyes of a leopard in a thicket.
Well, let be.
At the day of naming you will tell us.

O my child, now indeed I am happy.
Now indeed I am a wife—
No more a bride, but a Mother-of-one.
Be splendid and magnificent, child of desire.
Be proud, as I am proud.
Be happy, as I am happy.
Be loved, as now I am loved.
Child, child, child, love I have had from my man.
But now, only now, have I the fullness of love.
Now, only now, am I his wife and the mother of his first-born.
His soul is safe in your keeping, my child, and it was I, I, I, who have made you.
Therefore am I loved.
Therefore am I happy.
Therefore am I a wife.
Therefore have I great honour.

You will tend his shrine when he is gone.
With sacrifice and oblation you will recall his name year by year.
He will live in your prayers, my child,
And there will be no more death for him, but everlasting life springing from your loins.

You are his shield and spear, his hope and redemption from the dead.
Through you he will be reborn, as the saplings in the Spring.
And I, I am the mother of his first-born.
Sleep, child of beauty and courage and fulfilment, sleep.
I am content.

Didinga UGANDA

AURANOMOI'S SONG OF PRAISE FOR HIS BULL AKORIKONO

The reedbuck calls to the roan like a young man, the reedbuck calls like a young man on the far side of a valley.
Gather ye together.
The rhinoceros stands silent at the foot of the acacia, watchful, head swaying from side to side.
Gather ye together.
The leopard crouches in the rocks, the black leopard of the forest crouches, eyes flaming, poised.
Gather ye together.
The buffalo swings his horns this way and that, scattering the mud in the river.
Gather ye together.
Ho! Akorikono of the spreading horns!
Ha! Akorikono of the spreading horns!
Ha! Akorikono, red, red as the blood which bought thee, the blood which handselled my manhood's spear.
As the red lightning art thou, Akorikono, as the lightning which breaks over Taala at the time of sowing.
Red, swift, terrible art thou, swifter than the Leopard, stronger than the rhinoceros.
The reedbuck calls to the roan like a young man, the reedbuck calls like a young man on the far side of the valley.
Gather ye together.
Ho! Akorikono of the spreading horns!
Ha! Akorikono, deep-fronted, firm-footed!

Like the flame flower art thou, Akorikono, like the flame flower of the forest, red and passionate, Akorikono,
Brother to the buffalo art thou: what other bull may stand beside thee?
The buffalo goes with his head on high,
The buffalo goes with his horns swinging this way and that.
Ha! Akorikono of the spreading horns!
The buffalo scatters mud on his brow, he churns the muddy waters.
Young men, ha!
Warriors, ho!
Young men and elders of the people, ha! eya!
Gather ye together.
He splashes mud on his ears, as he wallows in the river.
He paws the ground furiously and is not afraid.
The breath from his nostrils is a storm of wind: he breathes the lightning, and the thunder is the sound of his bellowing.
Ha! Buffalo-brother, Akorikono, the fearless, the invincible, master of the herd!
Behold him! He lashes his tail like a lion, like a young lion bloody with combat.
Lashes his tail menacingly.
Look well, ye cows! Your lord the bull of bulls, Akorikono, the masterful, prepares him for battle.
Beware, ye lesser bulls! The days of your presumption are ending, for Akorikono the masterful prepares him for battle.
With locked horns and heaving flanks they wrestle in combat, and one by one they withdraw torn and bleeding.
But Akorikono stands alone, he paws the earth with his hooves, he bellows loud challenges, swinging his head this way and that.
He lowers his head and charges and none may withstand him.
Froth falls from his mouth, he plunges and snorts and tears up the ground, drunken with victory, delirious with desire.
Look well, ye cows! Behold him, your master!
Ha! Akorikono of the spreading horns!
Ho! Akorikono, herd-master!
Kapeta knows him and Lobititang. His voice is heard at Malala and he looms red in forested Kimodo.
Like the flame flower of the forest, red and passionate as the flame flower, red against black.
Gather ye together.

Young men and elders of the people, ha!
Maidens and warriors, ho!
Gather ye together.
The reedbuck calls to the roan like a young man, the reedbuck calls like a young man on the far side of the valley.
The reedbuck calls to the roan, for the sap is in the trees and the green corn sways with the wind and the spring has returned.
The buffalo goes with his head on high drinking the wind, in multitudes, in great herds.
The leopard crouches in his lair waiting his mate.
Look well, ye cows! for Akorikono cometh, Akorikono of the spreading horns.
Rending, tearing, frothing and champing, tossing his great horns, red-frontleted, triumphant, he comes, your master and possessor, bull of bulls, the incomparable.
Ha! Akorikono!
Ho! Akorikono!
Red, swift, terrible art thou, swifter than the leopard, stronger than the rhinoceros, brave as the buffalo, bull without peer, invincible.
Akorikono!

GIRLS' SONG FOR THE GAME OF "POTS"

Leader:
We mould a pot as our mothers did.
The pot, where is the pot?

Chorus:
The pot it is here.
We mould the pot as our mothers did.
First, the base of the pot.

Leader:
Strip by strip and layer by layer,
Supple fingers kneading the clay,
Long fingers moulding the clay,
Stiff thumbs shaping the clay,
Layer by layer and strip by strip,
We build up the pot of our mother.

Chorus:
We build up the pot of our mother,
Strip by strip and layer by layer.
Its belly swells like the paunch of a hyaena,
Of a hyaena which has eaten a whole sheep.
Its belly swells like a mother of twins.
It is a beautiful pot, the pot of our mother.
It swells like a mother of twins.

Leader:
Oh, clay of the river, bend to our hands,
Curve delicately.
See the strong shoulder and narrow neck.
(In, children, in)
Strip by strip and layer by layer,
Supple fingers kneading,
Long fingers moulding,
Stiff thumbs shaping,
The beautiful pot, the pot of our mother.

All:
The pot, the pot of our mother.

Dinka NILOTIC SUDAN

CHANT[30]

In the time when Dendid created all things,
He created the sun,
And the sun is born, and dies, and comes again;
He created the moon,
And the moon is born, and dies, and comes again;
He created the stars,
And the stars are born, and die, and come again;
He created man,
And man is born, and dies, and never comes again.

[30] This song was already "old" when Beltrame (see Sources) collected it in 1854.

HERDER'S SONG

My bull is as white as the silvery fish in the river; as white as the egret on the river bank; as white as new milk.
His bellowing is like the roar of the Turk's cannon from the great river.
My bull is dark as the rain-cloud, that comes with the storm.
He is like Summer and Winter; half of him dark as the thundercloud; half of him as white as sunshine.
His hump shines like the morning star.
His forehead is as red as the ground hornbill's wattles,
His forehead is like a banner; seen by the people from afar.
He is like the rainbow.
I shall water him at the river, and drive
My enemies from the water with my spear.
Let them water their cattle at the well;
The river for me and my bull.
Drink, O Bull, of the river. Am I not here with
My spear to protect you?

Nuer NILOTIC SUDAN

BEGINNING OF A GIRLS' SONG[31]

The wind blows *wirawira;*
Where does it blow to?
It blows to the river.
The shorthorn carries its full udder to the pastures;
Let her be milked by Nyagaak;
My belly will be filled with milk.
Thou pride of Nyawal,
Ever-quarrelling Rolnyang.

[31] "Free translation of the first verses of a song sung by girls as they sit together in the evening after the day's work is done" (E. E. Evans-Pritchard, as cited. See Sources).

This country is overrun by strangers;
They throw our ornaments into the river;
They draw their water from the bank.
Blackhair my sister,
I am bewildered.
Blackhair my sister,
I am bewildered.
We are perplexed;
We gaze at the stars of God.

Amhara ETHIOPIA

KING TEKLA HAIMANOT LEARNS THAT HIS DAUGHTER MENTUAB HAS BEEN CAPTURED BY THE ENEMY

Is he not there? Is he not there? Is Belau not there?
Had Belau been there, he would never have let his sister go.
"My ox has died," the peasant complains to me,
"My mule has died," the soldier complains to me.
What afflicts me is Mentuab's fate.
Woe, woe, and woe! is no man spared?

Carries its full udder: the cow has refused to suckle its calf or be milked before going to graze. *Nyagaak:* the poet's sister. *Pride:* the dance-name of the girl Nyawal. *Rolnyang:* a youth's ox-name. *Strangers:* government forces. *Blackhair:* a girl's name. *We are perplexed:* the Nuer are perplexed by foreign invasion; the last line is a prayer to God to help them.

Belau: Princess Mentuab's brother and general of the army.

Galla SOUTHERN ETHIOPIA

THE VICTORIOUS FIGHTING MAN'S HOME-COMING

The *guččí*-vulture loves the sun.
I have descended to the narrow valley
And I have pulled down the horsemen!
My god-father will dress my hair;
The beautiful girls will adorn my comb;
My friends will kiss my mouth.
The children will say to me, "You have killed well!"
Fourteen invitations.
"Do not leave off [coming] for a week.
Sit down here on the right hand!"
War-songs mingled with hydromel. . . .
This is what I am thinking of!
As to my life, what have I thought of it?

CARAVANERS' SONG[32]

In summer they even make the dust rise;
In winter they even trample the mud!
If they talk with the dark maiden,
And smile upon the red maiden,
Poverty will never leave them.
Poverty is a terrible disease;
It penetrates the sides,
It bends the vertebrae,
It dresses one in rags,
It makes people stupid;
It makes every desire remain in the breast;

Guččí: a small vulture with red, transparent wings and tail. Its red feathers are used by warriors as a crest.

32 "The caravaners used to sing songs in praise of commerce" (E. Cerulli, as cited. See Sources) .

Those who are long, it shortens;
Those who are short it destroys wholly.
Not even the mother that has borne [the poor man] loves him any longer!
Not even the father who has begotten him any longer esteems him!

LOVE SONGS

I

If I might be an ox,
An ox, a beautiful ox,
Beautiful but stubborn;
The merchant would buy me,
Would buy and slaughter me,
Would spread my skin,
Would bring me to the market.
The coarse woman would bargain for me;
The beautiful girl would buy me.
She would crush perfumes for me;
I would spend the night rolled up [around her];
I would spend the afternoon rolled up [around her].
Her husband would say: "It is a dead [skin]!"
But I would have my love!

II

A javelin without blood is not a javelin!
Love without kisses is not love!

III

That which they have killed is the old cow;
The shegoat has died suddenly.
That which weeps is the mind;
The heart has died because of sorrow!

IV *Lament of a Woman Separated from Her Lover*

O merchant of merchandise
Who is at mount Burê!
The eyes have no axe;
The mind has no sickle
To cut down mountains.

Somali SOMALIA

SONGS TO HORSES

I

My broad-chested beast,
how to praise him I know not.
Like grass-covered Haud?
Like the pattering
rain from last evening's sky?
Like the cubs of a
lion roaring afar?
Like the foals of the
camels, Gedo and Lan?
Like my own song,
of Ged and Hohad?
His four hoofs
clatter over the ground,
like a grown girl,
who has been given her husband,
and has received great flocks,
who, with most costly robe,
and silken raiment,
and dress, has clothed herself,
and at the time of mid-day shadows,
to her sleeping husband,
brings his food,
as with shoes of cow's hide
she clatters?

Ged: the spring winds. *Hohad:* the summer wind.

II *To His Horse, Before a Battle*

We wait at Burao,
has the scout brought answer?
Lo, wiry dun,
the time to march is upon us.
I have sharpened spears,
and cut a thong from an oryx,
I have tied on a dagger.
I go on a crusade,
and start in the early morning,
in order to hasten.
We are of the same mettle.

LOVE SONG

Truly faultless you are, you are like your mother!
Truly faultless, such that no mother could bear you! . . .
Truly, yonder in Aden there are Arab women in plenty,
Or yonder in Harar there are Galla girls in plenty,
Or yonder in the West there are women in plenty.
True—but the Arab women, they have faults,
Or the Galla girls, they have faults,
Truly, the women of the West, have they not faults?

Malagasy MADAGASCAR

THE LOCUST

What is a locust?
Its head, a grain of corn; its neck, the hinge of a knife;
Its horns, a bit of thread; its chest is smooth and burnished;

Its body is like a knife-handle;
Its hock, a saw; its spittle, ink;
Its underwings, clothing for the dead.
On the ground—it is laying eggs;
In flight—it is like the clouds.
Approaching the ground, it is rain glittering in the sun;
Lighting on a plant, it becomes a pair of scissors;
Walking, it becomes a razor;
Desolation walks with it.

THE SONG OF THE BOTTLE

Let us sing the song of the bottle, aaa!
Its belly is clear like water,
But you can't see its heart.
Its mouth is on the top of its head, aaa!
Listen, listen, o men!
To lift it, you take it by the neck.
Its fathers laid on it a nasty "fadi";
You cannot knock one against another,
For their bellies would be cut
To punish them.
Who touches their wounds
Will be torn by a sharp tooth.
When put in water, a bottle breathes quickly,
Like a drowning man.
The vasahas fill it with rum
Up to its shoulders
And then bring it to us.
This is the song of the bottle, aaa!

Clothing for the dead: particolored like some mourning garments.

Vasahas: white men.

IMPROVISED SONG AGAINST A WHITE MAN

I will tell you a terrible truth, aaa!
I've seen a girl at Tamatava,
She had her mouth eaten;
It had been devoured by a vasaha,
Her white lover.
I've seen another girl at Fenerive,
With a big wound instead of a breast:
Her white lover had devoured her breast, aaa . . .

The vasaha does not love like other men, aaa!
When he makes love,
He slavers and bites like a dog.
Go to him, Benachehina,
And return without a mouth!
Go to him, Rasoa,
And return without a breast!
D'you know why the vasaha has a golden tooth?
The dog barks before he bites,
The vasaha bites with his golden tooth
Before he makes love . . .
A calf sucks the milk of a cow,
The vasaha sucks blood from a girl's mouth!
Do you believe me, aaa?

Merina MADAGASCAR

DIALOGUES

I

Man: May I come in, Rasoa-the-well-spoken?
Woman: Come in, honored sir,
I will spread a clean mat for you.
Man: I do not want to sit on a clean mat,
I want a corner of your robe.

II

Man: May I perish, lady!
I passed by your husband's house.
I greeted him, he did not answer;
I asked him the way, he did not speak.
What does it mean?
Woman: Do not be disturbed.
I will keep day and night apart.
The night will be his,
Daylight will be yours.

GIRLS' SONGS

I

Speak to Him-who-receives-fair-praise,
The young Prince to the east of Namehana.
If I call him, I fear people will hear.
If I get up, I fear they will see me.
I wait: tell him my regret.
The skin of him whom I love is perfumed.

II

Tell the clouds to wait
For the wind is falling.
Tell the lake to forget
For the birds will not come there to sleep.
It is bad to forget all at once,
It is good to forget little by little.

III

I am the child without friends
Who plays alone with the dust,
I am the chick fallen into the ditch:
If it calls, its voice is small,
If it flies, its wings are weak,
If it waits, it fears the wild-cat.

Do not make our love a love of stone
Whose pieces cannot come together;
Make it a love of lips,
Even angry, they draw close and meet.

North Africa

Algerian (Arabic) ALGIERS

IF . . .

If . . . ah! if . . . youth were at my command,
I would plant a garden of lemons and pomegranates for you.
If you came, I would bring you home,
I would be your lover, you would be my mistress.

I met her today at the garden gate;
Her waist was a bamboo, her cheek a poppy.
I met her today at Suk-el-luh;
She had her handkerchief in her hand, she was weeping and sobbing.
I met her today at Suk-el-djema;
She had her handkerchief in her hand, she was weeping and sobbing.
I met her today at Sabat-er-ryh;
I asked who she was. They said: She is someone's mistress.

If . . . ah! if . . . I brought you home, queen of gazelles,
I would tell you what I desire.

Tunisian (Arabic) TUNIS

SONG

I have a rose over our well;
When the wind blows, it bends down.
I have a rose over our cistern;
When the wind blows, it answers my question.

Egyptian (Arabic) CAIRO

POEM SUNG AT A MYSTICAL EXERCISE

O gazelle from among the gazelles of El-Yemen!
I am thy slave without cost:
O thou small of age and fresh of skin!
O thou who art scarce past the time of drinking milk!
The phantom of thy form visited me in slumber:
I said, "O phantom of slumber! who sent thee?"
He said, "He sent me whom thou knowest;
He whose love occupies thee."
The beloved of my heart visited me in the darkness of night:
I stood, to shew him honour, until he sat down.
I said, "O thou my petition, and all my desire!
Hast thou come at midnight, and not feared the watchmen?"
He said to me, "I feared; but, however, love
Had taken from me my soul and my breath."

POPULAR SONG

A lover saw another afflicted [with love]: he said to him, "Whither art thou going?"
He stopped and told his story: they both wept together.
They went to the cadi of love, both together to complain.
The three wept, and said, "Whither is our love gone?"
The night! The night! O thou with sweet hands! holding the dewy peach!
Whence were ye, and whence were we, when ye ensnared us?

A lover says to the dove, "Lend me your wings for a day."
The dove replied, "Thy affair is vain": I said, "Some other day:
That I may soar through the sky, and see the face of the beloved:

I shall obtain love enough for a year, and will return, O dove, in a day."
The night! The night! O thou with sweet hands! holding the dewy peach!
Whence were ye, and whence were we, when ye ensnared us?

Bedouin ORAN, ALGERIA

WOMEN'S GRINDING SONG

Under the earth of your grave you are hidden from sight, O Kheira
You are imprisoned in a house where there is only darkness
You have left Ahmed and his sister Mahjuba
You are gone, O beautiful one with earrings, gone not to come again
Your leg was like a lily
O woman like a gazelle.

Bedouin EGYPT

SONG

We are the Fuqara
And the falcon leads us,
Not a kite!
The Fuqara are proud
From Bornu to Egypt.
They do as they will.
And if it came to killing the Pashas,
They would do that too.

Siwan SIWA OASIS, EGYPT

SONG ON DRUMS AND PIPES[33]

I do not admire anyone, either in Siwah or elsewhere, except you.
What am I going to do now? My love has left me. He loved me once; but it seemed that my beloved afterwards despised my love and changed.
Pity, pity, O my love! I cannot say that you are not my love!
I belong to you my love! I, my sons and my property, all are under your command.
I have made my couch and waited, but my beloved boy did not come.
By Allah, I love this lad. This lad has fine rings on his fingers, and a charming beauty in his face.
My love, I cannot leave you! If it is fated that you must go away, hasten to return again.
The hair of my love is very long; my love's neck is two cubits' length.

Berber: Shluh WESTERN MOROCCO

GNOMES

I

O you whose eyes are painted, O girls,
You and the rifle—what you command is done.

II

The ball from ambush is the bitterest.
The tears of a weeping friend are bitter.
The rose-laurel is bitter—who ever ate it and found it sweet?
Yet I ate it for my friend, and it was not bitter.

[33] The song is a man's.

III

What makes you proud, cloth? you cover lepers.
What makes you proud, pearl? whores wear you.
What makes you proud, fortress? the lame climb on you.
What makes you proud, fountain? camels drink of you.

BALLAD

One day I traveled,
The second day I found
A sheaf of lavender
Above a spring.
"In God's name, you who draw water,
Give me a sip to drink."
"Come down, stranger,
Drink from the hollow of your hands."
"God has given me an impediment,
I cannot drink so."
"Come home to my house,
There is honey and tea."
The trickster went to the village,
He spent a week there.
She brought a jar
Full of honey.
He put his finger in it,
He had not time to finish.
Suddenly there comes a soldier,
It was her husband
Riding a gray horse
Worth a hundred *douros* cash.
He stabbed me, the traitor,
I lay where I fell.
Carry me to the mosque,
Measure me with a reed,
A shroud to cover my head.
Set water to heat.

Dig my grave, friends;
Weep, all of you.
O Mother, my Mother,
If anyone says:
"God keep your son,"
Answer: So be it.
He was not stabbed in a corner.
He did not steal cattle.
Eyes painted with antimony
Did him to death.

Berber: Ait Ndhir MIDDLE ATLAS, MOROCCO

MEMORIAL[34]

O you who ride to Segotta, the fighting men who set out for there full of life have not come back.

LOVE SONGS

I

When I make love with my lover, it is as if I were cleaning grain to feed myself: I eat and eat, a whole field full, yet my heart is not satisfied.

II

I wish I could put pain in the pans of a scale, to divide it equally between my lover and me.

III

O my dead lover! as when children put a candle in a lantern, light comes through the stones of your tomb.

[34] On a battle between Berbers and French, fought in 1911.

Berber: Ait Uriaren RIF, MOROCCO

ON A VICTORY[35]

Gunpowder spoke between sunset and the dinner-hour prayer.
The tribe of the Beni-Uriaren, O my mother!
How many of them lie dead!
How many wounded! Why?

Berber: Ait Temsaman RIF, MOROCCO

MEN'S SONG AT A WEDDING[36]

O my Yamma!

I followed the stream
To the pomegranate spring.
I picked a pomegranate
To assuage my desire.

Its master was watching
From inside the house,
He shouted to me: "Drop it, drop it!
Help! Stop thief!"

God preserve me from such ignominy!
What! I a thief?
I did not eat enough to satisfy me,
I did not carry any away on my back.

I only picked one
To assuage my desire.

[35] On a battle in 1910 in which the Ait Uriaren defeated two neighboring tribes.
[36] When the song is sung, the refrain "O my Yamma" precedes every line.

GIRLS' SONG AT A WEDDING

A lalla ia lalla! a lalla buiani!
I will never forgive my mother, who painted me for the wedding!
I will never forgive my father, who married me to this husband.
He married me to a widower, so that it is sin for me to be with a young man.
He has given me to an old man whose neck-veins stand out like knotted strings.
His beard is like a handful of alfalfa.
His belly is like the bottom of a grain sack.
O Muh, O my blood cousin!
O Muh, whose face is as white as the face on a silver coin.
We will run away on a moonless night.
With my arms around your neck, O my lover, what can happen to me?
O Muh, O splendid horseman!
O true son of the Rif, O my brother! I die for you.

Berber: Gzennaia RIF, MOROCCO

TO A YOUNG GIRL

Do not trample down the furrows, little gazelle.
I am ready now to show you
The path that you do not know.

Berber CENTRAL MOROCCO

LOVE SONGS

I

Saliva of my lover, you wash my heart as if there were soap in you.
You refresh my bones as rain waters the grass.

II

I wish I could die for two days, then come back to life;
I should see, my lover, if your eyes would shed tears.

III

I left him without saying good-bye to him:
O parting that I did not foresee,
You come like the day of my death.

Berber: Ait Abbas, Ait Aydel KABYLIA, ALGERIA

PILGRIMS' SONG

This is the day when they dig my grave;
They shape its walls with picks.

They make two pillows of mud,
One for my feet, one for my head.

O my loved body, they will let you down;
Lay your head on the earth, where corruption will take you!

SONG OF EXILE

My mother, O my sweet mother,
My mind is twisted like a grape-stock.

When I came to myself
The crowd was already gone,
And I knew my loneliness.

Behind the mountains the sun has gone down,
Toward the past the bridges are cut.

DANCE SONG

She burst into the dance.
None of us knows her name.
A silver amulet
Swings between her breasts.

She sprang into the dance,
Rings tinkling at her ankles,
Silver bracelets.

For her I sold
An apple orchard.

She burst into the dance,
Her hair streamed loose.

For her I sold
A field of olive-trees.

She sprang into the dance,
Her necklace of pearls glittered.

For her I sold
My grove of fig-trees.

She sprang into the dance,
With a flower of a smile.

For her I sold
All my orange-trees.

LOVE SONGS

I

Who told you, my brother, to follow
The emigrants in their exile?
Your absence is so long to me!
You have left me all alone in my bed.

If I had been old and chilled,
I should have laughed at the Demon,
He would not have prowled about me.

But I have just passed out of childhood,
It is only two months since I was first allowed to fast.
And my fruits are already ripening.

II

I weep; you weep.
No one can console another.

You are like emerald-green silk
Brought from far away in boxes.

We are destined for each other:
We have not come together.

Berber: Kabyle JURJURA MOUNTAINS, ALGERIA

LEARNING FRENCH

The day they taught us *bonsoir,*
We got a hit on the jaw,
We got our bellyful of prisons and locks.

The day they taught us *bonjour,*
We got a hit on the nose,
All blessings ended for us.

The day they taught us *merci,*
We got a hit on the throat.
A sheep inspires more fear than we do.

The day they taught us *cochon,*
A dog's honor stood higher than ours.
The peasant bought himself a mule.

The day they taught us *le frère,*
We got a hit on the knee;
We walk in shame up to our necks.

The day they taught us *diable,*
We got a beating that drove us mad.
We have become carriers of offal.

Tuareg SAHARA

OLD WAR SONG

I shoulder my sword.
Spears pierce.
The brave fall.
Mothers wail.

SONG COMPOSED BY A FIGHTING MAN LYING WOUNDED IN THE DESERT

I think of my beautiful wife.
I see her necklace,
Her bracelet,
The carpet spread ready.

ON THE TUAREG VIOLIN

I humbly adore the acts of the Most High
Who has given the violin more than a soul
So that when it plays, men fall silent
And their hands reach for their veils to draw them down to hide their emotion.
The griefs of love would soon have put me in the grave,
But by the power of the violin, O son of Aiclum,
God has restored me to life.

KOUKAA

Koukaa sits among the women
Like a grape-vine shoot among tamarisks.
Koukaa sits among the women
Like a date palm rising among *iraks.*
Koukaa sits among the women
Like a riding camel from Iguedalem among riding camels.
Koukaa sits among the women
Like a shield from Tarma among shields.
Koukaa sits among the women
Like a tunic from Ghati among other tunics.
Koukaa sits among the women
Like a javelin among lances thrust into the ground.

REMONSTRANCE[37]

May your father perish, Matalla! you are possessed by a demon if you believe that these people are not men! Yet they can ride camels; they march in the morning, they march in the evening. They know how to travel, they can gallop if need be, they know the way to give drink to a rider on his mount, how to take a strong, brave man unawares at night. Happy and rich, he sleeps without a suspicion, and his camels are on their knees. These men run him through with a lance as pointed as a thorn, and leave him to gasp until his soul flees his body; the eagle devours his guts. Before the Arab woman's time of mourning is passed, poverty will have taken her and thrown her on the dung-heap.

Tuareg: Kel Ahaggar SAHARA

AN OLD MAN'S NIGHT THOUGHTS

I stayed until the moon showed over the pass;
I took my leather pouch, I struck fire;
I took a vessel, I drew milk, I drank it
Until the one in the middle was satisfied.
Sleep spoke to me: "I will not make you wait,
For [at your age] there are no desires in you to do what you cannot."
I said to sleep: "May your mother perish! There are any number.
In the days when no light was mixed with my dark [hair],
Nothing could keep me from the courts of love, I went to every one.
My companions were none but young men of high birth,
We walked together openly, hiding nothing."

The one in the middle: the belly. *Any number:* literally, "ten."

[37] By Rotman ag El-hadj Bekri.

DROUGHT[38]

Our sacks are light, our she-goats are dry;
A poor man comes and squats on his heels,
No one cares—let him die if he likes!
The drought weighs on the countryside like Mount Oudan;
It licks its lips, satisfied, it does not fall back a step;
It is determined to strip us even of our face-veils
And our trousers, so that we cannot attend the courts of love.
The she-camels and the yearling calves are so exhausted that they cannot move from where they stand,
The he-camels stop in the middle of the desert from weakness;
What, then, will happen to the old she-goats' kids
Which can scarcely yet bend their joints?

FIGHTING FRENZY[39]

I sleep until the beginning of the last night watch;
I hear a woman asking to speak with me;
She tells me news that kills my soul.
I take my saddle by the pommel and girths,
I grasp the handle of my shield where it is fixed in it,
I make it vibrate to the point of splitting,
It gives an even, long-drawn sound, like the sounds that are sometimes heard high in the air,
I feel the vibration echo in all my bones,
I draw my shield lightly along my leg.

IN PRAISE OF ABAZZA AG MEKIIA[40]

He who arrived here last night—I think of him constantly.
Mokammed and Salek are like him,
But not like him in charm;

[38] By Kamid agg Afiser (1825–1900).
[39] By Ebbeki ag Bouken (1825–1902).
[40] By the poetess Tekadeit oult Ag-Eklan (born 1860).

He is smooth with the smoothness of a reed
That stands straight in the water, bright green, and sways;
His white riding-camel kneels, a silver collar around its neck;
Its master—the moon we see there is the substance of which he is made.

THE POETESS REPROACHES MOKAMMED AG MEKIIA FOR HAVING PASSED NEAR THE PLACE WHERE SHE WAS WITHOUT VISITING HER[41]

Mokammed, my anger shall begin with you,
You who passed close to me without stopping when I was having my herd pastured in the valleys of Iroubar,
By the village of Esali-sekin over there and the Tighal hills.
My rancor will spring at your neck and your nostrils.
I, a woman, am able to go to Aouheggak,
How much the more could you come here to Igentar!

Tuareg: Taitok SAHARA

GIRL'S SONG[42]

O my cousin, my beloved,
Once I thought I did not love you.
When they came back saying they had left you dead,
I went up on the hill where my tomb will be.
I gathered stones, I buried my heart.
The odor of you that I smell between my breasts
Shoots fire into my bones.

[41] By the poetess Eberkaou oult Beleou (born 1870).
[42] "Very old" (C. E. de Foucauld, as cited. See Sources).

AT A NOON HALT ON A JOURNEY[43]

Toward midday my thoughts became many,
I thought of what one had said to me:
"You will have no more of your meetings,
You and Tiheiaouin's brother."
The camels waited on in the sparse shade of the gum trees.

[43] By the poetess Kanimana oult Ourzig (1800–60).

INDONESIA

Borneo

Dusun

DRINKING SONGS

I

The squirrels are chattering
In the top of the mogombizau,
We chatter too,
For we are full of life.

II

The solimpogun grows
On waste ground.
Men eat what comes from earth,
Earth eats men.

LOVE SONG

The seashell is transparent,
The banana is good to eat.
You are beautiful, girl!
And your breasts are still soft.

Murut

CHANT ON THE RETURN FROM A SUCCESSFUL HEAD-TAKING RAID[1]

Men of the raiding party:
Koi, Koi.
The scarlet seeds lie thick
On the boulders of the Tagul,
Of the Tagul,
Koi, Koi.
We have hacked the rice-mortars
At the foot of the house-steps,
Of the house-steps,
Okoi, Koi.
The blood lies in clotted pools
Around the house,
The house,
Koi, Koi.
We throw down the scarlet fruit
In the midst of our dancing-floor,
Of the dancing-floor,
Koi, Koi.

Women of the house:
Behold our men folk:
Skilled are they to smite:
A row of tough bamboo.
With what blood shall we anoint them?
O men folk of ours,
Where did ye pluck them,
These red hibiscus flowers?

Men:
O ye women,
We went forth into the forest,

[1] "In the actual singing, some words are repeated . . . and the raiding cry *Koi* or *Kukoi* is introduced. The first stanza is given in full: in the following ones the repetitions are omitted" (O. Rutter, as cited, p. 193. See Sources).

We have picked the red hibiscus flowers.
What did ye expect of us,
A flock of the crested hornbills?

Women:
We raise the chant duly
Over these coconuts from the upper reaches.
Wearied are our lads,
They are back from the forest.
Their lives hung by but a single strand of hair.
Where did ye pluck these?
We are not presumptuous,
Give us the coconuts.

Men:
O ye women,
We are accustomed to journey in the forest,
And to carry nuts in our hands.
Only let us not be shamed before others:
We are all as the hard bamboo from which fire is struck:
Vain would be our return
Without the red hibiscus flowers.

Women:
Behold our men,
None can surpass them.
Clever are they to smite.
From daylight to dark will we sing.
They toiled to seek revenge:
Our bamboo boxes can now rest in peace.
How can we repay,
How set at ease the hearts of our men?
Up to the headwaters of our rivers will we go
In search of a recompense.
(*To the heads*)
Thus are your ill deeds to us repaid,
And over you now do we raise the chant.
Your long locks are tangled,
And men brought you by swift marches over the hills.

Men:

O ye women,
Till night succeeds the day
Raise chants over these nuts,
Nuts from the upper reaches of the river.
We feared lest we should get no share,
Or have to chant over a trophy divided with others,
Our life had all but left us:
They were like tigers that were gathered there.

Women:

Our men have found their quarry;
The tail-feathers of the hornbills are broken.
Many were the footprints on the river sandbanks,
On the place where the men fought.
Strewn on the stony banks
Lie the fallen scarlet flowers.
What is it that floats there
Slashed like meat on a bamboo grid?
The ants are the sole mourners over
The men from the upper reaches.
Do not, then, men of the upper reaches,
Seek our bamboo boxes.

Men:

Our spears gave many a thrust
There on the stony banks:
With their aid
We bring the red rattan head-rings.
See, O ye women,
Why do ye lie asleep?
The nuts are here.
The men went forth to the jungle
To seek the hornbills:
We had word of them,
We feared naught but the mocking laugh.
Your hornbills flew
Seeking a chance to sweep upon
The timid swallow

In the midst of the clearing.
We are young and strong,
We can give you cause for the chant. . . .[2]

INVITATION TO DRINK AND THE REPLY

I

Come, brothers,
Shame will fall on you:
Ye are slow to drink.
Follow in quick succession at the jar,
All ye that are in the house.
Else will ye, brave warriors,
Earn laughter and mockery
From us, your equals in age.
See now, brothers,
Thus do we drink,
We that are men.

II

Nay, we wish not to drink deep.
Neither are these bodies of ours
Like those of great warriors.
These bodies of ours—
We are old now,
We men.
When we were young,
None could point the finger of scorn at us
In drinking.
As for these bodies of ours,
Truly we were great warriors in former days:
The red fruit lay scattered thick:
Have ye not heard how it was,
In the days of old?

Scarlet seeds: blood. *Rice-mortars:* the bodies of the enemy. *Scarlet fruit, red hibiscus flowers, coconuts, nuts, scarlet flowers, head-rings:* the taken heads. *Crested hornbills:* great warriors. *Bamboo boxes:* men.

2 Six more stanzas follow.

We were as combs that smooth out the long hair:
And these bodies of ours,
Impenetrable as the tangled clump of the imbalua-rotan,
Stubbon rings that cannot be loosed;
These bodies of ours,
Like the hard sumbeling-bamboo that wounds those that touch it:
When we were in our prime
Even so did we slay,
We, in the days that are past.
All the village then
Were as the pounded grains of roasted rice
Spread out on a broad mat.

Dyak

SHAMANS' SONG OVER THE CONSECRATED RICE AT A FUNERAL CEREMONY

We know the origin of your life,
We know the ground of your being,
You are a creation of the god Djata
Who reigns at the golden door;
You are a work of Hatalla
Who guards the spaces of the sky.
You were created from drops of the dew
Which hangs up there in the heights,
From drops of the misty fragrance
Which drifts in the air.
You drip from the garing-tree which is rich in shade,
From the sihon-tree with wide-spreading branches.
A high man took you and stored you safe,
He who is like an eagle guarded you in a decorated vessel.

A high man: the priest.

Ngadju Dyak

VOYAGE OF THE BENEVOLENT SPIRITS[3]

The Sangiang start, push off from the lunok-tree,
the sea-snakes push off from the sandbar;
their feet swarm on the stone, the threshold of the house,
their feet swarm on the stone of the coming of the sea-snakes;
great the din of the glorious ones,
loud the noise of the glorious ones,
amid the sound of drums and gong,
fired are cannons mighty as sea-snakes,
often fired are great cannons.
They push off the prow,
they push off the stern with its rudder,
shouting they push off the sword-ship,
with a din they push off the ship of the sword-hilt.
And he rises, he stands, Dohong kiting tambon,
he rises, he stands, Pulang pampang rawing,
one of his ringed legs, held stiffly out, stands on the carved ship's beak,
his second leg steps bent on the tiger figurehead.
Great the din of the glorious ones, their din in the ship, in the
sword-ship,
loud the noise of the glorious ones in the ship of the sword-hilt.
Braceleted arms swarm on both sides of the ship's planks,
they rule the thin rudder, thin as the hornbill's tail feather,
it has a tiller of gold, round as the sawang-bush,
has a bent handle of gold, bent like the shoulders of the swallow.
Very fast the sword-ship, roaring it cuts through the water, the ship of
the sword-hilt,
the waves roll up, hurry toward the prow,
a whirlpool bubbles up behind the rudder beam of the sword-ship;
pointed out too late with the striped lance-shaft, pointed at too slowly,
they are already at the mouth of the river.
On now, on! you crew of the ship, of the sword-ship!

[3] Extract from a long chant of the shaman at a ceremony for the dead.

On now, on! you Sangiang in the ship of the sword-hilt,
enter, enter the mouth of the river,
go on to the mouth of the stream,
push on through the waves of the Sea-of-Mist, sail through the billows of mist,
hasten through the place of the rolling of thunder, sail through the site of heaped up lightning,
skirt the living wood, the staff of the mass of the sun,
sail to the living wood, the staff of the roundness of the moon!

Sea Dyak

EVENING QUIETNESS

[Section II of the
Chant of the Flowers of the Year]

The cricket
sings its evening song,
telling the eye of day
has sunk and gone.

The young ngingit
trumpets
from the waving branch,
for the sun
has sunk
in the glowing west.

The young otter
has ceased its gambols,
chasing its prey
on the ripples of the pebbly beach.

The young mouse deer
now slinks away
from its search for cane,
in the deserted garden.

The chicks
with noisy chirp
have found their coop.

The great white fowls
side by side
have sought their roost.

The great fat pig
grunting
has sought its sty.

The jutting poles
tremble
with the weight of speckled fowl.

The sky
is serried and painted,
like the fringe
of the petangan head-dress.

The sky
is oval and white,
like a plate
of a banquet-house.

The sky
is dark and red,
like the tail
of the perching hornbill.

The sky
is spotted and barred,
like the scales
of the mengkarong lizard.

The sky
is parded and red,
like the painted skin
of the tree leopard.

Black cloud-piles
slowly sail
and roll away.

The yellow star
now twinkles
near the circle
of the moon.

The Pleiads, one by one,
shine out
in their wonted place.

The three stars
proudly sail
chasing one another.

The evening star
shines beautiful,
like the budding
kenunsong flower.

The Mlanau star
trembles
in the vault of the deep, dark sky.

The star Perdah
pursues its course
on its mighty way.

The verandah grows
dark as though wrapped
in the blantan blanket.

And our house loft,
friend Budi Nsirimbai, grows
dark as though covered
with a paia pakan.

The whole house
trembles buried in gloom.
And now our resin lamps,
friend Nyeni Budi Mejah,
make glowing spots
in the village pathway.

The children
have ceased
their noisy games and quarrels.

The mothers
have ceased to nurse
their latest born.

The widows
have sought the secluded couch
up the low ladder.

The village maids
with giggle and noisy laugh
have sought the cot
in the loft above.

The old men
have ceased to feed
the evening fire.

INCANTATION UTTERED OVER A LOVE PHILTRE BY A WOMAN WHO DESIRES A MAN NAMED JAWA

You are no common or useless potion,
You are a potion I obtained in my sleep when I went to a solitary place.
I did not take you as I would have taken anything else,
I asked to have you and gave an offering for you.

Ngingit: a cicada; its trumpet-like note is heard only a little after sunset. *The three stars:* Orion. *Paia pakan:* a woven blanket of a certain pattern.

You were given to me by Kumang and Lulong Bintang,
By the mother of Abang and Sapantang Mayang,
By Puyu, by Kechu.
Now I smoke you with menyan, with coconut milk,
With flowers, with scented things.
And now be not false or ineffective,
Be not barren or impotent.
Fly like a bird, like a mynah,
Like the rhinoceros hornbill, like the black and white hornbill.
Be as quick as the lightning flashes before the face of night,
Be as swift as the bullet made of lead.
Be as rapid as the blowpipe of straight bore,
Go as far as the pith-wad can carry the blowpipe arrow.
Praises have been sung to you by Kumang and Lulong Bintang,
You have been praised by Jawai and the mother of Ngelai,
Both Puyu and Kechu have found out your efficacy.
Indeed you are no useless or common philtre,
You are a philtre of direct aim, a philtre of the spirits.
You are more deadly than the tuba root that has been dug up,
You are more fatal than the upas poison taken from the topmost branch
of a neighbouring tree.
You are more rancid than Kapayang fruit soaked for one morning. . . .
I am like this because I have become mad, and I am enamoured.
My heart is distressed, sunk down and will not forget Jawa.
He does not pity or love me,
Because there are those who prevent and forbid him.
I ask you to settle on and to sink into Jawa,
Cause him to be unsettled, cause him to be in suspense,
Cause him to be anxious, cause him to be restless,
Cause him to be mad, cause him to be enamoured,
Cause him not to sit down, cause him not to sleep,
Cause him not to eat, cause him not to cook,
Cause him to be dispirited, cause him to be anxious,
Cause him to be vexed, cause him to blame himself,
Cause him not to work on his farm, cause him not to weed it,
Cause him to be stupid, cause him to be foolish,
Cause him to weep, cause him to cry out loud.
Now seven days from this cause him to come to my room and wed me.

KLIENG'S WAR-RAID TO THE SKIES[4]

Klieng: "Let us three Ngelai and Bulan Menyimbang get bird-lime."
Ngelai: "To-day? Shall we return in a day?"
Klieng: "Nay, we spend nights away, and take as provision three pasus of rice."
Ngelai: "Where shall we collect the bird-lime?"
Klieng: "Say nothing: let us start and fell the pempan-tree of Ngelai of the Rain Chestnut, where we can arrange our weapons:
Arrange the plumes of hair like shoots of the lemiding-fern;
Put on the ancient war cap, the well fitting one;
Take the war charms to gird the loins;
Take the shield cut in slanting curves;
Gird on the horn-hafted weapons;
Take the plumes of hair thickly studding the sheaths;
Carry the sumpitan of tapang-wood."
And away they marched with feathers of the hornbill tossing in the sheaths.
Away down the ladder of evenly notched steps,
Holding the long rails converging at the bottom.
So started the three setting forth from thence.
In the day time they pushed on following the sun.
By the night they used flaming torches of light.
But weak was Bulan Menyimbang, weaker than a scorched leaf;
The strength was gone from the midst of his loins.
He fell to the right but was caught by the horn-hafted sword.
He fell to the left, but was held up by the barbed spear handle.
Spirit of the Winds: "O dead is our friend, beloved of heart!
O dead is our husband, beloved of body!"
And up rose Bunsu Entayang from the spout of the leaping waterfall.
Up rose Bunsu Rembia from the top of the bee-trees;
And touched him with the knuckles of the fingers of the hands,
And dropped upon him oil sweetly perfumed;
And there was a twitching in the soles of his feet,
A throbbing of the pulse in the region of the heart:
And Bulan Menyimbang stood up.
He smelled an odour like the scented gharu of the hills;

[4] Extract from a long narrative poem.

He inhaled a perfume as of pressed cardamon-flowers.
And lo! there was cooked rice, a bambu-full,
And dried fish a basket full.
"Whether for life or for death I will eat this rice," says he.
And he ate to his satisfaction.
He smoked, holding the fumes in his mouth,
He ate pinang, throwing the refuse away,
And Bulan Menyimbang started to walk.
He walked slowly holding on to the wing feathers of the swallow.
He marched on holding to the beak of the hornbill.
And there was heard a booming sound like the roar of the tidal bore,
A rushing and crushing as of pelting rain.
And Ngelai Bujang Pedar Umbang looked behind.
Ngelai: "O you are alive, friend! our friend lives!"
And the three went forward, and came to the highway like the breast of the land turtle,
A path already made clear and good.
Looking they saw a long house which a bird could only just fly through in a day.
A short house through which a little tajak flies in a day.
Ngelai: "O that is an enemy's house, friend."
And he donned his coat of hair woven by a woman of Sempok with deformed shoulder.
He put on his war-cap of jungle fowl feathers.
And girded on his sword tufted with hair, as big as an empty paddy bin.
And set on his shoulder a sumpitan.
And grasping the shield with slanting ends Ngelai started to advance.
"Stop, friend," says Bungkok Arok Papong Engkiyong Bujang Pengema Ribis Basong,
"That is not an enemy's house, it is my farm lodge,
My house the worth of a rusa-jar."
The three advanced, and saw a house of one door, a single row of posts,
A beautiful house in the midst of a wilderness.
Bulan: "Whose sleeping place is this?"
Klieng: "That is the sleeping place of Laja, brother of Dara Lantang Sakumbang.
This belongs to Ngelai Bujang Pedar Umbang,
That to Tutong Bujang Lemandau Gendang."

Bulan: "And where is mine?"
Klieng: "You have none, Bulan Menyimbang."
Bulan: "You who have sleeping places are not more brave than I.
In fighting with spears never did I run away.
In fighting with swords never did I fear death." . . .

Sumpitan: blowpipe used for propelling poisoned arrows.

Sumatra

Batak TOBA REGION

DIALOGUE

Girl:
Shall I fish?
Shall I not fish?
Yes, I will fish,
Will have fish to cook.
Shall I marry?
Shall I not marry?
Yes, I will marry.
Then I will have a son to carry,
To carry around on my back,
To take around on my shoulder,
I will rock a son in my arms,
So that his father will laugh too.

Youth:
Shall I till a field?
Shall I not till a field?
Yes, I will work,
Then I will have a field to cultivate.
Shall I marry?
Shall I not marry?
Yes, I will marry,
Then I will have a daughter to carry,
To carry around on my back,
To take around on my shoulder,
I will rock a daughter in my arms
So that her mother will laugh too.

COMPLAINT OF A WIDOW OVER HER DYING SON

O my young shoot,
do not dare
to leave me, a rice-husk.
In your place I will go into the ground.
My son must live on,
live in this world.
I want to joke once again
with my companions.
If you die
ah, then I shall be like a hen let fly,
like a horse turned loose.
My young shoot wants to leave me.
me, untimely born,
who am like a heated pot
that will not hold together
like forged iron.
I must hang my head,
turn my eyes to the ground
when I see women who have children about them.
My mouth is like a tied bag,
like closed tongs,
when I think of the body of my dear
failing there.
Yes, it snatches me up,
it throws me like a lid
when I remember your mouth
that still could not answer
to the words of its mother
who stands alone. . . .
If you die, I must drown,
drown myself in the River Sitjumallan,
if you fall into the depths,
into the deep pit,
which cannot be climbed.
I will do this:
I will make a twisted rope
the road to death.

COMPLAINT OF A FISHERMAN'S WIDOW

You went in a little boat through the great water,
your seat a palm-branch,
and caught the big fish
so that it should be a dainty for the rich,
should be for the bellies of those who do not want to die.
You are he whose fingers never rested,
who threw the big net
and the net of cords into the great water
across which none can swim.
And now I am pitiable,
forsaken by my husband,
so that I am like straw.

The big fish: the text has "the roots of the big fish" (unexplained).

≺ 159 ≻

Nias

Niassan

CREATION MYTH[5]

He arose, Uwu Lowalangi,
He arose, high Luo Zaho.
He went to bathe, to paint his body,
He went to bathe and to reappear again
Up there by the spring that is like a piece of mirror,
Up there by the spring that is like a piece of glass.
He took earth, one handful,
He took earth, the size of an egg,
When he saw his shadow in the water,
When he saw his shadow in the deep water.
He carried it to the village, under the council house,
He carried it to the village, under the dwelling house,
His earth, one handful,
His earth, the size of an egg.
He shaped it like the figure of an ancestor,
He shaped it in the form of a child,
His earth, one handful,
His earth, the size of an egg.
He brought out the pans of the balance,
He brought out the pans for weighing,
He brought out the weight shaped like a hen,
He brought out the weight in the likeness of a cock,
He laid it in the pan of the balance,
He laid it in the pan for weighing,

[5] Beginning of a chant sung at the funeral ceremonies of chiefs.

He weighed the wind like gold,
He weighed the wind like gold-dust.
When he laid it in the pan of the balance,
When he laid it in the pan for weighing,
He laid it on the lips of its mouth,
He laid it by the breath of its breathing,
Thereupon it spoke like a man,
Thereupon it spoke like a child,
Up there before Uwu Lowalangi,
Up there before high Luo Zaho.
He gave him a name,
He gave him a name there:
Sihai, up there, who has no offspring,
Sihai, up there, who has no children.
And he arose, Uwu Lowalangi,
He arose, high Luo Zaho,
He gave a place to what he had made,
He gave a place to his handiwork,
To Sihai, who has no offspring,
To Sihai, who has no children.
And he thought, he reflected,
He thought, he began to move,
Up there, Uwu Lowalangi,
Up there, high Luo Zaho,
Having now one like him in shape,
Having now one like him in body.
There was yet no sun, to guide the thousands,
There was yet no moon, to guide the many.
It was still dark, the land of Uwu Lowalangi,
It was still dark, the land of high Luo Zaho,
And Uwu Lowalangi established him,
High Luo Zaho established him,
Sihai, up there, who has no offspring,
Sihai, up there, who has no children:
"Walk upon the earth, which is shaken by the northwind,
Walk upon the earth, which is shaken by the blast."
A house was built for him of tree-fern,
A house was built for him of tuhu-wood,
Uwu Lowalangi had established him,

High Luo Zaho had established him,
Tuha Sihai, who has no offspring,
Tuha Sihai, who has no children. . . .

SONGS AT A WEDDING

I *The Bride to her Brothers*

O brothers, how have I wronged you
That you are in such haste to bury me,
That gold, O brothers, is more precious to you than I am?
This cannot bring you good fortune, brothers,
Nor bring food for the pigs.
So long as I was among you, brothers,
I willingly did as you said
Whenever you gave me a command
And I have satisfied you in all things.
Why do you give me away to serve strangers?

II *Dialogue: Bride and Mother*

"The words began as if a cannon had been fired.
The people are hurrying by as if driven by the devil.
Countless people are coming. Mother, O Mother,
Where are you sending your child, Mother?"
"You are going into poverty,
Under the house of the rich man is your place,
Be content with your lot,
Do not fear, do not draw back—
The word is spoken as if a cannon had been fired."

Its mouth: the mouth of the figure he has molded.

THE CHIEF MEN OF A VILLAGE ANSWER THE GREETING OF TRAVELERS

As if the sun were rising
Our guests come up;
See them there on Mount Bawo,
The whole land is dazzled.

Like a very great chieftain
Our guests come up.
Why have you come to make alliance
With so small a chieftain?

The country was so dark
Here among us of this place.
Only now does the sky grow bright
For Hoeloe boro dano is come.

Many guests have come
From a kindred tribe,
But not until now guests like these,
Like the risen sun.

Many guests have come,
But not until now guests like these
Who bring a speaking letter.

Like the coming of English ships
Is the coming of these guests,
Like a ship as big as the earth.
Why would you anchor it
In water so shallow?

Once it was in deep water,
The village of those who live here,
But it is not so today;
It is sanded up to the deck
After nine generations.

SONG FOR GIRL DANCERS[6]

The golden eagle rejoices,
The ganowo-bird plays.
In the house of the noble chieftain,
The hastening dancing girls do even as they.

O you who swing your arms, you dancing-girls,
O you who draw the end of the rambudi,
Do not hurry, do not press on one another,
Do not press on one another as you dance!
There are no head-hunters behind us,
There are no traitors before us.
For this is how dancing delights me:
Like a hawk breasting the wind,
Like driftwood slowly moving in the river.
What are they about, the dancers, swinging their arms,
While they curve the end of the rambudi?
As if the source of the wind were rejoicing,
The hearts of the audience are refreshed.
What are they about, while they sway, while they dance,
While the end of the rambudi swings?
It is as if the corners of the mirror-floor in the house were swept and brushed,
Swept and brushed the upper side of the golden platform in the house,
The house of the chieftain, the counsellor,
In the house against which gold is heaped.
And what are they like, the ornaments, the ends of the rambudi,
The garments of the male dancers and the dancing-girls;
And the sotora, which costs thousands,
Which changes its color there like a lagasi-fish,
Which is marked like a homi-eel,
Which is like the glittering stars
At which men delight to look?
So shines the rambudi.
And what are they about, they who swing their arms, the dancers,
While they bend their rounded bodies this way and that,
While they reach out their arms that are like the homi-eel?

[6] Beginning of a long poem.

Look! their fingers are like fusi-crabs,
While they bend their necks, while they dance.
Their golden ear-pendants strike together,
Light their cheeks on either side of their faces.
And the ornaments, the snake-rings strike together;
And so the spectators are astonished
And so we are filled with wonder
At those who swing their arms, the dancing-girls,
Here in the house, in the middle of the mirror-floor,
Here in the house of the chieftain, the counsellor. . . .

EPILOGUE TO A NARRATIVE POEM

The earth is all twisted and turned,
The world is upside down.
The nobility is impoverished,
The nobles live in want.
Everyone drifts like driftwood.
The edge of the sky on either side
Has flown up like a bat,
Has passed like a whirlwind.
The village gate has fallen to pieces
The village common is full of moss.
Even if those yet unborn grow old,
Even if babies still carried on the back grow gray,
They will never see the beauty that was.
It is like an areca nut turned inside out:
The kernel is where the rind was.
Men are estranged from one another, the world is too old
To be a dancing-ground.
When the earth was new
All ornaments were beautifully made.
The breadth of a necklace is no longer fixed.
The world is on the point of perishing:
The ubi does not thrive as before,
Maize-culture has declined,
The whole nobility is impoverished,

Rambudi: a fabric and a garment made from it. *Sotora:* a fabric.

Pig-breeding has fallen off.
Once again: It is like an areca nut turned inside out,
The kernel is outside, the shell is inside.

The edge of the sky, etc.: in the youth of the world the edges of the sky came down so near to the earth that men had only to reach up and pick the heavenly food that grew there.

Lesser Sundas

Do Donggo SUMBAWA

SONGS

I *Girl's Song: Refusing a Lover*

The tree is big, good to lean against,
Its broad leaves are good shade,
Very good to give shade. But I
Would rather stand in the sun.

II *Bride's Song*

Whatever you say and whatever you do,
Whatever happens—not for as long as it takes a sirih-plug to dissolve in the mouth,
Not for a moment do I forget your face.

III *Song of the Sirih-Leaf*

Even withered and dry, withered and dry,
Dried up and only fit to burn—
Everything is sweet from the touch of your hand.

*Leloba Village, East Flores**

DIRGE[7]

You have gone away, where are you?
We who are alive must go too, where?
Your eye sees nothing now, your ear hears nothing now,
we who are alive are alone in the village,
we who are alive walk alone through the land.
You dead who left us before this day,
take stones and throw them at him,
take earth and throw it at him.
We who remain alive are like the cock sitting alone on its perch,
like a dog that lies rolled up before the hearth.
You lie dead there on the mat, alas!
you enter the boat and travel over the sea,
never to come back,
your hand holds the sail, you travel over the sea.
You have gone away, where are you?
We too must go, where?
To the land of the dead, alas!
To the land of the dead, alas!

You dead . . . take stones, etc.: to show the dead man that the dead do not want him, so that he will return. *You enter the boat,* etc.: the soul sails across the sea to the island of the dead.

* People not identified.
[7] An "old song," sung over the dead man's body by his daughter and sister.

*Ili Mandiri, East Flores**

PRAYER AT BURNING OFF A NEW COMMUNAL FIELD

The Lord-over-the-land calls the hotspurs and fighting cocks of the village together.
They bring a split bamboo cane,
They bring the bamboo fire-saw,
They bring a dry palm-leaf as a torch,
They go, they wait for the right time,
They wait till the sun begins to go down.
They are in the field, they knock a hole in the bamboo,
They saw back and forth across the hole, they shave off chips for tinder.
Now the fire flames up, it licks up,
They have the strong fire:
It must burn hot, so that the ashes of the trees will be white as flowers,
It must lick like the arms of the cuttle-fish in the sea,
It must flame up as fast as the eel shoots through the water.
They kindle the palm-leaf torch and fire the field:
The smoke must gather like black storm clouds,
The flames must dance bright like red holiday sarongs fluttering in the wind,
The tree stumps must be black as crows,
The ashes must spread out evenly like a great white cloth,
The fire must eat upward to where the ax stopped cutting.
Then the hotspurs and fighting cocks dance,
They go home to the village and tell the Lord-over-the-land.
He has fowl roasted and rice boiled for them,
He gives them the feast-day rice to eat,
He chooses a goat big as a buffalo and a giant pig as a sacrifice
And then he puts the bamboo fire-saw safely away.

Lord-over-the-land: not its owner but its overseer on behalf of the village which owns it.

* People not identified.

Wetar Island*

CURSE TABOOING A LAKE

Whoever may come, from all lands,
from the head or the foot of an island,
from the east of the island
or from the west of the island,
looking for pigs,
hunting for wildcats,
or to fish or to gather fruit,
they are all one to me—
only one thing: strike them dead!
Set out, kill them all to the last man,
so that the island will be purified.
The evil spirit shall enter the crocodile.
If the stranger is sitting in his boat,
may the crocodile eat him!
If he tries to run on land
or to climb a tree, he shall fall.
If not, then let pigs eat him!
If not, the tree he has cut down
shall fall and kill him!

* People not identified.

Celebes

Minahasa*

SONG OF A DYING GIRL

O Mother, when I am dead,
Comb my hair smooth and braid it.
When you dress me, Mother, put a fine white dress on me,
A fine white dress, Mother, and linen from Semarang.
And when I am carried to the grave, O Father,
See that my kinsmen accompany my corpse;
When I am lowered into the grave,
O Father, let me down gently.

SONG AT THE DEPARTURE OF A BEAUTIFUL GIRL

O Star of Tonsea, where are you going?
You were always the pattern of gaiety to your companions.
Now you are leaving Tonsea;
Ah, your companions have fallen silent.
For the shining star has gone.
She went to Kema, never to come back,
She will never come back, for she went there for love.

* People not identified.

SONG OF A GIRL TO BRING BACK HER UNFAITHFUL LOVER

Be happy, my lover, I love you so dearly;
I love you so dearly, but you listen to those who are my enemies,
You hear those who are angry with me—what am I to do?
What am I to do to justify myself?
Ah, we shall never be one!
We shall never be one in this world!

Toradja CENTRAL CELEBES

HARVEST-SEASON SONGS

I

Wind, where are you?
The leaves of the trees hang still.
Where are you, wind?
The leaves of the trees do not move.

II

The level of the sea has gone down,
The sand flats glitter in the sun.
The water has gone down in the river,
The sand banks shine in the light.

Kabajana Island*

SONG AT A HEAD-HUNTING FESTIVAL

Tongimpuu, ruler of the world,
Is of a mind to make war
On Bilangiano, the lightning,
On Lintuano, the thunder.

He summons his brothers,
Tongimpuu, ruler of the world,
And bids them put on war-dress.
They come, wearing armor,
Armed with sword,
Lance, and shield.

They come down to the coast,
Put their ship in the water,
Pushing off from the beach in the shallow water;
They moor it in the roadstead, ready to sail.

With a leap thirty yards long
He springs in.
Scarcely stooping, already he stands straight
In the bow of the ship,
Ordering them to sail,
Tongimpuu, ruler of the world.
Small as a pigeon, so far away it is,
Like an oil-nut, the ship dances.

One day they travel,
Eight days more the ship sails,
Until they see land,
Shaped like a lute.
The ship has reached it,

* People not identified.

Lies well anchored in the harbor.
He calls to the crowd
Rejoicing on the beach.

Now he goes ashore,
Tongimpuu, ruler of the world,
Makes his way
To the peak of the mountain.
Below him he sees the villages,
Bilangiano, the lightning,
Gathering his people
To celebrate the great festival.

Bilangiano, the lightning
Hastens up,
With hurried steps
He comes to the village.
Now they sound the alarm-drum,
Bilangiano, the lightning,
Lintuano, the thunder,
To summon the men from the festival.

They come to the fore-hall,
Breathless they climb
To the dancing platform.
They fan with the ends of their coats
To cool the great heat,
To dry their sweat.

All hurry off,
Hasten up to the village.
Bilangiano, the lightning,
Comes down to lead them.
Down he goes
To fetch his sword,
His lance and shield,
Loud sounds his war-cry.

Tongimpuu, ruler of the world,
Challenges him to come out,

Minded to kill him.
All one day they fight
Then he is killed
Bilangiano, the lightning.

He has fallen.
His head carried off,
Dead he lies.
Bilangiano, the lightning.

Down the mountain he leads his brothers
That they may go back,
Tongimpuu, ruler of the world.
"Let us hasten home
And summon the men to a feast,
Let us celebrate
For eight days and eight nights!"

Lute: so the German translation, though the lute is not an Indonesian instrument.

Moluccas

Buru*

SONG

Passing a bay where there are many kinar trees,
You see a leaf fall, then it turns another way.
Two meet to give each other back their love-presents; but they laugh.

Patasiwa or Patalima CERAM

SONG FOR A KACHUA DANCE

Little Timora,
A girl with a face that shines like oil,
A girl with cheeks full of dimples,
A girl with eyebrows like a frigate-bird,
A girl with teeth polished smooth,
Goes out one day, fools her mother, fools her father,
She goes down to the brook, she goes down hiding pinang in her dress,
She goes to the water, she goes down hiding sirih in her dress.

Hiding pinang . . . sirih: the pinang and sirih are presents for her lover.

* People not identified.

BOATMEN'S SONG

There are many hens in Papua,
Many hens there,
If one dies, there's another instead,
There are many hens in Papua.

You saw her everywhere, like a coconut,
If anyone tried to hug her, she protested,
And her screeching was heard like a flute.
Now the gentleman has another woman,
Now he can hug and kiss.

Near Nusa island
He stands by the prow,
Djapara raises her anchor,
And he is sad at heart.

The two hundred gulden he is wasting on the woman
Go round in his head,
While he stands with his right foot already on Djapara
And his left foot still on the yawl.

He plants a new hedge
And a pomegranate in his garden.
He marries again
Because they love each other.

You are like the moon, the moon,
You are like the stars and the sun.
You want to leave already, Sir,
I will keep you till early morning.

She is like a stinging nettle,
So he turns her away,
He has wasted two hundred gulden,
He makes a wry face.

Whose daughter is this girl
Who is wearing the shell-ring?
He has taken her
And now he marries her.

Whose daughter is this girl
With the pearl-embroidered bodice?
He has her now
And presses her tenderly to his heart.

Malay of the Moluccas

LINKED PANTUNS

Whose cock is that,
The black cock with a broken foot?
Whose daughter is that,
She who is like a jewel?

The black cock with a broken foot
Sits on a wheel-barrow.
She who is like a jewel
Makes my heart glad.

It sits on a wheel-barrow,
The rice-bird flies to the river.
She makes my heart glad,
Kissing on the cheek is like incense.

The rice-bird flies to the river,
I blow out an arrow and break its foot.
Kissing on the cheek is like incense,
Kissing on the mouth revives the heart.

≺ 178 ≻

Philippines

Ifugao LUZON

THE MYTH OF NUMPUTUL, THE SELF-BEHEADED

1

Kanadih Balitok of Dalegdeg,
When the sun is half way,
He sees his enemies at Dalegdeg,
That they're raging against him,
Urging each other against him,
Won't give him another night.
In the darkness of night time,
The kindred confer together.
On the morn of the morrow,
They take down their food basket,
Begin to eat and finish.
They put things away,
Change to betel chewing.
When the sun is half way,
Ngalan-da the kindred,
"Let us go find strong sorcery."
They pack for the journey,
Tuck on their hipbags,
Next belt on their bolos,
Take their spears in hand,
Descend from their houses.
They cross their outskirts at Dalegdeg,
Go downstream and arrive at
The lake of the Downstream Region.

Kanadi diye they see it,
Turn their spears around and plunge into it,
Come to the bottom and arrive at
The village of Ghoul and Facer-Against-Enemies,
Ringed-Nose, and Drooped-Over,
And Sound-of-Crunched-Bones.

2

They, it is said, enter,
Thrust their spears into the ground,
They give each other betels,
And turn them red-spittled.
Said the Ghouls of the Underworld,
"What is the reason for your coming
To our village in the Underworld?"
Spake Balitok of Dalegdeg,
"The reason we have come is:
Our creditors urge each other against us,
Likewise our enemies at Dalegdeg.
We've come," he says, "to seek for
Strong Sorcery,
Expulsion and Counteraction."
Said Ghoul of the Underworld,
"Wait a while," says he,
"Till our youngest-born comes home."
In a little while in the Underworld,
When the sun marks mid-afternoon,
Ngalana Self-Beheaded of the Underworld,
Comes homeward bound.
They see Self-Beheaded of the Underworld,
He's rejoicing and rejoicing,
He's dancing and dancing,
His neck-stump is bubbling,
He goes grabbing all kinds of snakes,
And all kinds of centipedes,
And thrusting them down his neck-stump.
And increasingly he rejoices,
Accelerates his dancing.
Nothing else than that Balitok be seized with fear,

And up spake Ghoul of the Underworld,
"Don't be afraid, Balitok,
For that is the one you'll take back with you,
So get ready to go, Balitok."

3

Soon they rise to the top of the lake,
The lake of the Underworld,
Leave the water and go upstream,
Nothing else than that Balitok look side-wise,
And *ah nakayang!* Self-Beheaded,
Is seen to be rejoicing,
Dancing along as they go,
Reaching out and grabbing
All kinds of snakes and centipedes
And thrusting them into his neck-stump!
They go not noting time's passage,
And pass through the outskirts of Dalegdeg.
They ascend and enter Dalegdeg.
Balitok wastes no time,
He catches a large pig and ties it,
Trammels it and invokes this Obtainment. . . .
He sees and "faces" Self-Beheaded
And feeds him raw meat.
Kanadih his Obtainment
Is pointed against their enemies.
Mala, it is said, Self-Beheaded,
Gathers his strength for an onslaught,
He sees their enemies at Dalegdeg,
Descends on both sides of their families.
He sees their enemies at Dalegdeg,
And includes their boy-babes.
As if skeletonized—there's left no remainder.
He sees the sorcery and *kanadi*
The eaves have grown lighter and risen!
And there's nobody talking.
Balitok sees his enemies at Dalegdeg,
They become like kinsmen, some of them,
Become like uncles the others.

Their debts against him are lost,
Their omens against him are broken.
He sees those he's speared at Dalegdeg,
And no one comes out to avenge them.

That is the reason, in Dalegdeg,
That they farm and their crops are fruitful,
And ripen, and there's no crop-failure.

Nabaloi Igorot BENGUET, LUZON

FROM AN *ANGBA*[8]

Chorus:
Head takers we, brave;
Fighters we, brave.
Therefore we awoke;
Therefore we were rich;
Therefore we were powerful;
Therefore we lived long.

The civet cat is brave,
The civet cat is active.
It climbs the daguay,
It climbs the sabwan.
It eats raw meat;
It eats it bloody.
(*Chorus:* Head takers we, etc.)

The civet cat travels at night.
It fights the enemy;
It fights the enemy.
It eats raw meat;
It eats it bloody.
(*Chorus*)

[8] Sung at a *bindayan,* formerly head-hunting celebration, now given to cure sickness or in fulfilment of a vow.

Clouds of the mountain,
Hide us, the pursuers.
You cause the moving stones, moving stones,
To roll down, head taker.
(*Chorus*)

Crow flying,
Go north to Loo;
Go look down at
The hanging head.
Croaking crow,
What are you looking at?
Go look down at
The body we beheaded,
The body we beheaded.
(*Chorus*)

The wild boar coming from the west,
Walking from side to side,
Was cutting off
The gabi I planted.
Oh! There is the torch of Sagod,
Traveling in line,
The light shining.
You can see, probably,
The body we beheaded,
The body we beheaded.

SONG

Brighter, brighter, shine you moon; brighter, brighter, shine you moon.
I will follow the trail to the hot lands; I will follow the trail to the hot lands.
Rocks, rocks to step on; rocks, rocks to step on.
Bamboo, bamboo to hold to; bamboo, bamboo to hold to.

Tinguian ABRA PROVINCE, LUZON

SONG FOR A CEREMONIAL DANCE[9]

The young leaves of the coconut wave.
Wave, wave, they wave.

The leaves of the aba are not alike.
Alike, alike, are not alike.

The leaves of the nonang turn back and forth.
Back and forth, back and forth, turn back and forth.

The leaves of the lamay quake.
Quake, quake, they quake.

The leaves of the bangon arise.
Arise, arise, they arise.

The leaves of the rattan cut and twist.
Twist, twist, cut and twist.

The leaves of the oling rustle and rattle.
Rattle, rattle, rustle and rattle.

The leaves of the bakan fall before time.
Fall, fall, fall before time. . . .

Bamboo of Podayan, ever living, ever living.
Ever living, ever living, bamboo of Podayan.

Bamboo of Baliweyan go "wey" when the wind blows.
Go "wey," go "wey," bamboo of Baliweyan.

[9] Extracts. The lines are sung alternately by the girls and the boys.

Bamboo of Bataan like the sunshine.
Sunshine, sunshine, bamboo of Bataan.

My cane of Bamboo gives out a clang.
Clang, clang, gives out a clang.

Bamboo of Palai wave up and down.
Wave, wave, wave up and down.

MELANESIA

New Guinea

Kurelu BALIEM VALLEY

DIRGE FOR A SON KILLED IN BATTLE

THE FATHER	CHORUS OF WOMEN
The warriors went to the Tokolik	*Ai-i-e-eo*
And moved slowly past the ponds.	*Ai-i-e-eo*
He, all alone, went forward.	*Ai-i-e-eo*
Now he is gone	*E-eo*

Our child is dead
And this is very sad.
Our land can be here no more
We will go far away.

Shall we go northward, to the spring of Elesi?
Or south into the Southern Valley?
Shall we go to the peoples in the west,
Or shall we start a new life, far away?

YOUNG MEN'S SONG

Where are all the young girls gone?
We danced with them at the Liberek
And now they are all married.
Well, what can be done,
When the kains take all the women?

Kains: leaders.

Kuman CENTRAL HIGHLANDS

SONG AT A PUBLIC COURTSHIP CEREMONY

Where is the site [about which we are going to sing]?
Here it is: the open place is here.
Where you see the binga and koiya flowers grow on top of the stone
Where the leaves of yomga and dande trees are shining.

What is the name of the place over there?
It is Kumbu Kambu down in the valley.
Where the tsirandie and tarandie flowers bloom
Where the bogonwan tree grows.
Its fruits are ripe and the kagl and wagua birds feed.
They came from beyond the water, from the hillside they came.

On top of the Kuglbagl and Darua ridges go see
The muglua and agula birds are sweetly singing
The gande and wena birds are nodding their heads.
Quietly on hand and foot go, see.

On top as high as the Mauge and Waiya our song shall go
Over the Kuglbagl and Darua ridges it shall go
As far as Numbu and Maugl it shall be heard
Although we stay here the spirit of our song goes on.

WOMEN'S SONG AT A GIRL'S INITIATION

Go fetch water from the well, cut the leaves and bring the food
Chop the firewood and heat the stones
Unfold the mats, spread out the leaves,—
Men and women are coming, children arrive.
Let us give room to them.

Ascend to the top of the mountain Chaumau
See the nice woods
Climb up the kundombo and gandia trees
See their white and red-hued flowers open.

Watch the birds kinde, wendo, dire assemble on a branch.
Listen to the songs of kagl, waugl, and dilu as they sing in pairs.
They have all gone now, over the river, over the hills.
There is a hole in the tree; you go see how nice the child of the rainbow hides like the oyien-flower.
Go see and find the lightning and thunder's children, how beautiful they are:
On top of the Pindaude plains they dwell and stay
May they descend; we wish to see them;
We want to know and hold them.

Mbowamb MOUNT HAGEN REGION

CHARM TO RESTORE A DYING MAN

Heart alive, alive, alive!
Liver alive, alive, alive!
Kenenena-banana alive, alive, alive!
Jara-tree alive, alive, alive!
The kundkunt-bird sits on the keraip-tree and beats its wings.
He is full of life!

LAMENT OF A WIDOW FOR HER DEAD HUSBAND

In Mund lived the man Petlimb!
He went to war and drove the enemy east and west!
ejo we e e e eje
In the eyes of the people of Mund are tears!
owe e e e ejo
He lived in Mund and now he has gone into the east *ijo we*
In the eyes of the people of Mund are tears!
owe eje, e e e e ejo.

Into the east: to the land of the dead.

LOVE SONG

elelo elelo elelo le—e pajo wapajo we wapajo lole
Where can Ken of Pokatl have gone to?
I sit on the bank of the Klomant River and call to her!
I just want to hear her voice, then I will go away.

WOMAN'S SONG[1]

i ruwema ruwema elka wia wai
If you're fond of that redhead from Kopetl,
Why! there in the west the wench is lying in the men's house!
If you're fond of your big cymbium snail,
You ought to give it to me and hang it on me yourself!
I don't like lying in the sun alone.
I feel too hot under the mat.
Oh, must I long and loiter around for nothing?
Wakl, I embrace you; Wutle Wakl, embrace me!

COURTING SONG AND REPLY[2]

I

The girl:
Oh, my handsome boy!
You think I ought to say something nice to you?
Just you listen, and I'll tell you something!
You act like Kokon Morok himself,
My handsome boy!
You want me to tell you something more!
Now just you listen!
The way the snail twines, put your arm around me that way,
My handsome boy!
Haven't you had enough yet?

[1] "The wife of Jamka Letlimb sang this song about Koipe Wakl" (Vicedom, as cited. See Sources).

[2] Vicedom (see Sources) calculates that these songs from a courtship ceremony no longer in use date back to 1840–60.

As men throw themselves into the rushing stream, so you may handle me,
My handsome boy!
Say more to you than that?—what makes you think so?

II

The boy:
Oh, you beautiful girl!
You think I ought to say something to you, too.
Just you listen!
What do you mean by jeering at me like that?
Oh, you beautiful girl!
Do you want to hear something else nice?
Just you listen!
As the flood carries stones away with it, so you carry me away,
You beautiful girl!
I had to say something to you—it was you who wanted it!

Wogeo Island*

SONGS

I

He has two ear-rings,
Two ear-rings which shine like two suns.
He gazes at himself in the looking glass.
Yes, his sweetheart likes him.

II

My sweetheart has soft skin,
Skin soft and smooth.
Her skin glows like sunset on the waters,
Like the sunbeams through the palm leaves.

Kokon Morok: a Don Juanesque figure of legend.

* People not identified.

Fuyughé SUFALAN, PAPUA

THE DANCER[3]

Ou-é . . .
A diadem of feathers on my brow,
Diamonds, diadems of the bird of paradise,
Ou-é . . .
This beautiful diadem on my brow . . .

Ou-é . . .
This beautiful diadem on my brow,
Lightly I touch this country with my feet,
Ou-é . . .
Lightly I touch it with my feet.

Ou-é . . .
This beautiful diadem on my brow,
Gracefully I touch this soil:
Ou-é . . .
Everybody throng around me! . . .

SONG[4]

In the distance, the *Okélé* bird,
Over there, how sad he is,
Over there, the little *Okélé* . . .

Over there, the *Okélé* bird
Perhaps he sees the rain falling?
He sees the rain and sings of it,
Over there, the little *Okélé*.

[3] Dance song, composed by Koma Doubé Pio, "the great poet of the district." The title is his own.
[4] Composed by Koma Doubé Pio.

He sees the rain and hails it . . .
Ah! . . . You sing, and my own heart,
My bitter heart is so dejected . . .

SONG OF OLD AGE AND A WHITE HEAD

The cicada of the forest
Ghélélé has sung.
A cloud on Mount Ghumé,
A cloud has covered its head.

O my sons and daughters,
Come down and see
The shadow over our land
This shadow which descends . . .

Will I ever be able to climb again?
I am too old, and worn out,
My body too feeble,
Far too feeble has become.

The cicada of the forest
Ghélélé has sung.

Koita CENTRAL DIVISION, PAPUA

SONG SUNG WHILE FENCING A GARDEN[5]

On an iri we sleep, on another iri we sleep,
we with somebody, on an iri we sleep,

Ghélélé: this large Papuan cicada sings at nightfall.

[5] Literal translation (punctuation added).

we with girls, on a bed of iri we sleep,
on another pile we sleep, we sleep in couples,
we sleep, we sleep together on an iri, we sleep,
we sleep in couples, we sleep, we sleep together,
we sleep.

Mekeo PAPUA

"SING-SINGS" OF NATURE

I *A Bird That Calls Before Dawn*

1

The world is day-breaking! The world is day-breaking!
My dawn bird is singing!
The world is day-breaking! The world is day-breaking!
My cock bird is singing!
The world is day-breaking! The world is day-breaking!

2

The bird is singing!
My heart is throbbing!
Dawn bird is singing!
My heart is throbbing!

II *An Unknown Land*

I have now come to the land of unknown,
Where thunder rolls and where water flows down,
Sweeping through villages on its way,
Where lightning flashes and the flood flows down,
Flooding the whole world upon its way.

Iri: the Koita sunblind, made of dried banana leaves, which makes a comfortable mattress.

III *The World Calling on Dawn*

Come o my dawn!
And dawn on me.

Come o my morn!
And gaze on me!

IV *Asking Where the Thunder Peals*

Where is the sky beating?
Above my home beating!
Where is the sky beating?
Above my land beating!

D'Entrecasteaux Islands

Dobuan DOBU

INCANTATION AT FIRST TWINING YAM VINES

Kapali! kapali
twisting around!
he laughs with joy!
I with my leaves
my shoot long in the budding point
my shoot broad in the leaf.
Kapali, kapali
twisting around
he laughs with joy.
I with my garden darkened with foliage
I with my leaves.
Kapali, kapali
twisting around
he laughs with joy.

Kapali: a species of spider. "The suggestion is that the yam vines continue to work up and around the sticks as a *kapali* web-weaving" (R. F. Fortune, as cited. See Sources).

CHARM AT A CEREMONIAL BATHING TO MAKE ONE BEAUTIFUL AND IRRESISTIBLE

Dawn over Woodlark Island, the sun casting off its coating of night,
your breaking forth from covering as the sun breaking forth from darkness,
my breaking forth from covering as the sun breaking forth from darkness,
your fine skin breaking forth from the evil peeling from your body,
my fine skin breaking forth from the evil peeling from my body.
my skin is that of a man of rank.
long bagi
bagi closed and kept long in the bound up basket.
your fine skin breaking forth from the evil peeling from your body,
my fine skin breaking forth from the evil peeling
from my body
from my hip
from the skin of my skull
peeling off
to my feet it descends
I hurl it from me,
to the tips of my hand it descends
I hurl it from me.

SONG OF THE DEPARTED SPIRIT[6]

I go hillwards to Bwebweso
By Dokwabu's white pandanus flower
I go hillward to Bwebweso.

The white, white pandanus flower,
From the palm I have climbed
I look out upon the path behind me,
I mourn for Dobu.

Your breaking forth, etc.: the "you" is a supernatural. *Bagi:* shell necklace.

6 Dance song of the first dance after mourning is over.

LOVE SONGS

I

Tell her to bear in mind
        at Badilai bay
my sweetheart tell her
tell her to bear in mind.

Tell her to bear in mind
with her child confidant
let him bring a canoe and embark
that we meet on the way
my sweetheart tell her.

II

From the cliff of the north-east
the cave booms seawards
from the cliff of the north-east.

My sister-in-law sleeping
his red hair
I slept dreaming of it
from the cliff of the north-east.

III *To a Mountain Woman*

My speech goes to your house floor
your flute you breathe to singing
you breathe to singing, singing,
I cry unto your house floor.

The speech of the mountain
refreshes like wind rising and falling
your flute you breathe to singing
my speech goes to your house floor.

DANCE SONGS

I

The cock is crowing
my sweetheart embrace me
dawn breaks hitherward
your embraces are sweet to me
my sweetheart embrace me.

II

The east wind is blowing
fish hawk he swoops down hither
swoops, swoops down hither
the east wind is blowing

don your red dance skirt
your young breasts come newly
the tabu will rend them
fish hawk he swoops downward.

III

He is singing, singing inland
from the straits of Natuwa
black satin bird singing inland.

At Kelologea one lies dead
Mwarebu, the maiden
her mourning sweet sounding
he is singing, singing inland
black satin bird singing inland.

IV

I wander without a mother
the village darkens I sleep
wandering alone motherless
I wander without a mother

would I were with our sister
soup she'd pour for my drinking
wandering alone motherless
the village darkens I sleep
I wander without a mother.

V

You had me awake night long
Budia woman
flute playing arousing me
you had me awake night long

our basket you carry and
we shall dip up sand
sea water we'll drink
flute playing arousing me.

VI

Kuyoni child Kuyoni
undress that I may see
undress that I see, see.

Kuyoni her mons of Venus
white as the white pandanus flower
undress that I may see.

VII

A man must tell the mother.
Yawaula is cold
a deep sea and cold.

The slain man is brought back
O that Kaburigi might remain
and mourn me, dying before him.
Yawaula is cold
a man must tell the mother.

Tabu: here, "disfiguring spell." *Sea water,* etc.: a way of refreshing the body after a night of love-making. *Kaburigi:* the dead man.

Bwaidogan GOODENOUGH ISLAND

LOVE INCANTATION[7]

Hibiscus, my hibiscus
Hibiscus, my hibiscus,
Let us go
Would that we might go
To Wafalo Point
My husband we lie down and rest.

MARRIAGE SONG

I Nedoiyasi my husband is Walabeyana
I Nedoiyasi my husband is Walabeyana
Walabeyana your ways of living of old
You have laid them aside
I Walabeyana my wife is Nedoiyasi
Nedoiyasi your husband is Walabeyana
I my husband is Walabeyana
I my wife is Nedoiyasi.

WAR SONG, SUNG BEFORE GOING INTO BATTLE

Hot spring makoko fish I sing
In my wild pig's home I sleep
My foes flee from me
I make my face like a wild man's
I make my face like a stranger's
I make my face I make my face like an evil spirit's
I make my face evil
My younger brothers my face it is vengeful
I make my face like an evil spirit's

[7] Literal translation, slightly altered (as are the next four songs).

I remain in my lair in the woods
My appearance is evil
I with my younger brothers
I courageous tremendously
The muscle of my upper arm it sinks it swells.

CANOE SONG

Buoyant it is buoyant
It speeds along and it travels fast
It speeds along and it travels fast
It flies like the butterfly that crosses the water
Like the firefly it flies like the garfish it flies
It speeds along.

SONG

In the deep forest
I go crying
He waves the fire-sticks he waves the fire-sticks.

Wild pig's home: the woods; the warrior is hiding there until dawn, waiting to make his attack.

The butterfly: a particular species of butterfly, which is often seen flying across the water.

Waves the fire-sticks: to light up the path.

Trobriand Islands

Trobriandan

SONG OF WAR[8]

1

O my mother, my own mother,
As I sit I weep,
As I walk I moan,
As the dancers weave their dance.
While we gather round
Our new ship to see.
In grief I stand
In tears I sit,
Moaning I go.

2

My own mother did neglect me.
'Twas my sister did befriend me,
Borne up on the waves,
At the farewell by the shore.
The women did farewell me,
Full of grief did farewell me
Clasping their breasts;
Lest Topileta might not know me,
Nor the father I brought,
To your shame and mine.
My own mother did neglect me,
'Twas my sister did befriend me,

[8] The theme is a fight, a death, and an exile.

Borne up on the waves,
At the parting by the shore.

3

You fled from Kuyawa;
Into exile you fled,
From the blind man you anointed,
From the beauty of measured words;
For you poetry was dead.
You took up words of anger,
That angered and distressed,
That incited to war,
When Mwayani fell.
With trouble in our hearts,
We inter our dead;
And you are in exile,
Who did the blind anoint.

4

I weep as I remember
Our parting by the pole;
The feeling of our fear,
The feeling of our love.
I weep on thy love token,
The little that you gave,
Standing by the slipway,
As I sat among the lashings.
I weep as I remember
Our parting by the pole.

5

The children cry in misery,
For I am gone,
While they gaze from the shore.
The children cry in misery,
For I am gone,
While they gaze from the shore.
In their misery they dance,

Gumakibu is gone,
While they gaze from the shore.
My mother too is wailing,
Call back, call back, my son.
The children cry in misery,
For I am gone,
While they gaze from the shore.

6

I'll think of a spirit boat,
I'll go and dance,
Where the waves break,
Where the foam swirls,
I'll gather the sea weed,
And put it on my head;
And my boat is a spirit boat
Returned from the sea.
I'll think of a spirit boat,
I'll go and dance.

LOVE-MAGIC SPELL

Leaves of dirt and leaves of cleansing,
Leaves of dirt and leaves of cleansing,
Smooth as the bark of the reyava-tree
As the tail of the opossum.
My face shines in beauty;
I cleanse it with leaves;
My face, I cleanse it with leaves. . . .

Beautiful will my face remain,
Flashing will my face remain,
Buoyant will my face remain!
No more it is my face,
My face is as the full moon.
No more it is my face,
My face is as the round moon.

Topileta: ruler of the afterworld. *Gumakibu:* the exile himself.

I pierce through,
As the creamy shoots of the areca leaf,
I come out,
As a bud of the white lily.

Bismarck Archipelago

*Gazelle Peninsula, New Britain**

THIEF'S SPELL

Black concealment be about me! Black night be about me! May it be like black soot all about!

Let none be able to see! Let none be able to see me and recognize me! Let me be a leguan-lizard, that vanishes unseen! Let me be a ghost, that no one sees!

If the noise I make must be heard, let me remain concealed! Let me be like a ghost, the sound it makes is heard, but it is not seen!

Moanus ADMIRALTY ISLANDS

SONG OF A WOMAN NAMED HI PAK

I stood on the beach of Tjokele.
I waved.
I stopped waving.
My hand was tired.
The sails heading south disappeared.
My man is Koun.
I stood on the beach at Tjawokil.
I cried out.
I stopped crying out.
My jaw was tired.
The sails at the place where they are dragged inland had disappeared.
My man is Kamau.

* People not identified.

Duke of York Islands*

SONGS

I *Women's Song at a Wedding Feast*

He takes hold of her:
"A rainbow!"
They sing out
uin ueu.
She says: "Look!
a new stripe
in the rainbow."
With their most beautiful ornaments
on their bodies
they go bathing.
She bites him.

II *Song of a Men's Secret Society*

A woman sees the tumbuan-spirit's cock feathers.
She vomits,
cries: *Noi jaja;*
the spirit looks down,
moves like a snake in the water
and sings. One man beats the slit-drum,
all paint their foreheads,
all go into the bush,
all see the bush-spirit Leleo—
he comes down from a tree,
his body painted like a snake's skin;
all strike bells,
all put on feathers,
noise sounds over the sea.

III *Men's Song*

She cries out sobbing
as she sees

* People not identified.

the shadow
with a mouth: Stay there,
stay there, you ghost!
E au!

IV *Women's Song at a Dance Song Festival*

Good fire, good singing,
all the women are singing,
calling to their mothers,
beautiful feather ornaments in their hands.
Others, come as guests in a canoe,
watch the dancing,
they leave—a storm comes up.
Those standing in the canoe all conjure it
by singing.
The sea lies still and smooth.
All rejoice.

V *Men's Song*

She spins round dancing
before his eyes,
he waves to her with his hand
and turns to go away.
"You have such beautiful eyes."
io!
She, Lareijali, goes among the seaweed
and picks it.
"There! look! what a
man! what a fine body!" She sees
the other man and
calls sadly after her
own man.
Then she goes to the beach.

VI *Women's Song*

Strong wind,
the storm-spirit rages and roars
auinai au

all the women see him—his
head is bristly—
are startled
—they sit down and sing.
Then they all walk about
together.
One says: Now it is over—
we will go to the beach
and go out in a boat.

Solomon Islands

People of Buin SOUTHERN BOUGAINVILLE

SONG OF A SICK CHIEF

I have lain in the house,
My countrymen,
I whose fame fills the air!
Why did it have to happen
That I should remain in the house hidden from the world!
A messenger came to me and said:
"Already your elder brother
Is cutting down the wood there
For a fighting ground,
Longing for battle
And searching for you."

My countrymen,
I whose fame fills the air!
Why did it have to happen
That I should remain in the house hidden from the world!
A messenger came and said to me:
"Listen! your people are looking for you and grieving
There in the chiefs' house named 'Prison,'
They who sit there now
They would be off,
They would dart the spear
And raise their war-cry
In the wood cleared for battle!"

My countrymen,
I whose fame fills the air!

Why did it have to happen
That I should remain in the house hidden from the world!
My friend Chopper-Parrot came and wept.
My countrymen,
I whose fame fills the air!
And you have held me to be one
Who knows the sharpness of the javelin!

WOMAN'S SONG

Red Tuft-tree, come,
Slip into the hiding place
Here at the mouth of the brook,
Where the love-leaves are close by!
I will put you to sleep in a leaf.
And when you go, put a leaf
In your arm-band.

Red Tuft-tree, come,
Slip into the hiding place,
Into the taro-patch
Where the tongue-leaves are close by!
I will put you to sleep in a leaf,
And when you go, put a leaf
In your arm-band.

MAN'S SONG

I followed your track with anger in my heart.
When you become a widow,
I will take you home.—
I was still little
When you were made to go to your husband Tree-Stump.—
I followed your track with anger in my heart.

Red Tuft-tree: a parasitic plant with red flowers, growing high in trees. Here, the name the woman gives her lover. *Love-leaves, tongue-leaves:* the leaves from which her skirt is made.

When your dead husband bathes in the otherworld sea
I want to put a leaf from the fringe of your skirt in my arm-band.—
Your husband is short,
Tell him this: "You will yet come to know the spear.
He already has it in his hand for that."

MAN'S SONG: AGAINST A WOMAN

You smouldering twig, you are too good at asking for things!
You made me, Bast-tree, give you those beads,
But then you kept away from me.
You said: "If you gave me three lengths of gold cord
Then you could give me twin almonds.
We would hide away, you and I,
And lie by the smouldering-twig skirt.
When we had lain so,
I would pick leaves from the akakona-tree
And rub myself with them."

Your body is
The stinking swamp at night
In which strayed travelers weep until dawn.

Your body is
The foul river-mouth
Where I, Chopper-Parrot,
Could not sleep for flies.

Nasioi BOUGAINVILLE

WOMEN'S SONG

I wish, Tobereke, you had married me.
You went by, looking away; I am weeping.

Twin almonds: testicles.

*Sa'a Island**

KAHUTO, THE OWL

[A bedtime lullaby]

Hoot! wife of mine, owl wife
Hoot! roast for you and me
Hoot! let's go and see the dance
Hoot! at King Eagle's
Hoot! at Torowala on the hill
      A pig yam for me
Hoot! how are we to go?
Hoot! let's go by sea
Hoot! my feet will get wet
Hoot! or how are we to go?
Hoot! let's go by the path
Hoot! my feet will get dirty
Hoot! let's fly like birds
      Come on! Come on!

*San Cristobal Island**

CHARM FOR RAIN[9]

My dracaena, let the great storm come,
A great storm, surf rushing both ways.
My dracaena, let the lightning flash,
Let the thunder sound on the far horizon,
Let the thunder sound on the near horizon,
Lightning speed hither, waters of Maramara,

* People not identified.

[9] "Only the opening words of the [charm], which is a long and very fine description of a great storm on the coast" (C. E. Fox, as cited. See Sources).

Strike hard the source of the waters of Maramara:
Strike and tear out where the great rocks go deep,
Sweep down thence the great banyan,
Drag it to the far horizon,
Let it overshadow darkly the great sharks.
O red dracaena leaf, what is that? a great storm,
Roaring and pressing down;
Roaring and dragging out the trunk of the great fata-tree,
Carrying down the landslip from the great river,
Carrying its trunk down to Mara.

Banks Islands and New Hebrides

Lakona, Santa Maria, Banks Islands*

IN HONOR OF MAROS DURING HIS ABSENCE AT SEA[10]

(*The poet, speaking as Maros:*)
Leale! ale!
I am an eagle, I have soared to the furthest dim horizon.
I am an eagle, I have flown and lighted at Mota.
I have sailed with whirring noise round the mountain.
I have gone down island after island in the West to the base of heaven.
I have sailed, I have seen the lands.
I have sailed in circles, I have been strongly set.
An ill wind has drifted me away, has drawn me away from you two.
How shall I make my way round to you two?
The sounding sea stretches empty to keep me away from you.
You, Mother, you are crying for me, how shall I see your face?
You, Father, you are crying for me, how shall I see your face?
I only long for you, and weep; it is irksome to me; I go about as an orphan, I alone, and who is my companion?
Roulsulwar you are crying for me without the house.

* People not identified.

[10] Codrington (as cited. See Sources) prints this as prose. The line divisions given are based on his punctuation. The last five lines are repeated in performance.

(*The poet, addressing Maros:*)
Youths!
My friend, you have lingered; I have lingered over your song.
I have measured it, and lengthened out my voice, the sound of it has spread down hither to my place.
Ask, hear; who was it that measured the song of Maros?
It was the song-measurer who sits by the way to Lakona.

*Lepers Island, New Hebrides**

KITE-FLYING SONG

Wind! wherever you may abide, wherever you may abide, Wind! come hither; pray take my kite away from me afar. E-u! E-u! Wind! blow strong and steady, blow and come forth, O Wind!

Roulsulwar: Maros's little daughter.

* People not identified.

New Caledonia

Kanaka

LULLABY FOR A CHILD WHOSE MOTHER HAS GONE TO GATHER FOOD

Why these tears?
Why these tears
And these sobs
And these wails

Why are you crying in your basket
On your pillow
Your basket of bent lianas
Your rolled pillow?

Let us go out!
You are crying for us to go out
To slide the door open
To pass the mask
Holding onto the pole
To go to the sacred ground
And the walk

Up! Let us go!
Up on our feet!
Listen

Listen to the tree
It is singing u-u-h! u-u-h!
Listen to the water there
The water in the ravine

Listen to the forest up there
And the paperbark-trees
Look at the paperbark-trees down there
The furrow made by the wind
Driving them this way and that
Mingling them together.

SONG FOR A SEATED DANCE: VICTORY OF THE MEA

[On their repelling an attempted surprise night attack
by the fighting men of Moindu-Burai]

I *Omens of Victory*

I was lying stretched out,
Stretched out, lying,
Sound asleep.
Lying, with my head on my hand, in the barred bed,
I was stretched out and I dreamed,
I had a vision,
I was stretched out and I saw his spirit.
I saw him, that night,
I was stretched out, and I saw a god.
I saw the assegai god,
I saw the long god,
I saw Dadaio,
The ancestor god of the land,
Beyond this mountain.

II

I saw him make an oven,
I saw him go for wood.
I saw him set up the stones of the oven.
He broke bamboo, he broke it under his foot.
He made the spirit happy.
He made sure of the Right.

III *Introduction*

I will not go on at random.
I will begin a word and an action.
I ask an action for me there above.
I will begin an action,
That it may be long to my fame,
An action that I shall have spoken and performed,
That will surprise even myself.
May men long talk of this wood whose weight I have carried!

IV *Purpose of the Song: to send the news to the place of the ancestors at Mea.*

I will choose one and send him,
I will send one, by the power of this action which I am thinking.
I will send one or another, one from among you,
I will send one, by the power of this action which I am thinking!
Let him go far, let him carry this account,
Let him carry it beyond this mountain,
Let him carry it as a part of himself.
Let him carry it as far as Wawo,
Let him carry it down to Warha,
Carry it beyond Memara,
Let him go up the river Wawo
And carry it to the end of the valley of Mea.

V *Challenge to the Enemy*

Tell them to come,
Only to come,
To stand up and come,
Come all of them and fill the countryside,
Let them come at once, this very night,
Let them come in this very darkness,
Tonight,
In this twilight,
Fertile in bruises and groans.

VI *He Prepares to Give Orders*

I will discourse, I will speak.
Let me speak and harangue,
I will speak in a loud voice,
Forcefully, tirelessly,
With the words crowding into my mouth,
    Day and night.

VII *The Orders*

I will speak to give one group its task,
I will take another group and station it there,
To a family I will give such-and-such work,
To one kindred united by the same stone, another task;
I will share out their tasks to all the allied clans who come:
    To the Wari,
I will apportion tasks to them all,
To the Oirha,
To the Awairha,
To the Mewemea.

VIII

I will speak, I will order their sluice-gate closed.
I will choose men to bar the way,
To see that the channel is kept dry.

He addresses the fighting men on guard:
Stand where you are, keep strict watch!

IX *The Fighting Men Answer*

We are here, all of us, the clan of the Ba,
We, all of its men,
We are here to receive those who come,
Those who have begun.
We are here for those who have begun this thing,
Here to drive them out.

x *He Continues His Orders*

Let them be driven back,
Let them be routed,
Let them be driven back and thrown down
As one throws water.
Let them be pushed back into the crossroads,
Thrown back into the low places,
Into the hollows,
Into the defiles,
Into the gorges of Werha,
Into the narrow gorge of the river Nyavi,
The narrows of the Vajaraba,
The deep, narrow passages of Meude.
Let them be struck down!
Strike, strike down!
Strike, knock down!
Let them be like coconut-palms stripped of their leaves,
Like candlenut-trees beheaded,
Like the broken head of the rhawa-tree,
Or the shattered crown of the bejo-tree!

XI

Let them be struck among the vines,
Pushed back among the water herbs,
Thrashed in the brush.
Let them be struck among the marsh plants,
Let their hiding places be beaten and searched to capture them,
Strike at them, push aside the grass to bring them out,
Strike them, search, so that they will appear,
And make them run!

XII *The Enemy Will Be Eaten. He Gives the Orders and Describes the Scene*

Strike and choose, choose among them.
He will strike and take the one he chooses;
He will strike and choose the best!
"Take those who are shiny,

Choose those whose skin is smooth,
Choose those whose skin is well filled out
Or young!"

XIII

They are chosen. They are cut up.
"Take, feel, search, tear apart,
Choose them, cut, share.
Cut and keep your portion.
Share out their food to the fighting men,
Cut up the bodies and carry them,
Share out the limbs and drag them.
Dismember, load your shoulders.
Strike! Heap all these pieces in a basket,
Let those who carry the baskets be like
Those who carry soa-cakes,
Those who carry frogs,
Bent under their load of food,
Payment for building a house,
Or like those who return from a festival of exchanging gifts,
Or a summer festival."

XIV *He Speaks to the Fighting Men in the Distance*

You there!
Who is up above?
Up there on the mountain?
Have any of the enemy escaped
Through the meshes?
Are there any who have made off
Trampling down the grass in the other direction?

XV *The Fighting Men Answer*

We have been there,
We barred the way to some women,
Crossing the road,
We barred the way to some men.
Only three men among them escaped.

XVI *The Speaker Resumes—Praise of the Victors*

Happy the spirits of these warriors!
Raise their totems!
Let them come and tell it,
    Tell it.
Tell it at length,
Tell it to those who would not fight,
Who are at home,
To those who limp and shun war,
To the people of the house,
To those infected with tonga,
To those kept back by a wounded foot,
A splinter.

XVII *The Fleeing Enemy*

They have fled!
They have run away mourning,
    Howling and crying!
They have fled weeping as far as Wawe.
    Sobs at Boaja!
    Sobs in Aremu,
    Tears in Purupuni,
    Talk in Noanawara,
    Tears when they came to Nawi,
    Tears as they forded the Pueu
    Followed the Kasii,
    Came to the meeting of the streams,
        Tears all the way to Poerebaseno!

XVIII *Shame and Grief of the Vanquished*

They weep and gather ashes!
They weep, they arrive, they cut down coconut-palms!
They weep, they arrive, they tear down their houses!
They arrive and lay waste the countryside.
They strike till the ground rings where the sacred poles stand!

XIX

They come to Meru and bark an araucaria.
At Wauru they trample on coconut-palms,
Cut off their crowns at Nemoere,
Destroy them at Puavee,
Destroy them at Nejiaxa!
They arrive, they weep, they sit down,
        They weep together,
They weep huddled together
Like a string of fish,
Like things set in a row.

XX *The People of the Conquered Country Address Them*

Alas, my friends!
What of this thing that you were to do?
Where are the fighting men?
What has become of the things you said?
The decision you made?
This war that you began,
This plan that you carried within you
Meaning to lead it like water through an unknown channel?
You kept your plant from all,
        A secret, a deadly secret!
You carried on your action as through a water channel, you did not tell
The Boawe! You carried it on
        Far from the Auru,
        Far from the Teise,
        Far from the Onere,
        From the Buidaioru!
Did you carry it on thus for fear they would hear you?
Keep it apart, for fear they would learn your secret?

XXI *The Vanquished Answer*

Why should we have told them?
They are rats that gnaw into houses,
They are sultan-hens that break the cords around sugar-cane.

XXII *The Others Reply*

What of those who are not here?
What did you think to do?
Did you think you could do what you have done before?
Gather what is hard to gather?
Dig in ground only lately left uncultivated?
And you are surprised that you were defeated!
Well, the men on guard saw you,
They struck your hands,
They tore off the sign
Of your virility!

Barred bed: a special bed, hung round with weapons; lying in it inspires the spirit of war. *Broke bamboo:* a challenge to war. *Made sure of the Right:* made sure that the ancestral spirits would take their place on the right of the fighting men, and so bring them victory. *Tonga:* an infection causing ulcers of the foot. *Cut down coconut-palms,* etc.: the vanquished destroy what is the life of their village, in mourning for their dead comrades. *Break the cords,* etc.: sugar cane stems are tied together to promote their growth. *The Others Reply:* in the original, lines 3 and 4 of this section are metaphors, of which only the implied meaning is given in the translation. *Do what you have done before:* repeat a previous victory. *Dig in ground,* etc.: ground recently cultivated gives a poor yield.

Fiji Islands

Fijian

THE SHADES OF THE NEWLY DEAD TO THE GODS

My Lords! In evil fashion are we buried,
Buried staring up into the heaven,
We see the scud flying over the sky,
We are worn out with the feet stamping on us.
Our ribs, the rafters of our house, are torn asunder.
The eyes with which we gazed on one another are destroyed,
The nose with which we kissed has fallen in,
The breast to which we embraced is ruined,
The thighs with which we clasped have fallen away;
The lips with which we laughed at one another have decayed,
The teeth with which we bite have showered down,
Gone is the hand that threw the tinka stick,
The hawk's stones have rolled away,
Rolled away are the destroyers of razors.
Hark to the lament of the mosquito!
Well it is that they should die and pass onward;
But alas! for my conch shell that they have taken away!
Hark to the lament of the fly!
Well it is that they should die and pass onward,
But alas! They have taken away the eye from which I drank!
Hark to the lament of the black ant!
Well it is that they should die and pass onward,
But alas! for my whale's tooth that they have taken away!

Tinka stick: used in the game of reed throwing. *Hawk's stones:* testicles. *Destroyers of razors:* alluding to the custom of shaving the pubes. *Conch shell:* ear. *Whale's tooth:* penis.

ON THE PESTILENCE THAT SCOURGED THE FIJIANS AFTER THEIR FIRST CONTACT WITH WHITES *CA.* 1791

The great sickness sits aloft,
Their voices sound hoarsely,
They fall and lie helpless and pitiable,
Our god Ndengei is put to shame,
Our own sicknesses have been thrust aside,
The strangling-cord is a noble thing,
They fall prone; they fall with the sap still in them. . . .
A lethargy has seized upon the chiefs,
How terrible is this sickness!
We do not live, we do not die,
Our bodies ache; our heads ache,
Many die, a few live on,
The strangling-cord brings death to many,
The *malo* round their bellies rots away,
Our women groan in their despair,
The *liku* knotted round them they do not loose,
Hark to the creak of the strangling-cords,
The spirits flow away like running water, *ra tau e.*

SONG ON THE GREAT VISITATION OF MEASLES IN 1875

Our chiefs consult together,
They consult without being able to decide,
They consult about the ship that is being prepared
For Tui Viti to sail in. It was an evil consultation.

The house of death is opened,
That trouble may come to Viti
And destroy all our people.

Strangling-cord: "an allusion to the custom of strangling the sick" (B. Thomson, as cited. See Sources).

One side is already depopulated;
We are very near to the gates of hell.

SONG ON THE WAR IN THE MOUNTAINS OF VITI LEVU IN 1876

Who is the chief at Veitawatawa?
Lewatiakana is the chief at Veitawatawa.
What were the words of Lewatiakana?
"Let us be strong, children, and throw off the cloth;
I am your great governor of Na Nuyu Koro."
Who is the chief of Matawalu?
Na Gusundrandra is the chief there.
What was it he took in hand to do?
Na Gusundrandra said, "Government stores shall not go into the mountains";
And he turned them back at Koroisata.
Who is the chief of Naveiyaraki?
Katakataimoso is the chief there.
What was it that he proclaimed?
Katakataimoso said, "My name shall resound to the skies."
He said, "Let the Government at Nasauthoko be destroyed."
They are judged, they are judged, they are judged.
Let us sing about the prison;
There they eat the seeds of beans;
There Tui Timbiri is their gaoler;
There they are bound with withes of the walai-creeper.
With these bonds the sergeants drag them,
Drag them along the mountain paths, crying as they go,
Drag them to Waiwai, where they rest,
Thence on to Vatutoko, on the ridge,
And down to Nawaka, where they arrive in the evening,
And await the arrival of the steamer not yet come
Which is to take them to Levuka to break stones.
"Oh, I am utterly lost and done for, I am utterly lost and done for," they cry,
To Levuka to break stones.
"Oh, I am lost and done for; oh, I am lost and done for."

SONG[11]

1

Andi Vaverusa lies sleeping.
Is this the sleep of health or of death?
Her head hangs helplessly over the pillow.
Sleep on, woman, who will spare me no place in our husband's love.
Sleep on, woman, who dost not remember our sisterhood.
This sort of double-wifeship is painful as moli thorns to our flesh.
This kind of double-wifeship hurts us as sharp shells cut our feet.
I take out my paint and my finest dress,
I walk away over the plain,
I pass by under the shaking rock,
I wade across the river.
Two lads of Setura were playing there,
The children of Banisikulu.
I turn aside from the path to where a lemba tree grows.
I open my paint basket,
I paint both my eyes black
And one cheek with spots.
I open and unfold my coloured dress,
I tie it tight round my waist.
As I tighten it I sneeze.
What does that sneeze portend?
Is today the day of my death?
I then turn to the cocoa-nut tree.
Moistening my hands, I spring to climb it,
Halfway between the leaves and the root
I pause, and look round on the land.
My land looks mournful to me.
I see Setura lovely in the distance.
The house-tops are dimly grey in the distance,
I see the strand where I sauntered in life,
The white shell ornaments on the canoe-ends are blurred together in the distance.

[11] A chief married two sisters. One, Andi Vaverusa, had children and was beloved by him; the other, Andi Senikumba, was childless and neglected, and at length she determined to commit suicide. She speaks in the first part of the poem, her sister in the second.

I let go both my hands,
And my life is parted from me.
Ia nam bosulu.

2

Andi Vaverusa was lonely,
Her only sister was missing.
She had been missing for two days.
Pity that day touched Andi Vaverusa.
"Go call our husband," she said, "and take out my richly coloured dress."
To her husband she says, "Do you hold our child and take care of him; I will be back again in two days."
Then Andi Vaverusa set off to walk down towards the plain.
But her baby waved his hand to her, and Andi Vaverusa returned to kiss him. "Take care of our child," she says again; "in two days I will return."
Then Andi Vaverusa goes away again. But the baby waves both hands to her, and she turns back once more to kiss her boy.
Then she goes away again saying, "In two days I will return."
She goes away across the plain. She passes the shaking rock. She crosses the Dolondolu river; there are playing in it the two children of Banisikulu.
Andi Vaverusa asks them, "Did any one pass here two days ago?"
They answered her, "Do you perhaps inquire after that most beautiful lady—a lady beautiful even as you are—a lady whose hair hung down two fathoms, who passed by two days ago?"
She passed on, and under the red lemba tree she saw her sister's open paint basket.
She painted one eye black, and both cheeks with spots. She opened her painted liku and tied it round her.
As she tied it she sneezed. What does this sneeze portend? Is this the day of her death?
She turned to a cocoa-nut tree, and wetting her hands, she climbed it. Halfway between the leaves and the root she paused and looked below her.
What did she see below her? The long tresses of Andi Senikumba, the dead body of her sister.
"Is my best and only sister dead?" she cried.

For a while she remained looking over the land, Setura lying lovely in the distance, the houses grey in the distance, the strand where she had walked when living with her sister.
She let go with both hands, saying, "Our lives are parted from us both."
And their bodies lie together.

DANCE SONG

1

I sat on the beach in the evening,
I was in bad spirits, and heavy thoughts filled my mind,
When Andi Kulamatandra said to me,
"Where are all the young men gone! Let them come
And practise the song and dance of the bird of sweet voice, the kasi-kasi."
Baskets full of flowers are brought.
They pick the rich-scented flowers of the langakali,
They sever from the boughs the bright-coloured flowers of the ever-flowering mata.
The drums are pushed out of the house and brought into the midst of the square.
Let us form to dance the dance and sing the song of the kasi-kasi, and thus they pace the measure.

2

Chorus:
Has it not been heard at Thikombia,
How they killed the bird Kasi-kasi,
How they killed and how they cooked him,
How they cooked and how they ate him?
They have made away with Kasi-kasi,
And the singers lifted up their voices and clapped their hands,
Only to cease when the sun touched the sea.

3

Solo (Andi Kulamatandra speaks):
For a day Kasi-kasi has been missing,
For two days Kasi-kasi has not appeared.

My belly constrains me and I weep;
I cry aloud, "My awakener is lost."
Under the shade of the makosi-tree I stand and pine,
I cannot speak; my songs are only cries of pain.
I weep alone in my house.
The pigs grunt to be killed,
The fowls cackle and crow.
All these are mine, and no one else's,
Yet I lie awake till daylight,
Till the sky is painted by the coming day,
For the song of Kasi-kasi was sweet,
Like the notes of a bamboo-flute.
The voice that woke me sweetly in the morning is silent.
Oh, let a canoe be brought that I may go and seek him.
Oh, let a canoe be brought that I may at least go home.

4

Chorus:
"A canoe from whence, dear lady?" they reply.
"You are Vasu of Lauthala to windward
[You cannot leave your people]."
They bring to her two large tambuas,
"This is our atonement for your bird;
We sit down and offer it humbly, the atonement of all your people,
A propitiation to drive away your tears.
The fair island of Nukumasi too is offered to you,
Young men shall sing all day and dance all night;
The people of Thikombia shall make tappa for you, dear lady;
Men shall put up fences—fences at Lomai-e-cake, and bring pigs to fill them, [if only you will stop grieving].

THE EPIC OF DENGEI

Thus did Dengei weep tears of annoyance,
"One night, two nights have I lain awake,
Three nights, four nights have I lain awake,
Not once has Turukawa cooed,
Alas! my fowl, my noble fowl!
Alas! my fowl, my man-like fowl!

Sorrow has taken possession of my brain,
I am sick with it; I cannot eat,
Come, herald, run,
Run straight to Narauyamba,
Question the archers, and say,
"You, did you shoot Turukawa?
Not once did he coo at daybreak,
The 'Cave-dweller' is still fasting,
The tears are welling from his eyes;
The men are off to sleep on board."

The Herald speaks:
I am wearied with the labour of poling,
Dispatched with this message from the Cave-dweller,
"Come, herald, run,
Summon the two chiefs to me,
Why was my fowl slain?
I know of no evil that he did."
Thus the herald gave his message,
Nakausamba answers him boastfully,
"Herald, hold thy peace,
We are all the children of men,
I am the child of space,
I am the child of the rising moon,
Which Waithala made to rise,
This herald is full of questions,
My way would be to have thee roasted,
It would be a pity not to have thee eaten,
For thou art the worst of lowborn men;
I have confined the rising moon."
Then speaks Nathirikaumoli,
"Tell this to the Cave-dweller,
How came he by his pigeon?
Found he it in the water, or found he it on land,
Go, tell him that we will fight for it,
Turukawa is the root of the evil,
It is by him that Kauvandra is divided,
It is not well that we should live together,
Up with the flag and let us fight."
His spear lies ready on the shelf,

And his club can be snatched from the eaves,
Have you counted the spear-points of tree-fern?
Sit down and let us number them,
Ten times one hundred in all;
Let us hoist the pennants of war,
The welkin rings with the tumult.
The craftsmen are sitting in council,
They consult, each gives his opinion,
Rokola now speaks,
"Go and fit close a rampart of vesi,
Give special heed to the gate."
Ten days has the battle raged,
The rope has snared them; they are dismembered,
Lutunasombasomba is dishonoured,
He it is who is to be pitied,
Let us then recall his words,
"We are now in terrible plight,
You gloat over our corpses,
Thinking how ye will dismember them for the feast."
The poem is finished and there is silence.

Second Choir
Turukawa used to coo all the day long,
He did not coo at daybreak,
Ndengei wept for love of him,
Alas! my fowl, my noble fowl,
For a whole month I have eaten nothing,
For two months have I fasted for him,
Let one run to Narauyamba,
And question the two young chiefs,
Did ye shoot Turukawa?
He did not coo at daybreak,
"Joy possesses us,
We did injure the Awakener."
They joined battle at nightfall,
It is a war that can never be atoned.
Never atoned; go, storm the fortress,
Both sides joined battle,
Ah! one is clubbed, Ah! another is down,
The bodies of the Ului Ndreketi are piled high.

The war spreads even to the shore,
Aye, spreads even to the sea-shore,
The Kauvandra tribes are thrashed,
Whose was the word that set the battle going?
Lo! the death-dance for the ending of the war!
Crash goes the club into the thick of the chiefs!
We fight, we fight, we fight–i!

EPIC SONG[12]

I was sweating: then I hurdled the threshold.
Then I came outside; then I circled about.
I broke off the dangling uci-shrub
And I inserted it above my ear.
When the dangling uci-shrub is bruised,
It quivers like the tail feathers of the cock.
And now Lady Song-of-Tonga speaks:
"Why is the dangling uci broken?"
And now The-Eldest answers:
"Leaves for garlands have no worth as food;
I am using it just as an ornament."
I descended down to the shore.
I leapt into the bow of my canoe;
Its timbers were felled at The-Task-is-Complete,
The artist, Flaming-Moon, felled them;
Its name was The-Turmeric-of-the-Mother-and-Child.
And shells concealed the tying of its sennit.
The walls of the chief's house were hung with barkcloth.
And a large dentalium adorned the chief's house.
And there were four figureheads together.
And Lady Song-of-Tonga is weaving her fishnet.

The 'Cave-dweller': Dengei, whose home was a cavern.

[12] Lady Song-of-Tonga is angered when her husband, The-Eldest, injures her uci-shrub. Still irritable, she strikes their daughter, who cries bitterly. The-Eldest, feeling that Lady Song-of-Tonga has been unjust, tries to comfort the child in various ways with no success. At length he asks the dwarf to dance for her. The dance is vigorous, but she is amused only temporarily. When she continues to cry, The-Eldest carries her sorrowfully back to the house.

The "I" of the passages in italics is sometimes The-Eldest, sometimes Lady Song-of-Tonga; in the other lines the poet narrates.

And Fruit-of-the-Distant-Sleep crawls to her.
And she grasped the weaving hook from my hand.
I struck her with the handle of the net.
And the child is smothered black from weeping.
And now The-Eldest speaks:
"Lady Song-of-Tonga, what evil have you done?
You strike a helpless creature."
And I grasped the forearm of the child.
Then I slung her to my back and carried her.
And now The-Eldest speaks:
"O my child, for what blossom are you weeping?
Are you crying for the red leba?
Look there at the ripe ones on the branch."
I grasped the handle of my ray-spined spear.
Reaching upward I tapped a fruit in the cluster.
It fell and I halved it straightway.
And the red leba speaks in his hand:
"Why am I broken in half?"
And now The-Eldest answers:
"You are halved to no purpose."
Fruit-of-the-Distant-Sleep is weeping.
She sees, and now her thoughts are soothed.
Then I threaded the leba on a girdle cord.
And dangled it there before her.
And now the child is angry and refuses to look.
And she leaps down and scratches the earth;
And she scoops up a handful and casts it on her back.
And I grasped the forearm of the child.
And I slung her to my back and carried her.
"O my child, for what blossom are you weeping?"
And The-Eldest is looking about.
And my glance fell upon Clapping-Out-of-Time,
I saw him; then I shouted calling.
And now Clapping-Out-of-Time speaks:
"The-Eldest, why am I called?"
And now The-Eldest speaks:
"You are called for no purpose.
Fruit-of-the-Distant-Sleep is weeping.
Come dance to see if you can please her."

Leap to the mote on the landward side.
Leap to the mote on the seaward side.
And he twists bending in the dance and stands again.
Saliva drips forth from his mouth.
"Come, watch, Fruit-of-the-Distant-Sleep."
She looks but asks no questions.
And the child is smothered black from weeping.
And I grasped the forearm of the child
And I slung her to my back and carried her.
And Sailing-the-Ocean is sorrowful.
Returning I carried Fruit-of-the-Distant-Sleep;
Went to enter The-Grass-Strewn-Floor.
Nabosulu
Nabusele.

Sailing-the-Ocean: another name for The-Eldest.

AUSTRALIA

Australia

Yaoro KIMBERLEY DIVISION, WESTERN AUSTRALIA

CHANTS

I *Recited Before Going to the Beach To Fish*

The wind has calmed down.
The beach is quite dry.
Deserted the country lies.
The beach is quite dry.

Oh tide, you are staining the sea
Breakers stir up the mud.

II *Hunter's Chant Sung While Spearing Turtles*

Glowing like the sacred blood you appear.
Riding up and down on the waves,
Quickly the stranger arrives.

The turtle arrived
from the south
glistening and glimmering in the waves,
shining and glittering on the waves.

Bad KIMBERLEY DIVISION, WESTERN AUSTRALIA

A TRIPTYCH ON THE DUGONG

1

At Narel the dugong has stopped.
A loud noise it made when breathing.
At Narel the dugong was halted.
A hissing noise he made sucking the air
The dugong.

2

The tide has gone out, the sea will soon return.
The low tide has finished, the flow will soon come back.
A dugong calf has come, a young dugong has arrived.
A young dugong came in the bay, a dugong calf has arrived.

3

Hanging at its mother's tail
Down in the depth of the sea
The dugong calf swims with its mother.
With the old mother it dives.

Bathurst and Melville Islands*

SONG OF A WIDOW FOR HER DEAD HUSBAND[1]

"Why do you come here every day to my grave?"
"Because," she says, "your posts are painted and ready.
Come on, get up from that grave!

* People not identified.

[1] Sung "one morning when the posts had been painted and placed in position around his grave, ready for the ceremonial dancing" (C. H. Berndt, as cited, p. 303. See Sources). "To facilitate reading, such words as 'he says,' 'she says' have been included in the general translation . . . ; but it should be clearly understood that they are not, as a rule, part of the actual song itself. The singer makes it obvious [usually] by change of pitch and so on, just who is supposed to be speaking" (*ibid.*, p. 292).

I saw you there dancing just now,
Shaking yourself in the dance."
"Why not come to me here?" he asks.
"I'm not old, I'm too young," she tells him.
"Well, I'm waiting for you here . . .
I'm glad my wife's coming near me.
You'll be thirsty, I can't give you water;
I'm taking you to a dry and waterless country."

Northern Territory*

SONG[2]

Windmill turning turning goes *rrr . . . rrr*.

Mudbara WAVE HILL, NORTHERN TERRITORY

FROM THE SACRED DULNGULG CYCLE

The day breaks—the first rays of the rising Sun, stretching her arms.
Daylight breaking, as the Sun rises to her feet.
Sun rising, scattering the darkness; lighting up the land . . .
With disc shining, bringing daylight, as the birds whistle and call . . .
People are moving about, talking, feeling the warmth.
Burning through the Gorge, she rises, walking westwards,
Wearing her waist-band of human hair.
She shines on the blossoming coolibah-tree, with its sprawling roots,
Its shady branches spreading . . .

* People not identified.
[2] Literal translation.

Laragia NORTHERN TERRITORY

TRADITIONAL SONG

Waves coming up; high waves coming up against the rocks,
Breaking, shi! shi!
When the moon is high with its light upon the waters:
Spring tide; tide flowing to the grass,
Breaking, shi! shi!
In its rough waters, the young girls bathe.
Hear the sound they make with their hands as they play!

Northeastern Arnhem Land*

SONG OF A WOMAN CRYING FOR THE DEAD BABY SON OF HER DAUGHTER

The fire is burning at Birginbirgin, and Gamarala, and Nuga,
Burning out the wallaby and kangaroo . . .
Ah my daughter, my brother, my nephew, my grandchild, my cousins,
We came from our home, my daughter, my grandchild!
We travelled, and hither we came,
We came to this unfriendly place, my daughter, my grandchild!
My baby died here! . . .
Both of us came with our child, here we found sickness.
My country is far away, hither we came,
Travelling from place to place—my brother, my brother's child!
Crying I carried him, sick.
Who is watching and staring while father cries?
Ah my daughter, my daughter, my grandchild!

* People not identified.

SONG OF DEPARTURE AND FAREWELL[3]

The sail at the mast head dips from side to side,
As the boat comes up from the south . . .
The sail unfurled at the mast head flaps in the wind,
It stands upright and flaps, as the boat goes on.
The wind tosses the sail, up on the mast,
And the mast head moves, dipping from side to side.
The sail on the mast flaps, dancing, and "talks" in the wind . . .

THE GIDGID-BIRD[4]

The white gidgid-bird is hunting fish.
It stabs the fish with its beak, and calls as it flies . . .
It swoops low over the water, looking for fish,
And the fish leaps away in fear . . .
"You and I, mother seagull, we fly . . ."
The bird saw the east wind blow, as it hunted fish,
And the fish leapt forward in fear,
Leaping away from its beak, as the wind came blowing . . .

THE NARBA-BIRD[5]

The narba-bird flies crying (its eggs and young!),
It circles low, then soars up to the clouds and rain;
It calls, and the sound echoes up to the clouds.
It alights on the rock, and cries, watching the sea,
Cries from the rock as it stands, searching for fish.
It flies low, crying, eyes tearfully searching the water—
Rain from its tears! It spreads its wings on the water;
The east wind blows, and the clouds are dark with rain . . .

Gidgid-bird: a white sea bird a little smaller than the ordinary sea gull.

Narba-bird: a black bird which makes its nest near salt water and lives on fish; it figures prominently in rain-making ritual.

[3] From the Macassan cycle.
[4] From the *jiritja* moiety "Badu" cycle.
[5] From a large *dua* cycle.

FROM THE "GOULBURN ISLAND" LOVE CYCLE

The tongues of the Lightning Snakes flicker and twist, one to the other . . .
They flash among the foliage of the cabbage palms . . .
Lightning flashes through the clouds, with the flickering tongue of the Snake . . .
It is always there, at the wide expanse of water, at the place of the sacred tree . . .
Flashing above those people of the western clans,
All over the sky their tongues flicker: above the place of the Rising Clouds, the place of the Standing Clouds,
All over the sky, tongues flickering and twisting . . .
They are always there, at the camp by the wide expanse of water . . .
All over the sky their tongues flicker: at the place of the Two Sisters, the place of the Wauwalak.
Lightning flashes through the clouds, flash of the Lightning Snake . . .
Its blinding flash lights up the cabbage palm foliage . . .
Gleams on the cabbage palms, and on the shining leaves . . .

Wonguri-Mandjikai NORTHEASTERN ARNHEM LAND

SONG CYCLE OF THE MOON-BONE

I

The people are making a camp of branches in that country at Arnhem Bay:
With the forked stick, the rail for the whole camp, the Mandjikai people are making it.
Branches and leaves are about the mouth of the hut: the middle is clear within.

Lightning Snakes: "The Lightning Snakes play across the sky at the beginning of the monsoonal period" (R. M. Berndt and C. H. Berndt. See Sources).

They are thinking of rain, and of storing their clubs in case of a quarrel,
In the country of the Dugong, towards the wide clay-pans made by the Moonlight.
Thinking of rain, and of storing the fighting sticks.
They put up the rafters of arm-band-tree wood, put the branches on to the camp, at Arnhem Bay, in that place of the Dugong . . .
And they block up the back of the hut with branches.
Carefully place the branches, for this is the camp of the Morning-Pigeon man,
And of the Middle-of-the-Camp man; of the Mangrove-Fish man; of two other head-men,
And of the Clay-pan man; of the Baijini-Anchor man, and of the Arnhem Bay country man;
Of the Whale man and of another head-man: of the Arnhem Bay Creek man;
Of the Scales-of-the-Rock-Cod man; of the Rock Cod man, and of the Place-of-the-Water man.

II

They are sitting about in the camp, among the branches, along the back of the camp:
Sitting along in lines in the camp, there in the shade of the paperbark trees:
Sitting along in a line, like the new white spreading clouds;
In the shade of the paperbarks, they are sitting resting like clouds.
People of the clouds, living there like the mist; like the mist sitting resting with arms on knees,
In here towards the shade, in this Place, in the shadow of paperbarks.
Sitting there in rows, those Wonguri-Mandjikai people, paperbarks along like a cloud.
Living on cycad-nut bread; sitting there with white-stained fingers,
Sitting in there resting, those people of the Sandfly clan . . .
Sitting there like mist, at that place of the Dugong . . . and of the Dugong's Entrails . . .
Sitting resting there in the place of the Dugong . . .
In that place of the Moonlight Clay Pans, and at the place of the Dugong . . .
There at that Dugong place they are sitting all along.

III

Wake up from sleeping! Come, we go to see the clay pan, at the place of the Dugong . . .
Walking along, stepping along, straightening up after resting:
Walking along, looking as we go down on to the clay pan.
Looking for lily plants as we go . . . and looking for lily foliage . . .
Circling around, searching towards the middle of the lily leaves to reach the rounded roots.
At that place of the Dugong . . .
At that place of the Dugong's Tail . . .
At that place of the Dugong; looking for food with stalks,
For lily foliage, and for the round-nut roots of the lily plant.

IV

The birds saw the people walking along.
Crying, the white cockatoos flew over the clay pan of the Moonlight;
From the place of the Dugong they flew, looking for lily-root food; pushing the foliage down and eating the soft roots.
Crying, the birds flew down and along the clay pan, at that place of the Dugong . . .
Crying, flying down there along the clay pan . . .
At the place of the Dugong, of the Tree-Limbs-Rubbing-Together, and of the Evening Star.
Where the lily-root clay pan is . . .
Where the cockatoos play, at that place of the Dugong . . .
Flapping their wings they flew down, crying, "We saw the people!"
There they are always living, those clans of the white cockatoo . . .
And there is the Shag woman, and there her clan:
Birds, trampling the lily foliage, eating the soft round roots!

V

An animal track is running along: it is the track of the rat . . .
Of the male rat, and the female rat, and the young that hang to her teats as she runs,
The male rat hopping along, and the female rat, leaving paw-marks as a sign . . .

On the clay pans of the Dugong, and in the shade of the trees,
At the Dugong's place, and at the place of her Tail . . .
Thus, they spread paw-mark messages all along their tracks,
In that place of the Evening Star, in the place of the Dugong . . .
Among the lily plants and into the mist, into the Dugong place, and into the place of her Entrails.
Backwards and forwards the rats run, always hopping along . . .
Carrying swamp-grass for nesting, over the little tracks, leaving their signs.
Backwards and forwards they run on the clay pan, around the place of the Dugong.
Men saw their tracks at the Dugong's place, in the shade of the trees, on the white clay;
Roads of the rats, paw-marks everywhere, running into the mist.
All around are their signs; and there men saw them down on the clay pan, at the place of the Dugong.

VI

A duck comes swooping down to the Moonlight clay-pan, there at the place of the Dugong . . .
From far away. "I saw her flying over, in here at the clay pan . . ."
Floating along, pushing the pool into ripples and preening her feathers.
"I carried these eggs from a long way off, from inland to Arnhem Bay . . ."
Eggs, eggs, eggs; eggs she is carrying, swimming along.
She preens her feathers, and pulls at the lily foliage,
Drags at the lily leaves with her claws for food.
Swimming along, rippling the water among the lotus plants . . .
Backwards and forwards: she pulls at the foliage, swimming along, floating and eating.
This bird is taking her food, the lotus food in the clay-pan,
At the place of the Dugong there, at the place of the Dugong's Tail . . .
Swimming along for food, floating, and rippling the water, there at the place of the Lilies.
Taking the lotus, the rounded roots and stalks of the lily; searching and eating there as she ripples the water.
"Because I have eggs, I give to my young the sound of the water."

Splashing and preening herself, she ripples the water, among the lotus . . .
Backwards and forwards, swimming along, rippling the water,
Floating along on the clay-pan, at the place of the Dugong.

VII

People were diving here at the place of the Dugong . . .
Here they were digging all around, following up the lily stalks,
Digging into the mud for the rounded roots of the lily,
Digging them out at that place of the Dugong, and of the Evening Star,
Pushing aside the water while digging, and smearing themselves with mud . . .
Piling up the mud as they dug, and washing the roots clean.
They saw arm after arm there digging: people thick like the mist . . .
The Shag woman too was there, following up the lily stalks.
There they saw arm after arm of the Mandjikai Sandfly clan,
Following the stalks along, searching and digging for food:
Always there together, those Mandjikai Sandfly people.
They follow the stalks of the lotus and lily, looking for food.
The lilies that always grow there at the place of the Dugong . . .
At that clay-pan, at the place of the Dugong, at the place of the lilies.

VIII

Now the leech is swimming along . . . It always lives there in the water . . .
It takes hold of the leaves of the lily and pods of the lotus, and climbs up on to their stalks.
Swimming along and grasping hold of the leaves with its head . . .
It always lives there in the water, and climbs up on to the people.
Always there, that leech, together with all its clan . . .
Swimming along towards the trees, it climbs up and waits for people.
Hear it swimming along through the water, its head out ready to grasp us . . .
Always living here and swimming along.
Because that leech is always there, for us, however it came there:
The leech that catches hold of those Mandjikai Sandfly people . . .

IX

The prawn is there, at the place of the Dugong, digging out mud with its claws . . .
The hard-shelled prawn living there in the water, making soft little noises.
It burrows into the mud and casts it aside, among the lilies . . .
Throwing aside the mud, with soft little noises . . .
Digging out mud with its claws at the place of the Dugong, the place of the Dugong's Tail . . .
Calling the bone bukalili, the catfish bukalili, the frog bukalili, the sacred tree bukalili . . .
The prawn is burrowing, coming up, throwing aside the mud, and digging . . .
Climbing up on to the lotus plants and on to their pods . . .

X

Swimming along under the water, as bubbles rise to the surface, the tortoise moves in the swamp grass.
Swimming among the lily leaves and the grasses, catching them as she moves . . .
Pushing them with her short arms. Her shell is marked with designs,
This tortoise carrying her young, in the clay pan, at the place of the Dugong . . .
The short-armed Mararlpa tortoise, with special arm-bands, here at the place of the Dugong . . .
Backwards and forwards she swims, the short-armed one of the Mararlpa, and the Dalwongu.
Carrying eggs about, in the clay pan, at the place of the Dugong . . .
Her entrails twisting with eggs . . .
Swimming along through the grass, and moving her patterned shell.
The tortoise with her young, and her special arm-bands,
Swimming along, moving her shell, with bubbles rising;
Throwing out her arms towards the place of the Dugong . . .
This creature with the short arms, swimming and moving her shell;
This tortoise, swimming along with the drift of the water . . .
Swimming with her short arms, at the place of the Dugong . . .

XI

Wild-grape vines are floating there in the billabong:
Their branches, joint by joint, spreading over the water.
Their branches move as they lie, backwards and forwards,
In the wind and the waves, at the Moonlight clay pan, at the place of the Dugong . . .
Men see them lying there on the clay pan pool, in the shade of the paperbarks:
Their spreading limbs shift with the wind and the water:
Grape vines with their berries . . .
Blown backwards and forwards as they lie, there at the place of the Dugong.
Always there, with their hanging grapes, in the clay pan of the Moonlight . . .
Vine plants and roots and jointed limbs, with berry food, spreading over the water.

XII

Now the New Moon is hanging, having cast away his bone:
Gradually he grows larger, taking on new bone and flesh.
Over there, far away, he has shed his bone: he shines on the place of the Lotus Root, and the place of the Dugong,
On the place of the Evening Star, of the Dugong's Tail, of the Moonlight clay pan . . .
His old bone gone, now the New Moon grows larger;
Gradually growing, his new bone growing as well.
Over there, the horns of the old receding Moon bent down, sank into the place of the Dugong:
His horns were pointing towards the place of the Dugong.
Now the New Moon swells to fullness, his bone grown larger.
He looks on the water, hanging above it, at the place of the Lotus.
There he comes into sight, hanging above the sea, growing larger and older . . .
There far away he has come back, hanging over the clans near Milingimbi . . .
Hanging there in the sky, above those clans . . .
"Now I'm becoming a big moon, slowly regaining my roundness" . . .

In the far distance the horns of the Moon bend down, above Milingimbi,
Hanging a long way off, above Milingimbi Creek . . .
Slowly the Moon Bone is growing, hanging there far away.
The bone is shining, the horns of the Moon bend down.
First the sickle Moon on the old Moon's shadow; slowly he grows,
And shining he hangs there at the place of the Evening Star . . .
Then far away he goes sinking down, to lose his bone in the sea;
Diving towards the water, he sinks down out of sight.
The old Moon dies to grow new again, to rise up out of the sea.

XIII

Up and up soars the Evening Star, hanging there in the sky.
Men watch it, at the place of the Dugong and of the Clouds, and of the Evening Star.
A long way off, at the place of Mist, of Lilies and of the Dugong.
The Lotus, the Evening Star, hangs there on its long stalk, held by the Spirits.
It shines on that place of the Shade, on the Dugong place, and on to the Moonlight clay pan . . .
The Evening Star is shining, back towards Milingimbi, and over the Wulamba people . . .
Hanging there in the distance, towards the place of the Dugong,
The place of the Eggs, of the Tree-Limbs-Rubbing-Together, and of the Moonlight clay pan . . .
Shining on its short stalk, the Evening Star, always there at the clay pan, at the place of the Dugong . . .
There, far away, the long string hangs at the place of the Evening Star, the place of the Lilies.
Away there at Milingimbi . . . at the place of the Full Moon,
Hanging above the head of that Wonguri tribesman:
The Evening Star goes down across the camp, among the white gum trees . . .
Far away, in those places near Milingimbi . . .
Goes down among the Ngurulwulu people, towards the camp and the gum trees,
At the place of the Crocodiles, and of the Evening Star, away towards Milingimbi . . .

The Evening Star is going down, the Lotus Flower on its stalk . . .
Going down among all those western clans . . .
It brushes the heads of the uncircumcised people . . .
Sinking down in the sky, that Evening Star, the Lotus . . .
Shining on to the foreheads of all those head-men . . .
On to the heads of all those Sandfly people . . .
It sinks there into the place of the white gum trees, at Milingimbi.

Aranda CENTRAL AUSTRALIA; SIMPSON DESERT, NORTHERN TERRITORY

NATIVE-CAT SONGS

The great beam of the Milky Way
Sends out flashes of lightning incessantly.
The great beam of the Milky Way
Casts a flickering fire glow over the sky forever.
The great beam of the Milky Way
Gleams and shines forever.
The great beam of the Milky Way
Burns bright crimson forever.
The great beam of the Milky Way
Trembles with deep desire forever.
The great beam of the Milky Way
Quivers with deep passion forever.
The great beam of the Milky Way
Trembles with unquenchable desire forever.
The great beam of the Milky Way
Draws all men to itself by their forelocks.
The great beam of the Milky Way
Unceasingly draws all men, wherever they may be.

Bukalili: power name. *Cast away his bone:* he has shed his old bone ("he dies somewhere," in the sea) and gradually becomes visible again after his death.

The tnatantja pole rises into the air,—
The great beam of the Milky Way.
The kauaua pole rises into the air,—
The great beam of the Milky Way.
The great beam of the Milky Way
Strips itself bare like a plain.

"How the pole of the Milky Way is drawing me to itself—
How my own pole is drawing me to itself!"
"How the pole of the Milky Way is drawing me to itself—
From what a far country it is drawing me to itself!"
"Let the Milky Way be tied around with many bands;
Let the dweller in the earth-hollow be tied around with many bands!"
"The pole of the Milky Way has drawn me irresistibly—
The dweller in the earth-hollow has drawn me irresistibly."

The great beam of the Milky Way,
The dweller in the earth-hollow, is trembling with desire forever.

The narrowing sea embraces it forever,—
Its swelling waves embrace it forever.
The sea, ever narrowing, forever embraces it,—
The great beam of the Milky Way.
Its embracing arms forever tremble about it,—
The great beam of the Milky Way.
Set in the bosom of the sea it stands,
Reverberating loudly without a pause.
Set in the bosom of the sea it stands,
Sea-flecked with drifts of foam.
In the bosom, in the sea it stands,
Casting a flickering fire glow over the sky forever.

Let them sit down around the pole of the Milky Way,
Let them sit down around the dweller in the earth-hollow.
Around the pole of the Milky Way let them sit down,
Around the dweller in the earth-hollow let them sit down.
In their camp-hollow let them present gifts to each other,—
Let them sort out their bullroarers!

SACRED SONG OF THE AVOCET CULT

The avocets are coming,
Very many avocets are coming.

The avocets come one after the other,
The avocets come one after the other.

The avocets dive,
The tjirkoa-geese dive in the lake.

The avocets fly up,
The tjirkoa-geese in the lake fly up.

On the salt lake they fly up,
The cormorants on the lake fly up.

The avocets are slim,
The avocets are slim.

They stand on long legs,
The avocets stand there.

The avocets see the ocean,
Shading their eyes with their hands, they see the ocean.

The avocets see the ocean,
They see this very broad ocean.

The avocets see the ocean,
They see the green ocean-waves.

The avocets fly over the ocean-hills,
The avocets fly over the ocean-hills.

The avocets dive into the wet,
The avocets play tag.

The avocets move their shoulder-bones fast,
They move their wings and tails fast.

THE SONG OF ANKOTARINJA[6]

1 Red is the down which is covering me;
Red I am as though I was burning in a fire.

2 Red I am as though I was burning in a fire,
Bright red gleams the ochre with which I have rubbed my body.

3 Red I am as though I was burning in a fire,
Red, too, is the hollow in which I am lying.

4 Red I am like the heart of a flame of fire,
Red, too, is the hollow in which I am lying.

5 The red tjurunga is resting upon my head,
Red, too, is the hollow in which I am lying.

6 Like a whirlwind it is towering to the sky,
Like a pillar of red sand it is towering to the sky.

7 The tnatantja is towering to the sky,
Like a pillar of red sand it is towering to the sky.

8 A mass of red pebbles covers the plains,
Little white sand-rills cover the plains.

9 Lines of red pebbles streak the plains,
Lines of white sand-rills streak the plains.

[6] "Verses 1–5 describe Ankotarinja in his burrow at Ankota; he is decorated with red down. A great tnatantja stands on his head and shoots up to the sky (6 and 7). The country in the vicinity of Ankota is described in 8 and 9. After he has caught the scent an underground pathway opens before Ankotarinja (10 and 11). He follows up the scent (12 and 13). He devours the *tjilpa* men at Parr' Erultja (14). After being struck down, he sees his home at Ankota, and returns by the underground pathway (15–17). Once more he is back in his old home (18)." (T. G. H. Strehlow, as cited. See Sources.)

10 An underground pathway lies open before me,
Leading straight west, it lies open before me.

11 A cavernous pathway lies open before me,
Leading straight west, it lies open before me,

12 He is sucking his beard into his mouth in anger,
Like a dog he follows the trail by scent.

13 He hurries on swiftly, like a keen dog;
Like a dog he follows the trail by scent.

14 Irresistible and foaming with rage,—
Like a whirlwind he rakes them together.

15 Out yonder, not far from me, lies Ankota;
The underground hollow is gaping open before me.

16 A straight track is gaping open before me,
An underground hollow is gaping open before me.

17 A cavernous pathway is gaping open before me,
An underground pathway is gaping open before me.

18 Red I am, like the heart of a flame of fire,
Red, too, is the hollow in which I am resting.

Loritja CENTRAL AUSTRALIA

SACRED SONG OF THE JACKEROO CULT

The jackeroo, the jackeroo
Has bird's wings, has bird's wings.

The jackeroo has a crest,
The jackeroo has bird's wings.

Tjurunga, tnatantja: sacred pole.

The jackeroo with his crest was weeping with longing for a vagina,
The jackeroo, the jackeroo.

O jackeroo, be still,
Stop your whistling.

The jackeroo sits there,
Having whistled with the others.

The jackeroo sits there,
After he whistled, he flew away.

High in the air he flew, very far,
After he whistled, he flew away.

The jackeroo bird came flying,
He flew toward the sun.

I am sitting on the good fig-tree, I, the jackeroo,
I put my spear in the spear-thrower.

He spears the owl,
Their spears clatter as they fight.

The black lizard runs away tottering,
She has no knee left, she cannot run now.

A great smoke went up,
The jackeroo is cooking the lizard.

Narrinyeri SOUTH AUSTRALIA

SONG: THE RAILWAY TRAIN[7]

You see the smoke at Kapunda
The steam puffs regularly,
Showing quickly, it looks like frost,
It runs like running water,
It blows like a spouting whale.

Murring SOUTHEAST AUSTRALIA

UMBARA'S SONG[8]

Capsizing me striking me
the wind blows hard the sea long stretched
between striking hard hitting striking
me dashing up me striking.

7 Free translation.

8 Literal translation. "Umbara composed his songs when tossing about on the waves in his boat" (A. W. Howitt. See Sources).

Wurunjerri SOUTHEAST AUSTRALIA

WENBERRI'S SONG[9]

We go all the bones to all of them
shining white in this Dullur country
the rushing noise Bunjil father ours singing
breast mine this inside mine.

Bunjil: the tribal All-Father, here inspiring the poet's song.

[9] Literal translation. Composed to lament the death of his brother by evil magic, near Geelong in the Dullur country.

SOURCES

Sources

SYMBOLS USED

(*) Original text also given in the source cited.

(**) Original text and melody also given in the source cited.

FROM English translation taken from the source cited.

AFTER English translation by the Editor from the language of the source cited.

Sources are given in accordance with the original material from which the poems were taken and in accordance with the publisher's requirements. Every attempt was made to contact the copyright holders of the original material. Since some of the poems were published a long time ago, and a number of publications have since been suspended, it was not possible to obtain a written release for every poem in this volume. The phrase "with permission of the publisher" appears only when its inclusion has been requested.

THE FAR NORTH

Greenland

Page 3 "Magic Song for Him Who Wishes to Live." FROM: Knud Rasmussen, *Greenland by the Polar Sea: The Story of the Thule Expedition from Melville Bay to Cape Morris Jesup*, trans. Asta and Rowland Kenney (London, William Heinemann, 1921), p. 40. **Page 3** "Taunt Song Against a Clumsy Kayak-Paddler." AFTER: William Thalbitzer, "Eskimomusik und Dichtkunst in Grönland," *Anthropos*, VI (1911), 489. **Page 3** "A Salmon Trout to Her Children." *Ibid.*, pp. 490–91 (**, *ibid.*, p. 495.) **Page 4** "Lullaby." AFTER: Jean Malaurie, *Les derniers rois de Thulé* (Paris, Librairie Plon, 1955), p. 97. By permission of Thomas Y. Crowell Co., New York. **Page 4** "A Song from Arsut." FROM: Henry Rink, *Tales and Traditions of the Eskimo, with a sketch of their habits, religion, language and other peculiarities*, trans. from the Danish by the author (Edinburgh and London, William Blackwood & Sons, 1875), pp. 68–69. By permission of the publisher. **Page 5** "Another Song from Arsut." *Ibid.*, p. 69. By permission of the publisher.

Page 5 "Mutual Nith-Song Between Savdladt and Pulangitsissok." *Ibid.*, pp. 67–68 (slightly altered). By permission of the publisher. **Page 6** "Kayak Song in Dialogue." AFTER: William Thalbitzer, *Légendes et chants esquimaux du Groenland*, trans. Mme. Hollatz-Bretagne (Paris, Librairie Ernest Leroux, 1929), p. 38. **Page 7** "The Kayak Paddler's Joy at the Weather." FROM: William Thalbitzer, *The Ammassalik Eskimo: Contributions to the Ethnology of the East Greenland Natives*, Part II, No. 3: Language and Folklore (Copenhagen, Meddelelser om Grønland, Vol. XL, 1923), pp. 236–37 (*). **Page 7** "Paddler's Song on Bad Hunting Weather." *Ibid.*, p. 238 (*). **Page 8** "Songs at the Berry Picking on the Mountain." *Ibid.*, pp. 246–47 (*).

Canada

Page 9 "Magic Prayer." FROM: Knud Rasmussen, *Intellectual Culture of the Iglulik Eskimos* (Report of the Fifth Thule Expedition 1921–24, Vol. VII, No. 1), trans. W. Worster (Copenhagen, Gyldendalske Boghandel, Nordisk Forlag, 1929), p. 47. **Page 9** "Magic Words." *Ibid.*, p. 115 (*, *ibid.*, p. 195). **Page 10** "The Shaman Aua's Song to Call His Spirits." *Ibid.*, p. 119. **Page 10** "Sung by a Little Girl to Soothe a Crying Baby." *Ibid.*, pp. 163–64. **Page 10** "Old Dance Song." *Ibid.*, pp. 41–42. **Page 12** "Hunting Songs." *Ibid.*, pp. 236–39 (*). **Page 13** "Improvisation." *Ibid.*, p. 27. **Page 14** "Kibkarjuk Calls to Mind the Times When She was Her Husband's Favourite Wife and Was Allowed To Hunt Caribou Herself." FROM: Knud Rasmussen, *Observations on the Intellectual Culture of the Caribou Eskimos* (Report of the Fifth Thule Expedition 1921–24, Vol. VII, No. 2), trans. W. E. Calvert *et al.* (Copenhagen, Gyldendalske Boghandel, Nordisk Forlag, 1930), pp. 72–73 (*). **Page 15** "Akjartoq's Song of the Olden Days." *Ibid.*, p. 71 (*). **Page 16** "It Is Difficult to Put Words Together." FROM: Knud Rasmussen, *The Netsilik Eskimos: Social Life and Spiritual Culture* (Report of the Fifth Thule Expedition 1921–24, Vol. VIII, No. 1–2), trans. W. E. Calvert (Copenhagen, Gyldendalske Boghandel, Nordisk Forlag, 1931), p. 518 (*). **Page 16** "Uvlunuaq's Song." *Ibid.*, pp. 16–17 (* [and interlinear translation], *ibid.*, pp. 329–30). **Page 17** "Orpingalik's Song: My Breath." *Ibid.*, pp. 321–23 (* [and interlinear translation], *ibid.*, pp. 324–27). **Page 20** "Religious Hymn to be Sung Wearing a Head Decoration of the Skin of the Great Northern Diver." FROM: Knud Rasmussen, *Intellectual Culture of the Copper Eskimos* (Report of the Fifth Thule Expedition 1921–24, Vol. IX), trans. W. E. Calvert (Copenhagen, Gyldendalske Boghandel, Nordisk Forlag, 1932), pp. 138–39 (* [and interlinear translation], *ibid.*, pp. 159–60). **Page 21** "Dead Man's Song." *Ibid.*, pp. 136–38 (* [and interlinear translation], *ibid.*, pp. 184–85). **Page 23** "Men's Impotence." *Ibid.*, pp. 131–32 (* [and interlinear translation], *ibid.*, pp. 162–63). **Page 24** "The Song of Ulipshialuk's Wife." *Ibid.*, p. 135 (* [and interlinear translation], *ibid.*, pp. 168–69). **Page 25** "Hunger." *Ibid.*, pp. 132–33 (* [and interlinear translation], *ibid.*, pp. 151–52). **Page 26** "Song of Caribou, Musk Oxen, Women, and Men Who Would Be Manly." *Ibid.*, pp. 133–34 (* [and interlinear translation], *ibid.*, pp. 155–57). **Page 27** "Song." FROM: H. Ostermann, ed., *The Mackenzie Eskimos. After Knud Rasmussen's posthumous notes* (Report of the Fifth Thule Expedition 1921–24, Vol. X, No. 2) (Copenhagen, Gyldendalske Boghandel, Nordisk Forlag, 1942), p. 8. **Page 28** "Dance Songs." FROM: Helen H. Roberts and D. Jenness, *Songs of* *the Copper Eskimos* (Report of the Canadian Arctic Expedition 1913–18, Vol. XIV: Eskimo Songs) (Ottawa, F. A. Acland. 1925), pp. 504, 440, 463–64, 480 (*). By permission of Roger Duhamel, Queen's Printer. **Page 30** "Song from a Story." H. Ostermann, ed., *op. cit.*, pp. 74, 113–14 (*).

Alaska

Page 31 "Song Composed at the Beginning of an Autumn Festival in Honor of the Ribbon Seal." FROM: Knud Rasmussen, *Across Arctic America: Narrative of the Fifth Thule Expedition* (Copyright © 1927 G. P. Putnam's Sons, New York), p. 353. **Page 31** "Song for a Christmas Celebration." FROM: Robert Marshall, *Arctic Village* (New York, Harrison Smith and Robert Haas, 1933), p. 323. By permission of the estate of the late Robert Marshall.

Europe

Page 33 "Hymn to the Southern Mountains." AFTER: Eliel Lagercrantz, *Lappische Volksdichtung: IV. Seelappische Gesangsmotive des Varangergebiets* (Mémoires de la Société Finno-Ougrienne, 120) (Helsinki, Suomalais Ugrilainen Seura, 1960), pp. 30–31 (**). **Page 33** "Songs." *Ibid.*, pp. 32, 34–35 (**). **Page 34** "Complaint." AFTER: O. Donner, *Lieder der Lappen* (Helsingfors, 1876), p. 127 (*).

AFRICA

Western Africa and the Congo

Page 37 "Song After Defeat." AFTER: M. Brévié, "À propos d'une chanson bambara," *Annuaire et Mémoires du Comité d'Études Historiques et Scientifiques de l'Afrique Occidentale Française* (1917) (Gorée, Imprimerie du Gouvernement Général, 1918), pp. 219–20. **Page 38** "Song Encouraging a Masker Dancing the Part of a Girl." AFTER: M. Griaule, *Masques Dogons* (Institut d'Ethnologie de l'Université de Paris, *Travaux et Mémoires de l'Institut d'Ethnologie,* XXXIII) (Paris, Institut d'Ethnologie, 1938), pp. 538–41 (*). **Page 39** "Herder's Song." AFTER: Amadou Hampaté Bâ, "Poésie peule du Macina," *Présence Africaine,* VIII–IX (1950), 177–79. **Page 40** "War Song." AFTER: Maurice Delafosse, *Le Pays, les Peuples, les Langues, l'Histoire, les Civilisations: Haut-Sénégal–Niger (Soudan Français),* 3 vols. (Paris, Emile Larose, 1912), Vol. I, pp. 383–84. By permission of Éditions G.-P. Maisonneuve & Larose. **Page 41** "Love Song." *Ibid.*, p. 382 (*).

By permission of Éditions G.-P. Maisonneuve & Larose. **Page 41** "Drum Song." AFTER: F. Froger, *Étude sur la langue des Mossi (Boucle du Niger) suivie d'un vocabulaire et de textes* (Paris, Ernest Leroux, 1910), p. 221 (*). By permission of Presses Universitaires de France, Paris. **Page 42** "Song to the Xylophone at a Fighting Man's Funeral." AFTER: Stephen Chauvet, *Musique nègre: Considerations—Technique—Instruments de musique—Recueil de 118 airs notés* (Paris, Société d'Éditions Géographiques, Maritimes et Coloniales, 1929), p. 122 (melody given but not the original text). **Page 42** "Girls' Song." FROM: Northcote W. Thomas, *Anthropological Report on the Ibo-speaking Peoples of Nigeria,* Part III: *Proverbs, Narratives, Vocabularies and Grammar* (London, Harrison & Sons, Ltd., 1913), p. 51 (*). **Page 42** "Devices." AFTER: Roger Rosfelder, *Chants Haoussa* (Paris, Éditions Pierre Seghers, 1952), pp. 20, 23. **Page 43** " 'Praise-Song' by a Woman Possessed by a Spirit." FROM: M. F. Smith, *Baba of Karo: A Woman of the Muslim Hausa* (London, Faber & Faber, Ltd., 1954; reproduced in New York, Philosophical Library, 1955), p. 223. By permission of Frederick A. Praeger, Inc. **Page 43** "Song." AFTER: Joseph Brun, "Recueil de fables et de chants en dialecte *Hal-Poular,*" *Anthropos,* XIV–XV (1919–20), p. 208 (*). **Page 44** "Girls' Song." *Ibid.*, p. 209 (*).

Page 44 "Prologue to a Yomeh Ballad." FROM: K. L. Little, "A Mende Musician Sings of his Adventures," *Man,* XLVIII (1948), pp. 27–28. **Page 45** "Home-Sick Songs." FROM: F. W. H. Migeod, "Mende Songs," *Man,* XVI (1916), p. 186 (*). **Page 45** "Love Song." FROM: R. Lewis, *Sierra Leone: A Modern Portrait* (London, Her Majesty's Stationery Office, 1954), p. 148, quoting E. E. Sayers' translation in "A Few Temne Songs," *Sierra Leone Studies,* No. X, Dec. 1927, p. 110. **Page 46** "Song of a Wandering Story-Teller." AFTER: Hans Himmelheber, *Auru Poku: Mythen, Tiergeschichten und Sagen, Sprichwörter, Fabeln und Rätsel* ("Das Gesicht der Völker," Westafrikanischer Kulturkreis. Dichtung der Baule) (Eisenach, Erich Röth-Verlag, 1951), p. 7. **Page 46** "Song of a Woman Whose Husband Had Gone to the Coast to Earn Money." *Ibid.* **Page 46** "Women's Song." AFTER: Maurice Delafosse, *Essai de manuel de la langue agni parlée dans la moitié orientale de la Côte d'Ivoire* (Paris, Librairie Africaine et Coloniale, 1900), pp. 178–79 (*). **Page 47** "Dirges (I)." FROM: J. H. Nketia, in D. C. Osadebay, E. L. Lasebikan, J. H. Nketia, "West African Voices," *African Affairs,* XLVIII (1949), 157 (*). By permission of the Royal African Society, London. **Page 47** "Dirges (II)." FROM: J. H. Nketia, *Funeral Dirges of the Akan People* (Achimota, 1955), p. 121. **Page 47** "Address on the Talking Drums to Asase Yaa, the Spirit of Earth." FROM: K. A. Busia, "The Ashanti," in Daryll Forde, ed., *African Worlds: Studies in the Cosmological Ideas and Social Values of African Peoples* (London, The International African Institute, 1960), p. 195. **Page 48** "Song to Instruments." FROM: T. Edward Bowdich, *Mission from Cape Coast Castle to Ashantee* (London, John Murray, 1819), pp. 368–69 (slightly altered). **Page 49** "The Dead Man Asks for a Song." AFTER: Jakob Spieth, *Die Religion der Eweer in Süd-Togo* (Religions-Urkunden der Völker, Part IV, Vol. II) (Leipzig, Dieterich'sche Verlagsbuchhandlung, 1911), p. 237. **Page 50** "Death Song." AFTER: P. Wiegräbe, *Das Alte und das Neue Lied im Eweland* (Bremen, Norddeutsche Missionsgesellschaft, 1934), p. 6. **Page 50** "Dirge." AFTER: Josef Schönhärl, *Volkskundliches aus Togo: Märchen und Fabeln, Sprichwörter und Rätsel, Lieder und Spiele, Sagen und Täuschungsspiele der Ewe-Neger von Togo* (Dresden, C. U. Kochs Verlagsbuchhandlung, 1909), p. 156 (*). **Page 50** "Song." AFTER: Diedrich Westermann, *Grammatik der Ewe-Sprache* (Berlin, Dietrich Reimer [Ernst Vohsen], 1907),

p. 153. **Page 51** "Song to the *Sikeli* Drum." AFTER: J. Schönhärl, *op. cit.*, pp. 184–85 (**). **Page 51** "Song of the Telegraph" *Ibid.*, p. 189 (*). **Page 52** "Girls' Song Deriding White Men's Ewe Serving Boys." AFTER: F. Witte, "Lieder und Gesänge der Ewhe-Neger (Gĕ-Dialekt)," *Anthropos,* I (1906), 72 (**).

Page 52 "To the Sun-God." FROM: Frances Herskovits, "Dahomean Songs," *Poetry: A Magazine of Verse,* XLV (1934–35), 75–76. By permission of Mrs. Herskovits. **Page 52** "For the Earth God." *Ibid.*, p. 76. By permission of Mrs. Herskovits. **Page 53** "To the Envious." *Ibid*, p. 75. By permission of Mrs. Herskovits. **Page 53** "Song for the Dead." FROM: Frances Herskovits, "Dahomean Songs for the Dead," *The New Republic,* LXXXIV (1935), 95. By permission of Mrs. Herskovits. **Page 54** "Song in Praise of Bow and Arrow." AFTER: Maurice Delafosse, *Manuel Dahoméen* (Paris, Ernest Leroux, 1894), pp. 167–70 (*). By permission of Presses Universitaires de France, Paris. **Page 55** "The Song of King Agongolo." FROM: Melville J. Herskovits, *Dahomey: An Ancient West African Kingdom,* 2 vols. (New York, J. J. Augustin, 1938), I, 381–82. **Page 55** "Mock Lament over a Dead Slave." AFTER: Bufe, "Die Poesie der Duala-Neger in Kamerun," *Archiv für Anthropologie,* XLI (1915), 60 (*). **Page 56** "Drum Song in Three Parts from the Funeral Ceremony for a Hero." AFTER: Théodore Tsala, "Moeurs et Coutumes des Ewondo," *Études Camerounaises,* No. 56, 1958, pp. 107–9 (*). By permission of Institut de Recherche Scientifiques du Cameroun, Yaoundé. **Page 57** "Song at a Deathbed." AFTER: H. Trilles, *Les Pygmées de la forêt équatoriale* (Paris, Bloud & Gay, 1932), pp. 424–25. **Page 58** "Song of the Last Moments." AFTER: H. Trilles, *Le Totémisme chez les Fân* (Collection Internationale de Monographies Ethnologiques, Bibliothèque-Anthropos, I, 4) (Münster i. W., Aschendorffsche Verlagsbuchhandlung, 1912), pp. 275–76 (**). **Page 59** "Fire Song at an Expiation Ceremony." *Ibid.*, pp. 278–79 (**). **Page 59** "Song of the Will-o'-the-Wisp." AFTER: H. Trilles, "Les Légendes des Bena Kanioka et le Folk-lore Bantou," *Anthropos,* IV (1909), 965 (*). **Page 60** "Ombrure Calls Up the Forest Spirits." AFTER: H. Trilles, *Le Totémisme . . .* , pp. 190–92 (** in part). **Page 60** "The Honey Bird's Song." AFTER: H. Trilles, "Proverbes, légendes et contes fang," *Bulletin de la Société Neuchateloise de Géographie,* XVI (1905), 147 (*). **Page 61** "Song." FROM: E. E. Evans-Pritchard, *Witchcraft, Oracles and Magic Among the Azande* (Oxford, The Clarendon Press, 1937), p. 182 (*). By permission of The Clarendon Press, Oxford. **Page 61** "*Kimpa* (Rhythm)." AFTER: J. van Wing, *Études Bakongo. Histoire et Sociologie* (Bibliothèque-Congo, No. 3) (Brussels, A. Goemaere, 1921), p. 170. By permission A. Goemaere, Editor and Printer of H.M.S. the King. **Page 61** "Song of a Mother Whose Child Has Been Left Behind on the Caravan Trail." *Ibid.*, p. 309 (*). By permission of the same. **Page 62** "Song of a Marriageable Girl." AFTER: O. de Labrouhe, in André Leroi-Gourhan *et al., Ethnologie de l'Union Française (Territoires extérieurs),* 2 vols. (Paris, Presses Universitaires de France, 1953), I, 421. **Page 62** "Ritual Song." AFTER: H. Trilles, *Les Pygmées . . .* , p. 68 (* first stanza only). **Page 63** "Invocation to the Rainbow." *Ibid.*, p. 79. **Page 64** "Song of Expiation." *Ibid.*, p. 141. **Page 64** "Dirge in Dialogue." *Ibid.*, p. 424. **Page 64** "Song." *Ibid.*, p. 34 (*). **Page 65** "Song Sung by a Woman While Giving Birth." AFTER: H. Trilles, *L'Ame du Pygmée d'Afrique* (Paris, Les Editions du Cerf, 1945), p. 228. **Page 65** "Satire Improvised Before Whites Against the Tribe's Negro Overlords." AFTER: Alexandre LeRoy, *Les Pygmées: Négrilles d'Afrique et Négritos d'Asie* (Paris, Beauchesne et ses Fils, n.d.), pp. 123–24. **Page 66** "Song of the Animal World." *Ibid.*, pp. 122–23. **Page 67** "Elephant Song." AFTER: H. Trilles, *Les Pygmées . . .* , pp. 334–35.

Southern Africa

Page 69 "Home-Coming Song of Fighting Men After a Raid." AFTER: August Pettinen, "Lieder und Rätsel der Aandonga," *Zeitschrift für Eingeborenen-Sprachen,* XVII (1926–27), 207 (*). **Page 69** "Love Praise." *Ibid.,* pp. 220–23 (*). **Page 70** "Song of a Bridegroom in Praise of His Bride." *Ibid.,* pp. 223–25 (*). **Page 71** "The Rain-Man's Praise-Song of Himself." AFTER: *Idem,* "Sagen und Mythen der Aandonga," *Zeitschrift für Eingeborenen-Sprachen,* XVII (1926–27) p. 129. **Page 72** "Lament of a Widow over Her Dead Husband." AFTER: H. Vedder, *Die Bergdama,* Part II (Hamburgische Universität, Abhandlungen aus dem Gebiet der Auslandskunde, XIV, ser. B: Völkerkunde, Kulturgeschichte und Sprachen, 8) (Hamburg, L. Friederichsen & Co., 1923), pp. 64–65 (*). **Page 74** "Journey Song." *Ibid.,* p. 101 (*). **Page 74** "Leave-Taking." *Ibid.,* p. 103 (*). **Page 74** "Desperation." *Ibid.,* p. 104 (*). **Page 75** "The Ostrich." *Ibid.,* pp. 97–98 (*). **Page 76** "The Broken String." FROM: W. H. I. Bleek and L. C. Lloyd, *Specimens of Bushman Folklore* (London, George Allen & Co., Ltd., 1911), p. 237 (*). **Page 76** "Invocation." FROM: Theophilus Hahn, *Tsuni-||Goam: The Supreme Being of the Khoi-khoi* (London, Trübner & Co., 1881), pp. 58–59 (slightly altered) (*). **Page 77** "Prayer of a Hunter at a Grave of Heitsi-eibib." *Ibid.,* p. 69. **Page 77** "A Mother Praises Her Baby." AFTER: Theophilus Hahn, "Die Nama-Hottentoten," *Globus,* XII (1867), p. 278. **Page 78** "Praise Songs for the Baboon." FROM: W. H. I. Bleek, *Reynard the Fox in South Africa; or, Hottentot Fables and Tales* (London, Trübner & Co., 1864), pp. 33, 37. **Page 79** "Song of a Lioness Warning Her Cub." AFTER: T. Hahn, "Die Nama-Hottentoten," *loc. cit.,* p. 278. **Page 79** "Song of Greeting to a Missionary's Wife." *Ibid.*

Page 79 "In Honor of Senzangakona." FROM: Lewis Grout, *Zulu-Land; or, Life Among the Zulu-Kafirs of Natal and Zulu-Land, South Africa* (Philadelphia, Presbyterian Publication Committee, 1864), p. 197. **Page 80** "Song at Separation." FROM: H. Tracey, *"Lalela Zulu": 100 Zulu Lyrics,* collected and trans. from the original Zulu by Hugh Tracey (Johannesburg, African Music Society, 1948), p. 41. By permission of Hugh Tracey. **Page 80** "Love Song." *Ibid.,* p. viii. **Page 81** "Song of the Unburied." FROM: Hugh Ashton, *The Basuto* (London, Published for the International African Institute by the Oxford University Press, 1955 [second impression]), p. 104 (*). **Page 81** "Hymn of the Affiicted." AFTER: Thomas Arbousset, *Relation d'un voyage d'exploration au nord-est de la Colonie du Cap de Bonne-Espérance* (Paris, Maison des Missions Évangéliques, 1842), pp. 472–73. **Page 82** "Satirical Song on a Missionary." AFTER: Karl Endemann, *Versuch einer Grammatik des Sotho* (Berlin, Wilhelm Hertz, 1876), pp. 197–98. **Page 82** "War Song of Goloane." AFTER: Eugène Casalis, *Les Bassoutos; ou vingt-trois années de séjour et d'observations au sud de l'Afrique* (Paris, Ch. Meyrueis et Cie., 1859), pp. 346–47. **Page 84** "Old Praise Song of the Crocodile." FROM: S. K. Lekgothoane, "Praises of Animals in Northern Sotho," *Bantu Studies,* XII (1938), pp. 199, 201 (*). By permission of the Witwatersrand University Press, Johannesburg. **Page 85** " 'National Song' of the Matabele." AFTER: C. Croonenberghs, "La fête de la Petite danse dans le Haut Zambèse," *Les Missions Catholiques,* XIV (1882), pp. 220–21 (*). By permission of Oeuvres Pontificales Missionaires, Lyon. **Page 86** "A Song Made by Dancers on Hearing a Woman Mourning for Her Child."

FROM: Erwin W. Smith and A. M. Dale, *The Ila-Speaking Peoples of Northern Rhodesia,* 2 vols. (London, Macmillan & Co., 1920), II, p. 276. By permission of the authors (*). **Page 86** "Lament." FROM: Natalie Curtis, *Songs and Tales from the Dark Continent* (New York, G. Schirmer, 1920), pp. 42–43 (** *ibid.,* pp. 120–21). **Page 87** "Praise Song for a Chief." FROM: Henri A. Junod, *The Life of a South African Tribe,* 2 vols. (Neuchatel, Attinger Frères, 1912–13), Vol. I, 399–400. By permission of the late author's son, Henri Philippe Junod. **Page 88** "Dance Song in Praise of a Dancer." *Ibid.,* Vol. II, 183 (*). By permission of the late author's son, Henri Philippe Junod. **Page 88** "Complaint of a Jilted Lover." *Ibid.,* p. 172. By permission of the late author's son, Henri Philippe Junod. **Page 89** "War Song of the Nkuna Clan." *Ibid.,* p. 261 (**). By permission of the late author's son, Henri Philippe Junod.

Eastern Africa and Madagascar

Page 90 "The Pregnant Woman." FROM: Audrey I. Richards, *Chisungu: A Girls' Initiation Ceremony Among the Bemba of Northern Rhodesia* (New York, Grove Press, 1956), p. 210 (*). By permission of Faber and Faber, Ltd., London. **Page 90** "Mother and Slave Raiders." FROM: J. Torrend, *Specimens of Bantu Folk-lore from Northern Rhodesia: Texts . . . and English Translations* (New York, E. P. Dutton & Co., 1921), p. 156 (**). **Page 91** "Plaint." AFTER: A. Capus, "Contes, chants et proverbes des Basumbwa dans l'Afrique Orientale," *Zeitschrift für Afrikanische und Oceanische Sprachen,* III (1897), 376 (*). **Page 92** "Mugala's Song." *Ibid.,* p. 377 (*). **Page 92** "Song for a War Dance." FROM: O. F. Raum, *Chaga Childhood: A Description of Indigenous Education in an East African Tribe* (London, Published for the International Institute of African Languages and Cultures by the Oxford University Press, 1940), p. 223. By permission of the International African Institute. **Page 93** "Her Sister-in-Law Answers the Greeting Song of the Returning Daughter of the Household." AFTER: Bruno Gutmann, "Grusslieder der Wadschagga," in *Festschrift Meinhof: Sprachwissenschaftliche und andere Studien* (Hamburg. L. Friederichsen & Co., 1927), pp. 231–32 (*). **Page 93** "Song Commemorating the Death of a Hunter." AFTER: H. Molitor, "La musique chez les Nègres du Tanganyika," *Anthropos,* VIII (1913), p. 721 (**). **Page 94** "Man's Dance Song." *Ibid.,* p. 725 (**). **Page 94** "Praise Song for a Chief." AFTER: R. Wolff, *Grammatik der Kinga-Sprache (Deutsch-Ostafrika, Nyassagebiet) nebst Texten und Wörterverzeichnis* (Archiv für das Studium deutscher Kolonialsprachen, III) (Berlin, Georg Reimer, 1905), p. 160 (*). **Page 95** "Lament." FROM: Günter Wagner, *The Bantu of North Kavirondo* (London, Published for the International African Institute by the Oxford University Press, 1949), I, 465. By permission of the International African Institute. **Page 95** "Women's Song for Fighting Men Delayed on a Raid." FROM: A. C. Hollis, *The Masai: Their Language and Folklore* (Oxford, The Clarendon Press, 1905), pp. 351–52 (*). By permission of The Clarendon Press.

Page 96 "Hippopotamus Hunter's Song." AFTER: F. Würtz, "Lieder der Pokomo," *Zeitschrift für Afrikanische und Oceanische Sprachen,* I (1895), 327 (*). **Page 96** "A Caravan Porter's Song." FROM: Alice Werner, "The Voice of Africa," *Africa,* I (1928), 249 (*). By permission of the International African Institute.

Page 97 "Home-sick Song." FROM: Alice Werner, "Nature Poetry in East Africa," *Africa,* I (1928) p. 352 (*). By permission of the International African Institute. **Page 97** "Lullaby." AFTER: Bernard Zuure, *L'âme du Murundi* (Paris, Beauchesne et ses Fils, 1932), pp. 441–42 (*). **Page 97** "To the New King Mútara II Rwôgera." AFTER: Alexis Kagamé, *La Poésie dynastique au Rwanda* (Institut Royal Colonial Belge, Section des Sciences Morales et Politiques. Mémoires, Collection in 8°, XXII, 1) (Brussels, 1951), pp. 74–75. **Page 99** "Courtship and Wedding Songs." AFTER: Felix Dufays, "Lied und Gesang bei Brautwerbung und Hochzeit in Mulera-Ruanda," *Anthropos,* IV (1909), 855–57, 869–70, 877 (*). **Page 101** "Battle Hymn." FROM: Jack Herbert Driberg, *People of the Small Arrow* (New York, Payson & Clarke, Ltd., 1930), pp. 38–39. **Page 102** "Praise of King Mtesa." FROM: Charles Thomas Wilson and R. W. Felkin, *Uganda and the Egyptian Sudan,* 2 vols. (London, Sampson Low, Marston, Searle and Rivington, 1882), I, 215. By permission of Sampson Low, Marston & Co., Ltd., Great Missenden, Bucks. **Page 102** "Wedding Song." FROM: Joseph Kyagambiddwa, *African Music from the Source of the Nile* (New York, Frederick A. Praeger, 1955), p. 37 (**). **Page 102** "Song Composed Under a Tyrannical King." *Ibid.,* p. 90 (**). **Page 103** "Spear-Blessing." FROM: Jack Herbert Driberg, *Initiation: Translations from poems of the Didinga and Lango tribes* (Great Britain, The Golden Cockerel Press, 1932), pp. 5–6. By permission of A. S. Barnes & Company, Inc. **Page 104** "From the Rain-Making Ceremony." FROM: J. H. Driberg, *The Lango: A Nilotic Tribe of Uganda* (London, T. Fisher Unwin, Ltd., 1923), pp. 250–51 (*). **Page 105** "A Mother to Her First-born." FROM: J. H. Driberg, *Initiation . . . ,* pp 16–17. **Page 107** "Auranomoi's Song of Praise for His Bull Akorikono." FROM: J. H. Driberg, *People of the Small Arrow,* pp. 131–33. **Page 109** "Girls' Song for the Game of 'Pots.'" *Ibid.,* pp. 323–24. **Page 110** "Chant." AFTER: G. Beltrame, *Il Sènnaar e lo Sciangàllah,* 2 vols. (Verona, Drucker & Tedeschi, 1879), I, 243. **Page 111** "Herder's Song." FROM: S. L. Cummins, "Sub-tribes of the Bahr-el-Ghazal Dinkas," *Journal of the Royal Anthropological Institute of Great Britain and Ireland,* XXXIV (1904), p. 162.

Page 111 "Beginning of a Girls' Song." FROM: E. E. Evans-Pritchard, *The Nuer: A description of the modes of livelihood and political institutions of a Nilotic people* (Oxford, The Clarendon Press, 1940), pp. 46–47. By permission of The Clarendon Press. **Page 112** "King Tekla Haimanot Learns That His Daughter Mentuab Has Been Captured by the Enemy." AFTER: A. Klingenheben, "Zur Amharischen Poesie," *Rassegna di Studi Etiopici,* XV (1959), 13 (*). **Page 113** "The Victorious Fighting Man's Home-Coming." FROM: Enrico Cerulli, "Folk-Literature of the Galla of Southern Abyssinia," in *Harvard African Studies,* Vol. III (Cambridge, Mass., The African Department of the Peabody Museum of Harvard University, 1922), p. 102 (*). **Page 113** "Caravaners' Song." *Ibid.,* p. 146 (*). **Page 114** "Love Songs." *Ibid.,* pp. 107, 115, 117, 119 (*). **Page 115** "Songs to Horses." FROM: J. W. C. Kirk, *A Grammar of the Somali Language with examples in prose and verse* (Cambridge, The University Press, 1905), pp. 176–77, 197 (*). By permission of Cambridge University Press, New York. **Page 116** "Love Song." AFTER: A. W. Schleicher, *Die Somali-Sprache,* Part I: *Texte, Lautlehre, Formenlehre und Syntax* (Berlin, Verlag von Theodor Fröhlich, 1892), p. 45 (*). **Page 116** "The Locust." AFTER: A. Marre, in André Leroi-Gourhan *et al., Ethnologie de l'Union Française (Territoires extérieurs),* 2 vols. (Paris, Presses Universitaires de France, 1953), II, 711–12. **Page 117** "The Song of the Bottle." FROM: A. Fiedler, *The Madagascar I Love* (London, Orbis [London], Ltd., 1946),

p. 62. **Page 118** "Improvised Song Against a White Man." *Ibid.*, p. 140. **Page 118** "Dialogues." AFTER: Jean Paulhan, *Les Hain-teny merinas, poésies populaires malgaches* (Paris, Librairie Paul Geuthner, 1913), pp. 101, 137 (*). By permission of the author. **Page 119** "Girls' Songs." *Ibid.*, pp. 79, 247, 323 (*). By permission of the author.

North Africa

Page 121 "If . . ." AFTER: C. Sonneck, *Chants arabes du Maghreb: Étude sur le dialecte et la poésie populaire de l'Afrique du Nord,* 2 vols. (Paris, E. Guilmoto, 1902–4), II, 105 (*). **Page 121** "Song." AFTER: Hans Stumme, *Tunisische Märchen und Gedichte: Einer Sammlung Prosaischer und Poetische Stücke im Arabischen Dialekt der Stadt Tunis,* 2 vols. (Leipzig, J. C. Hinrichs'sche Buchhandlung, 1893), II, 155 (*). **Page 122** "Poem Sung at a Mystical Exercise." FROM: Edward William Lane, *An Account of the Manners and Customs of the Modern Egyptians, written in Egypt during the years 1833, –34, and –35,* 2 vols. (London, John Murray, 1871), II, 172–73. **Page 122** "Popular Song." *Ibid.*, pp. 82–83 (**). **Page 123** "Women's Grinding Song." AFTER: Edmond Doutté, *Merrâkech* (Paris, Comité du Maroc, 1905), pp. 106–7. **Page 123** "Song." AFTER: Anna Hohenwart-Gerlachstein, "Vom Wesen der Beduinen Ägyptens," in *Festschrift Paul Schebesta zum 75. Geburtstag* (Wien-Mödling, St. Gabriel-Verlag, 1963), p. 271. **Page 124** "Song on Drums and Pipes." FROM: Maḥmûd Moḥammad 'Abd Allah, "Sîwan Customs," in *Harvard African Studies,* Vol. I (Cambridge, Mass., The African Department of the Peabody Museum of Harvard University, 1917), pp. 26–27. **Page 124** "Gnomes." AFTER: L. Justinard, *Manuel de berbère marocain (dialecte chleuh)* (Paris, E. Guilmoto, 1914), p. 72 (*). **Page 125** "Ballad." *Ibid.*, p. 74 (*). **Page 126** "Memorial." AFTER: M. Abès, "Monographie d'une tribu berbère: Les Aïth Ndhir (Beni M'tir)," *Archives Berbères,* III (1918), p. 321. By permission of Presses Universitaires de France, Paris. **Page 126** "Love Songs." *Ibid.*, pp. 325–27. By permission of Presses Universitaires de France, Paris. **Page 127** "On a Victory." AFTER: S. Biarnay, *Étude sur les dialectes berbères du Rif* (Paris, Ernest Leroux, 1917), p. 354 (*). By permission of Presses Universitaires de France, Paris. **Page 127** "Men's Song at a Wedding." *Ibid.*, p. 339 (*). By permission of Presses Universitaires de France, Paris. **Page 128** "Girls' Song at a Wedding." *Ibid.*, p. 343 (*). By permission of Presses Universitaires de France, Paris. **Page 128** "To a Young Girl." AFTER: L. Justinard, *Manuel de berbère marocain (dialecte rifain)* (Paris, Paul Geuthner, 1926), p. 64 (*). **Page 129** "Love Songs." AFTER: M. Abès, "Chansons d'amour chez les Berbères," *France-Maroc,* III (1919), p. 221.

Page 129 "Pilgrims' Songs." AFTER: Jean Amrouche, *Chants berbères de Kabylie* (Paris, Charlot, 1947), p. 187. **Page 130** "Song of Exile." *Ibid.*, p. 73. **Page 130** "Dance Song." *Ibid.*, pp. 140–41. **Page 131** "Love Songs." *Ibid.*, pp. 95, 97. **Page 132** "Learning French." AFTER: Louis Adolphe Hanoteau, *Poésies populaires de la Kabylie du Jurjura: Texte kabyle et traduction* (Paris, Imprimerie Impériale, 1867), pp. 282–85 (*). **Page 132** "Old War Song." AFTER: Ludwig G. A. Zöhrer, "Studien über die Tuáreg (Ímohağ) der Sahara," *Zeitschrift für Ethnologie,* LXXII (1940), 147. By permission of Albert Limbach Verlag, Braunschweig. **Page 133** "Song Composed by a Fighting Man Lying Wounded in the Desert." *Ibid.*, p. 148. By permission of Albert Limbach Verlag, Braunschweig. **Page 133** "On the Tuareg Violin." AFTER: Georges-Marie Haardt and Louis Audouin-Dubreuil, *Le Raid Citroën. La première traversée du Sahara en automobile. De Touggourt à Tombouctou par l'Atlantide* (Paris, Plon, 1924) p. 217. **Page 133** "Koukaa." *Ibid.*, p. 220. **Page 134** "Remonstrance." AFTER: L. Hanoteau, *Essai de grammaire de la langue tamachek', renfermant les principes du langage parlé par les . . . Touareg* (Paris, Imprimerie Impériale, 1860), p. 211 (*). **Page 134** "An Old Man's Night Thoughts." AFTER: Charles Eugène de Foucauld, *Poésies touarègues—Dialecte de l'Ăhaggar,* ed. André Basset, 2 vols. (Paris, Ernest Leroux, 1925–30), I, 11-14 (*). By permission of Presses Universitaires de France, Paris. **Page 135** "Drought." *Ibid.*, pp. 61–63 (*). By permission of Presses Universitaires de France, Paris. **Page 135** "Fighting Frenzy." *Ibid.*, pp. 99–100 (*). By permission of Presses Universitaires de France, Paris. **Page 135** "In Praise of Abazza Ag Mekiia." *Ibid.*, pp. 331–33. By permission of Presses Universitaires de France, Paris. **Page 136** "The Poetess Reproaches Mokammed Ag Mekiia for Having Passed Near the Place Where She Was Without Visiting Her." *Ibid.*, pp. 449–50 (*). By permission of Presses Universitaires de France, Paris. **Page 136** "Girl's Song." *Ibid.*, II, 1 (*). By permission of Presses Universitaires de France, Paris. **Page 137** "At a Noon Halt on a Journey." *Ibid.*, pp. 7–8 (*). By permission of Presses Universitaires de France, Paris.

INDONESIA

Borneo

Page 141 "Drinking Songs." AFTER: J. Staal, "Dusun Drinking- and Love-Songs," *Anthropos,* XXI (1926), p. 183 (slightly altered) (*). **Page 141** "Love Song." *Ibid.*, p. 186 (slightly altered) (*). **Page 142** "Chant on the Return from a Successful Head-Taking Raid." FROM: Owen Rutter, *The Pagans of North Borneo* (London, Hutchinson and Co., Ltd., 1929), pp. 194–97. (* *ibid.*, pp. 277–79.) **Page 145** "Invitation To Drink and the Reply." FROM: G. C. Wooley, "Two Murut Pantuns from the Dalit District Keningau, British North Borneo," *Journal of the Malayan Branch of the Royal Asiatic Society,* V (1927), 366–67 (*). **Page 146** "Shamans' Song over the Consecrated Rice at a Funeral Ceremony." AFTER: Renward Brandstetter, "Die Hymnen der dajakischen *Tiwah*-Feier," *Festschrift. Publication d'Hommage offerte au P. W. Schmidt* (Vienna, Mechitharisten-Congregations-Buchdruckerei, 1928), p. 191. By permission of *Anthropos.* **Page 147** "Voyage of the Benevolent Spirits." AFTER: August Hardeland, *Versuch einer Grammatik der Dajackschen Sprache* (Amsterdam, Frederik Muller, 1858), pp. 292–94 (*). **Page 148** "Evening Quietness." FROM: E. Dunn, "The *Mengap Bungai Taun,* the 'Chant of the Flowers of the Year,' a sacred chant used by the Sea-Dyaks on the occasion of a sacrificial feast to invoke a blessing on the fruits of the field," Part I, *Anthropos,* VII (1912), 138–41 (*). **Page 151** "Invocation Uttered over a Love Philtre by a Woman Who Desires a Man Named Jawa." FROM: W. Howell and R. Shelford, "A Sea-Dyak Love Philtre," *Journal of the Royal Anthropological Institute of Great Britain and Ireland,* XXXIV (1904), 208–10 (*). **Page 153** "Klieng's War-Raid to the Skies." FROM: J. Perham, "Klieng's War-Raid to the Skies: a Dyak Myth," *Journal of the Straits Branch of the Royal Asiatic Society,* No. 16 (Dec. 1885), pp. 269–71.

Sumatra

Page 156 "Dialogue." AFTER: J. Warneck, "Studien über die Litteratur der Toba-Batak," *Mittheilungen des Seminars für Orientalische Sprachen an der Königlichen Friedrich Wilhelms-Universität zu Berlin,* II (1899), 105. **Page 157** "Complaint of a Widow over Her Dying Son." *Ibid.,* pp. 118–19. **Page 158** "Complaint of a Fisherman's Widow." *Ibid.,* pp. 120–21.

Nias

Page 159 "Creation Myth." AFTER: Wilhelm Schmidt, *Grundlinien einer Vergleichung der Religionen und Mythologien der Austronesischen Völker* (Vienna, 1910), pp. 77–78 (quoting H. Sundermann, *Die Insel Nias und die Mission daselbst,* Barmen, 1905). With permission Österreichischen (formerly Kaiserlichen) Akademie der Wissenschaften in Vienna, translated into the English language from P. W. Schmidt, *Grundlinien einer Vergleichung der Religionen und Mythologien der Austronesischen Völker,* Denkschriften der Kaiserlichen Akademie der Wissenschaften in Vienna, Vol. 80, pp. 77 f, 1910. **Page 161** "Songs at a Wedding." AFTER: F. M. Schnitger, "Lieder von Nias," *Zeitschrift für Ethnologie,* LXXIII (1941), 36–37 (*). By permission of Albert Limbach Verlag, Braunschweig. **Page 162** "The Chief Men of a Village Answer the Greeting of Travelers." AFTER: H. Sundermann, "Die Insel Nias und die Mission daselbst," Part II, *Allgemeine Missions-Zeitung,* XI (1884), 429–30 (*). **Page 163** "Song for Girl Dancers." AFTER: H. Sundermann, "Niassische Texte mit deutscher Übersetzung," *Bijdragen tot de Taal-, Land-, en Volkenkunde van Nederlandsch-Indië,* VII/4 (1905), 44–45 (* *ibid.,* pp. 10 f.). By permission of Koninklijk Instituut voor Taal-, Land-, en Volkenkunde. **Page 164** "Epilogue to a Narrative Poem." AFTER: W. L. Steinhart, *Niassische Teksten met nederlandsche Vertaling en Aanteekeningen* (Verhandelingen van het Koninklijk Bataviaasch Genootschap van Kunsten en Wetenschapen, LXXIII) (Bandoeng, A. C. Nix & Co., 1937), pp. 159–62 (*).

Lesser Sundas

Page 166 "Songs." AFTER: Johannes Elbert, *Die Sunda-Expedition des Vereins für Geographie und Statistik zu Frankfurt am Main,* 2 vols. (Frankfurt am Main, Druck und Verlag von Hermann Minjon, 1911–12), II, 73–74 (*).

Page 167 "Dirge." AFTER: Ernst Vatter, *Ata Kiwan: Unbekannte Bergvölker im tropischen Holland* (Leipzig, Bibliographisches Institut, 1932), pp. 85–86. **Page 168** "Prayer at Burning Off a New Communal Field." *Ibid.*, pp. 109–10. **Page 169** "Curse Tabooing a Lake." AFTER: J. Albert, *op. cit.*, p. 231 (*).

Celebes

Page 170 "Song of a Dying Girl." AFTER: T. J. Bezemer, *Volksdichtung aus Indonesien: Sagen, Tierfabeln und Märchen* (The Hague, Martinus Nijhoff, 1904), p. 288. **Page 170** "Song at the Departure of a Beautiful Girl." *Ibid.*, p. 288. **Page 171** "Song of a Girl to Bring Back Her Unfaithful Lover." *Ibid.*, p. 288. **Page 171** "Harvest-Season Songs." AFTER: N. Adriani and A. C. Kruijt, *De Bare'e-sprekende Toradja's van Midden-Celebes*, 3 vols. (Batavia, Landsdrukkerij, 1912–14), III, 507, 510 (*). By permission of Koninklijk Instituut voor Taal-, Land-, en Volkenkunde. **Page 172** "Song at a Head-Hunting Festival." AFTER: Johannes Elbert, *Die Sunda-Expedition des Vereins für Geographie und Statistik zu Frankfurt am Main*, 2 vols. (Frankfurt am Main, Druck und Verlag von Hermann Minjon, 1911–12), II, 14–16 (*).

Moluccas

Page 175 "Song." AFTER: K. Martin, *Reisen in den Molukken, in Ambon, den Uliassern, Seran (Ceram) und Buru* (Leiden, E. J. Brill, 1894), pp. 293–94 (*). **Page 175** "Song for a Kachua Dance." AFTER: Odo Deodatus Tauern, *Patasiwa und Patalima: Vom Molukkeneiland Seran und Seinen Bewohnern; Ein Beitrag zur Völkerkunde* (Leipzig, R. Voigtländers Verlag, 1918), pp. 82–83 (*). **Page 176** "Boatmen's Song." *Ibid.*, pp. 86–87 (**). **Page 177** "Linked Pantuns." AFTER: W. Joest, "Malayische Lieder und Tanze aus Ambon und den Uliase (Molukken)," *Internationales Archiv für Ethnographie*, V (1892), p. 26 (**). By permission of Friedr. Vieweg & Sohn Verlag, Braunschweig, and Johnson Reprint Corp., New York.

Philippines

Page 178 "The Myth of Numputul, the Self-beheaded." FROM: Roy Franklin Barton, *The Mythology of the Ifugaos* (Philadelphia, American Folklore Society, 1955), pp. 80–84 (*). **Page 181** "From an *Angba*." FROM: C. R. Moss, "Nabaloi Law and Ritual," *University of California Publications in American Archaeology and Ethnology*, Vol. XV, No. 3 (Oct. 28, 1920), p. 291 (*). By permission of University of California Press, Berkeley. **Page 182** "Song." FROM: C. R. Moss and A. L. Kroeber, "Nabaloi Songs," *University of California Publications in American Archaeology and Ethnology*, Vol. XV, No. 2 (May 10, 1919), p. 192 (**). By permission of University of California Press, Berkeley. **Page 183** "Song for a Ceremonial Dance." FROM: Fay-Cooper Cole, *The Tinguian: Social, Religious, and Economic Life of a Philippine Tribe* (Field Museum of Natural History Publication No. 209. Anthropological Series Vol. XIV, No. 2) (Chicago, Field Museum of Natural History, 1922), pp. 456–60 (* *ibid.;* melody, *ibid.*, p. 445). By permission of Chicago Natural History Museum.

MELANESIA

New Guinea

Page 187 "Dirge for a Son Killed in Battle." FROM: Peter Matthiessen, *Under the Mountain Wall: A chronicle of two seasons in the Stone Age* (New York, The Viking Press, Inc., 1962), p. 48. By permission of The Viking Press, Inc., and William Heinemann, Ltd., London. **Page 187** "Young Men's Song." *Ibid.*, p. 179. By permission of The Viking Press, Inc., and William Heinemann, Ltd., London. **Page 188** "Song at a Public Courtship Ceremony." FROM: John Nilles, "The Kuman of the Chimbu Region, Central Highlands, New Guinea," *Oceania,* XXI (1950–51), 34. By permission of Emeritus Prof. A. P. Elkin, editor of *Oceania.* **Page 188** "Women's Song at a Girl's Initiation." *Ibid.*, pp. 32–33. By permission of Emeritus Prof. A. P. Elkin, editor of *Oceania.* **Page 189** "Charm to Restore a Dying Man." AFTER: Georg F. Vicedom, in Vicedom and Herbert Tischner, *Die Mbowamb: Die Kultur der Hagenberg-Stämme im Östlichen Zentral-Neuguinea,* Vol. II (by Vicedom): *(I) Gesellschaft, (II) Religion und Weltbild* (Monographien zur Völkerkunde herausgegeben vom Hamburgischen Museum für Völkerkunde, I) (Hamburg, Friederichsen, De Gruyter & Co., 1943), p. 378. By permission of Hamburgisches Museum für Völkerkunde und Vorgeschichte. **Page 189** "Lament of a Widow for Her Dead Husband." *Ibid.*, p. 279. By permission of Hamburgisches Museum für Völkerkunde und Vorgeschichte. **Page 190** "Love Song." *Ibid.*, p. 196. By permission of Hamburgisches Museum für Völkerkunde und Vorgeschichte. **Page 190** "Woman's Song." *Ibid.* By permission of Hamburgisches Museum für Völkerkunde und Vorgeschichte. **Page 190** "Courting Song and Reply." *Ibid.*, pp. 190–91. By permission of Hamburgisches Museum für Völkerkunde und Vorgeschichte. **Page 191** "Songs." FROM: H. I. Hogbin, "Puberty to Marriage: A study of the sexual life of the natives of Wogeo, New Guinea," *Oceania,* XVI (1945–46), p. 197. By permission of Emeritus Prof. A. P. Elkin, editor of *Oceania.* **Page 192** "The Dancer." FROM: André Dupeyrat, *Mitsinari: Twenty-one Years among the Papuans,* trans. Erik and Denyse de Mauny (London and New York, Staples Press, 1955), pp. 100–1 (*). **Page 192** "Song." *Ibid.*, pp. 101–2 (*). **Page 193** "Song of Old Age and a White Head." *Ibid.*, pp. 102–3 (*). **Page 193** "Song Sung while Fencing a Garden." FROM: C. G. Seligmann, *The Melanesians of British New Guinea* (Cambridge, The University Press, 1910), pp. 152–53 (*). **Page 194** "'Sing-Sings' of Nature." FROM: A. P. Allan Natachee, "Mekeo Poems and Legends," *Oceania,* XXII (1951–52), 153–54 (*). By permission of Emeritus Prof. A. P. Elkin, editor of *Oceania.*

D'Entrecasteaux Islands

Page 196 "Incantation at First Twining Yam Vines." FROM: R. F. Fortune, *Sorcerers of Dobu: The social anthropology of the Dobu Islanders of the Western Pacific* (Australasian National Research Council Expedition to New Guinea, 1927–28) (New York, E. P. Dutton & Co., Inc., 1932), p. 121. By permission of E. P. Dutton & Co., Inc., New York, and Routledge & Kegan Paul, Ltd., London. **Page 197** "Charm at a Ceremonial Bathing to Make One Beautiful and Irresistible." *Ibid.,* p. 230. By permission of E. P. Dutton & Co., Inc., New York, and Routledge & Kegan Paul, Ltd., London. **Page 197** "Song of the Departed Spirit." *Ibid.,* pp. 187 and 257 (*). By permission of E. P. Dutton & Co., Inc., New York, and Routledge & Kegan Paul, Ltd., London. **Page 198** "Love Songs." *Ibid.,* pp. 251, 253, 260 (*). By permission of E. P. Dutton & Co., Inc., New York, and Routledge & Kegan Paul, Ltd., London. **Page 199** "Dance Songs." *Ibid.,* pp. 242, 254, 255, 300, 301, 304 (*). By permission of E. P. Dutton & Co., Inc., New York, and Routledge & Kegan Paul, Ltd., London. **Page 201** "Love Incantation." FROM: D. Jenness and A. Ballantyne, *Language, Mythology, and Songs of Bwaidoga. Goodenough Island, S. E. Papua* (Memoirs of the Polynesian Society, Vol. 8) (Wellington, N. Z., The Polynesian Society, 1928), p. 187 (*). **Page 201** "Marriage Song." *Ibid.,* p. 210 (*). **Page 201** "War Song, Sung Before Going into Battle." *Ibid.,* pp. 193–94 (*). **Page 202** "Canoe Song." *Ibid.,* p. 209 (*). **Page 202** "Song." *Ibid.,* p. 215 (*).

Trobriand Islands

Page 203 "Song of War." FROM: B. Baldwin, "Usituma! Song of Heaven," *Oceania,* XV (1944–45), 224–27 (*). By permission of Emeritus Prof. A. P. Elkin, editor of *Oceania.* **Page 205** "Love-Magic Spell." FROM: Bronislaw Malinowski, *The Sexual Life of Savages in North-Western Melanesia: An Ethnographic Account . . .* (London, George Routledge & Sons, 1929), p. 308. By permission of Routledge & Kegan Paul, Ltd., London.

Bismarck Archipelago

Page 207 "Thief's Spell." AFTER: Joseph Meier, "Die Zauberei bei den Küstenbewohnern der Gazelle-Halbinsel, Neupommern, Südsee," Part III, *Anthropos,* VIII (1913), 701 (*). **Page 207** "Song of a Woman Named Hi Pak." AFTER: R. Parkinson, *Dreissig Jahre in der Südsee: Land und Leute, Sitten und Gebräuche im Bismarckarchipel und auf den deutschen Salomoinseln* (Stuttgart, Verlag von Strecker & Schröder, 1907), p. 409 (*). **Page 208** "Songs." AFTER: Börnstein, "Ethnographische Beiträge aus dem Bismarckarchipel," *Baessler-Archiv,* V (1916), 250, 251, 253, 254, 256, 256 (*). By permission of B. G. Teubner, Leipzig.

Solomon Islands

Page 211 "Song of a Sick Chief." AFTER: Richard Thurnwald, *Forschungen auf den Salomo-Inseln und dem Bismarck-Archipel,* Vol. I: *Lieder und Sagen aus Buin* (Berlin, Dietrich Reimer [Ernst Vohsen], 1912), 48–49 (*). By permission of Dietrich Reimer (Andrews & Steiner), Berlin. **Page 212** "Woman's Song." *Ibid.,* pp. 289–90. (*). By permission of Dietrich Reimer (Andrews & Steiner), Berlin. **Page 212** "Man's Song." *Ibid.,* pp. 223–24 (*). By permission of Dietrich Reimer (Andrews & Steiner), Berlin. **Page 213** "Man's Song: Against a Woman." *Ibid.,* pp. 161–62 (*). By permission of Dietrich Reimer (Andrews & Steiner), Berlin. **Page 213** "Women's Song." AFTER: Ernst Frizzi, *Ein Beitrag zur Ethnologie von Bougainville und Buka mit spezieller Berücksichtigung der Nasioi* (Baessler-Archiv, Beiheft VI) (Leipzig and Berlin, B. G. Teubner, 1914), p. 51 (*). **Page 214** "Kahuto, the Owl." FROM: W. G. Ivens, *Melanesians of the South-East Solomon Islands* (London, Kegan Paul, Trench, Trubner & Co., 1927), p. 106 (*). By permission of Routledge & Kegan Paul, Ltd., London. **Page 214** "Charm for Rain." FROM: C. E. Fox, *The Threshold of the Pacific: An Account of the Social Organization, Magic and Religion of the People of San Cristoval in the Solomon Islands* (New York, Alfred A. Knopf, 1925), pp. 101–2. By permission of Routledge & Kegan Paul, Ltd., London.

Banks Islands and New Hebrides

Page 216 "In Honor of Maros During His Absence at Sea." FROM: R. H. Codrington, *The Melanesians: Studies in Their Anthropology and Folklore* (Oxford, Clarendon Press, 1891), pp. 335–36. **Page 217** "Kite-Flying Song." *Ibid.,* p. 336.

New Caledonia

Page 218 "Lullaby for a Child Whose Mother Has Gone to Gather Food." AFTER: M. Leenhardt, in André Leroi-Gourhan *et al., Ethnologie de l'Union Française (Territoires extérieurs),* 2 vols. (Paris, Presses Universitaires de France, 1953), II, 765–66. **Page 219** "Song for a Seated Dance: Victory of the Mea." AFTER: Maurice Leenhardt, *Documents Néo-Calédoniens* (Université de Paris, Travaux et Mémoires de l'Institut d'Ethnologie, IX) (Paris, Institut d'Ethnologie, 1932), 255–76 (* [and interlinear translation], *ibid.;* melody, *ibid.,* pp. 509–10).

Fiji Islands

Page 227 "The Shades of the Newly Dead to the Gods." FROM: Basil H. Thomson, "The Kalou-Vu (Ancestor-Gods) of the Fijians," *Journal of the Royal Anthropological Institute of Great Britain and Ireland,* XXIV (1894–95), 353. By permission of the Royal Anthropological Institute of Great Britain and Ireland. **Page 228** "On the Pestilence That Scourged the Fijians After Their First Contact with Whites ca. 1791." FROM: Basil H. Thomson, *The Fijians: A Study of the Decay of Custom* (London, William Heinemann, 1908), pp. 244–45. **Page 228** "Song on the Great Visitation of Measles in 1875." FROM: Sir Arthur Gordon, "On Fijian Poetry," in *Transactions of the Ninth International Congress of Orientalists,* 2 vols. (London, 1893), II, 752. **Page 229** "Song on the War in the Mountains of Viti Levu in 1876." *Ibid.,* pp. 752–53. **Page 230** "Song." *Ibid.,* pp. 746–48. **Page 232** "Dance Song." *Ibid.,* pp. 748–50. **Page 233** "The Epic of Dengei." FROM: Basil H. Thomson, *The Fijians . . . ,* pp. 138–40 (*). **Page 236** "Epic Song." FROM: Buell H. Quain, *The Flight of the Chiefs: Epic Poetry of Fiji* (New York, J. J. Augustin, 1942), pp. 85–88.

AUSTRALIA

Page 241 "Chants." FROM: E. A. Worms, "The Poetry of the Yaoro and Bad, North-Western Australia," *Annali Lateranensi,* XXI (1957), 216, 218 (* [and literal translations], *ibid.*). **Page 242** "A Triptych on the Dugong." *Ibid.,* pp. 222–23 (* [and literal translations], *ibid.*). **Page 242** "Song of a Widow for Her Dead Husband." FROM: Catherine H. Berndt, "Expressions of Grief Among Aboriginal Women," *Oceania,* XX (1949–50), 303 (*). By permission of Emeritus Prof. A. P. Elkin, editor of *Oceania.* **Page 243** "Song." FROM: Catherine H. Berndt, *Women's Changing Ceremonies in Northern Australia* (Paris, Hermann et Cie., 1950), p. 40 (*). **Page 243** "From the Sacred Dulngulg Cycle." FROM: Ronald M. Berndt and Catherine H. Berndt, *The First Australians* (Sydney, Ure Smith, 1952), p. 15. **Page 244** "Traditional Song." *Ibid.,* p. 136. **Page 244** "Song of a Woman Crying for the Dead Baby Son of Her Daughter." FROM: C. H. Berndt, "Expressions of Grief . . ." p. 317 (*). By permission of Emeritus Prof. A. P. Elkin, editor of *Oceania.* **Page 245** "Song of Departure and Farewell." FROM: Catherine H. Berndt, "A Drama of North-Eastern Arnhem Land," *Oceania,* XXII (1951–52), 283 (* [and interlinear translation], *ibid.,* p. 282). By permission of Emeritus Prof. A. P. Elkin, editor of *Oceania.* **Page 245** "The Gidgid-Bird." *Ibid.,* p. 285 (* [and interlinear translation], *ibid.,* pp. 284–85). By permission of Emeritus Prof. A. P. Elkin, editor of *Oceania.* **Page 245** "The Narba-Bird." *Ibid.,* p. 284 (* [and interlinear translation], *ibid.,* p. 283). By permission of Emeritus Prof. A. P. Elkin, editor of *Oceania.* **Page 246** "From the 'Goulburn Island' Love Cycle." FROM: R. M. Berndt and C. H. Berndt, *op. cit.,* p. 66.

Page 246 "Song Cycle of the Moon-Bone." FROM: Ronald M. Berndt, "A 'Wɔnguri-'Mandʒikai Song Cycle of the Moon-Bone," *Oceania*, XIX (1948–49), 23–50 (* [and interlinear translation], *ibid.*). By permission of Emeritus Prof. A. P. Elkin, editor of *Oceania*. **Page 254** "Native-Cat Songs." FROM: Catherine J. Ellis, *Aboriginal Music Making: A Study of Central Australian Music* (Adelaide, Librairies Board of South Australia, 1964), pp. 62–68 (** *ibid.*, pp. 69–109). **Page 256** "Sacred Song of the Avocet Cult." AFTER: Carl Strehlow, *Die Aranda- und Loritja- Stämme in Zentral-Australien* (Veröffentlichungen aus dem Städtischen Völker-Museum, Frankfurt am Main, I), Part III: *Die totemistischen Kulte der Aranda- und Loritja- Stämme* (Frankfurt am Main, Joseph Baer & Co., 1910–11), Section 1 (1910), pp. 59–60 (*). **Page 257** "The Song of Ankotarinja." FROM: T. G. H. Strehlow, "Ankotarinja, an Aranda Myth," *Oceania*, IV (1933–34), 190–92 (*). By permission of Emeritus Prof. A. P. Elkin, editor of *Oceania*. **Page 258** "Sacred Song of the Jackeroo Cult." AFTER: C. Strehlow, *op. cit.*, Part III, Section 2 (1911), pp. 24–25 (*). **Page 260** "Song: The Railway Train." FROM: George Taplin, "The Narrinyeri" in *The Native Tribes of South Australia* (Adelaide, E. S. Wigg & Son, 1897), p. 39 (*). By permission of E. S. Wigg & Son, Pty, Ltd. **Page 260** "Umbara's Song." FROM: A. W. Howitt, *The Native Tribes of South-East Australia* (London, Macmillan & Co., 1904), p. 423 (**). By permission of the Publisher. **Page 261** "Wenberri's Song." *Ibid.*, p. 422 (**). By permission of the Publisher.

INDEX OF PEOPLES

INDEX OF PEOPLES

Aandonga, 69–72
Acholi, 101
Ait Abbas, *see* Berber, Ait Abbas
Ait Aydel, *see* Berber, Ait Aydel
Ait Ndhir, *see* Berber, Ait Ndhir
Ait Temsaman, *see* Berber, Ait Temsaman
Ait Uriaren, *see* Berber, Ait Uriaren
Akan, 47
Algerian (Arabic), 121
Amhara, 112
Ammassalik Eskimo, *see* Eskimo, Ammassalik
Aranda, 254–258
Arnhem Land (unidentified people), 244–246
Ashanti, 47–49
Azande, 61

Bad, 242
Baganda, 102
Ba-Ila, 86
Bakongo, 61
Bambara, 37–38
Banks Islands (unidentified people), 216–217
Bantu Kavirondo, 95
Barundi, 97
Basumbwa, 91–92
Basuto, 81–83
Batak, 156–158
Bathurst and Melville Islands (unidentified people), 242–243
Baule, 46
Bedouin, 123
Bemba, 90
Berber, 124–132
  Ait Abbas, 129–131
  Ait Aydel, 129–131
  Ait Ndhir, 126
  Ait Temsaman, 127–128
  Ait Uriaren, 127
  Central Morocco, 129
  Gzennaia, 128
  Kabyle, 132
  Shluh, 124–126
Bergdama, 72–75
Buin, people of, 211–213
Buru (unidentified people), 175
Bushman, 76
Bwaidogan, 201–202

Caribou Eskimo, *see* Eskimo, Caribou
Central Morocco Berber, *see* Berber, Central Morocco
Chagga, 92–93
Copper Eskimo, *see* Eskimo, Copper

Dahomean (Fon), 52–55
Didinga, 105–110
Dinka, 110–111
Do Donggo, 166
Dobuan, 196–201
Dogon, 38–39
Duala, 55–56
Duke of York Islands (unidentified people), 208–210
Dusun, 141
Dyak, 146–155
  Ngadju, 147–148
  Sea, 148–155

East Flores (unidentified people), 167-168
Egyptian (Arabic), 122–123
Eskimo, 3–32
  Ammassalik, 6–8
  Caribou, 14–16
  Copper, 20–29
  Greenland, 3–8
  Iglulik, 9–13
  Mackenzie, 30
  Netsilik, 16–20

Nunivak Island, 31
Upper Koyukuk, 31–32
Ewe, 49–52
Ewondo, 56–57

Fang, 57–60
Fijian, 227–238
Fon, *see* Dahomean
French Guinea or Sudan, Former, (unidentified people), 42
Fulani, *see* Peul
Fuyughé, 192–193

Galla, 113–115
Gazelle Peninsula (unidentified people), 207
Gzennaia, *see* Berber, Gzennaia

Hausa, 42–43
Hottentot, 76–79

Ibo, 42
Ifugao, 178–181
Iglulik Eskimo, *see* Eskimo, Iglulik
Igorot, *see* Nabaloi Igorot
Ili Mandiri (unidentified people), 168

Kabajana Island (unidentified people), 172–174
Kabyle, *see* Berber, Kabyle
Kanaka, 218–226
Kel Ahaggar, *see* Tuareg, Kel Ahaggar
Kibende, 93
Kifimbwe, 94
Kinga, 94
Koita, 193–194
Kuman, 188–189
Kurelu, 187

Lakona (unidentified people), 216–217
Lango, 103–107
Lapp, 33–34
Laragia, 244
Leloba Village (unidentified people), 167
Lepers Island (unidentified people), 217
Loritja, 258–259

Mackenzie Eskimo, *see* Eskimo, Mackenzie
Malagasy, 116–118
Malay of the Moluccas, 177
Masai, 95
Matabele, 85
Mbowamb, 189–191
Mekeo, 194–195
Melville Island, *see* Bathurst and Melville Islands
Mende, 44–45
Merina, 118–120
Minahasa (unidentified people), 170–171
Moanus, 207
Mossi, 41
Mudbara, 243
Mulera-Ruanda, Former, (unidentified people), 99–101
Murring, 260
Murut, 142–146

Nabaloi Igorot, 181–182
Narrinyeri, 260
Nasioi, 213
Ndau, 86–87
Netsilik Eskimo, *see* Eskimo, Netsilik
New Britain, *see* Gazelle Peninsula
Ngadju Dyak, *see* Dyak, Ngadju
Niassan, 159–165
Nkuna, *see* Thonga, Nkuna
Northern Sotho, 84
Northern Territory, Australia (unidentified people), 243
Nuer, 111–112
Nunivak Island Eskimo, *see* Eskimo, Nunivak Island

Patalima, 175–177
Patasiwa, 175–177
Peul (Fulani), 39–41
Pokomo, 96
Pygmy, 62–68

Ruanda, 97–98

Sa'a Island (unidentified people), 214
San Cristobal Island (unidentified people), 214–215
Santa Maria Island (unidentified people), 216–217
Sea Dyak, *see* Dyak, Sea
Shluh, *see* Berber, Shluh

Siwan, 124
Somali, 115–116
Swahili, 96–97

Taitok, *see* Tuareg, Taitok
Temne, 45–46
Thonga, 87–89
  Nkuna, 89
Tinguian, 183–184
Tonga, 90–91
Toradja, 171
Trobriandan, 203–206
Tuareg, 132–137
  Kel Ahaggar, 134–136
  Taitok, 136–137
Tukolor, 43–44
Tunisian (Arabic), 121

Unidentified peoples
  Arnhem Land, 244–246
  Banks Islands, 216–217
  Bathurst and Melville Islands, 242–243
  Buru, 175
  Duke of York Islands, 208–210
  East Flores, 167, 168
  French Guinea or Sudan, Former, 42
  Gazelle Peninsula, 207
  Ili Mandiri, 168
  Kabajana Island, 172–174
  Lakona, 216–217
  Leloba Village, 167
  Lepers Island, 217
  Minahasa, 170–171
  Mulera-Ruanda, Former, 99–101
  New Britain, 207
  Northern Territory, Australia, 243
  Sa'a Island, 214
  San Cristobal Island, 214–215
  Santa Maria Island, 216–217
  Wetar Island, 169
  Wogoe Island, 191
Upper Koyukuk Eskimo, *see* Eskimo, Upper Koyukuk

Wetar Island (unidentified people), 169
Wogeo Island (unidentified people), 191
Wonguri-Mandjikai, 246–254
Wurunjerri, 261

Yaoro, 241

Zulu, 79–80